VIOLET PO

Within the Fa~~

AN AUTOBIOGRAPHY

HEINEMANN : LONDON

William Heinemann Ltd
15 Queen Street, Mayfair, London W1X 8BE
LONDON   MELBOURNE   TORONTO
JOHANNESBURG   AUCKLAND

First published 1976
Copyright © Violet Powell 1976
434 59955 7

Printed in Great Britain by
Richard Clay (The Chaucer Press), Ltd.,
Bungay, Suffolk

Contents

	Family Tree	viii
	Author's Note	xi
1	The Vale of Aylesbury	1
2	Restlessness and Rootlessness	18
3	Farewell to the Ghosts of Middleton	32
4	Two Dianas in the Irish Midlands	39
5	West Waterford	57
6	Julia Spreads her Wings	66
7	Bavarian Rhapsody	81
8	The Family Circle Widens	100
9	The Practice of Deception	116
10	East End, West End	135
11	By the Waters of Dynevor	144
12	Bats and Brickbats	150
13	Inept at Economics	157
14	The Rufus Stone	171
15	The Beetle's Droning Flight	180
16	The Blue Train	187
17	An Ending	204
18	Beginning Again	213
19	The Family Gets a Fright	222
	Index	239

for Ty

FAMILY TREE. CHART A. *marriages and children not directly referred to in the text have mostly been omitted.*

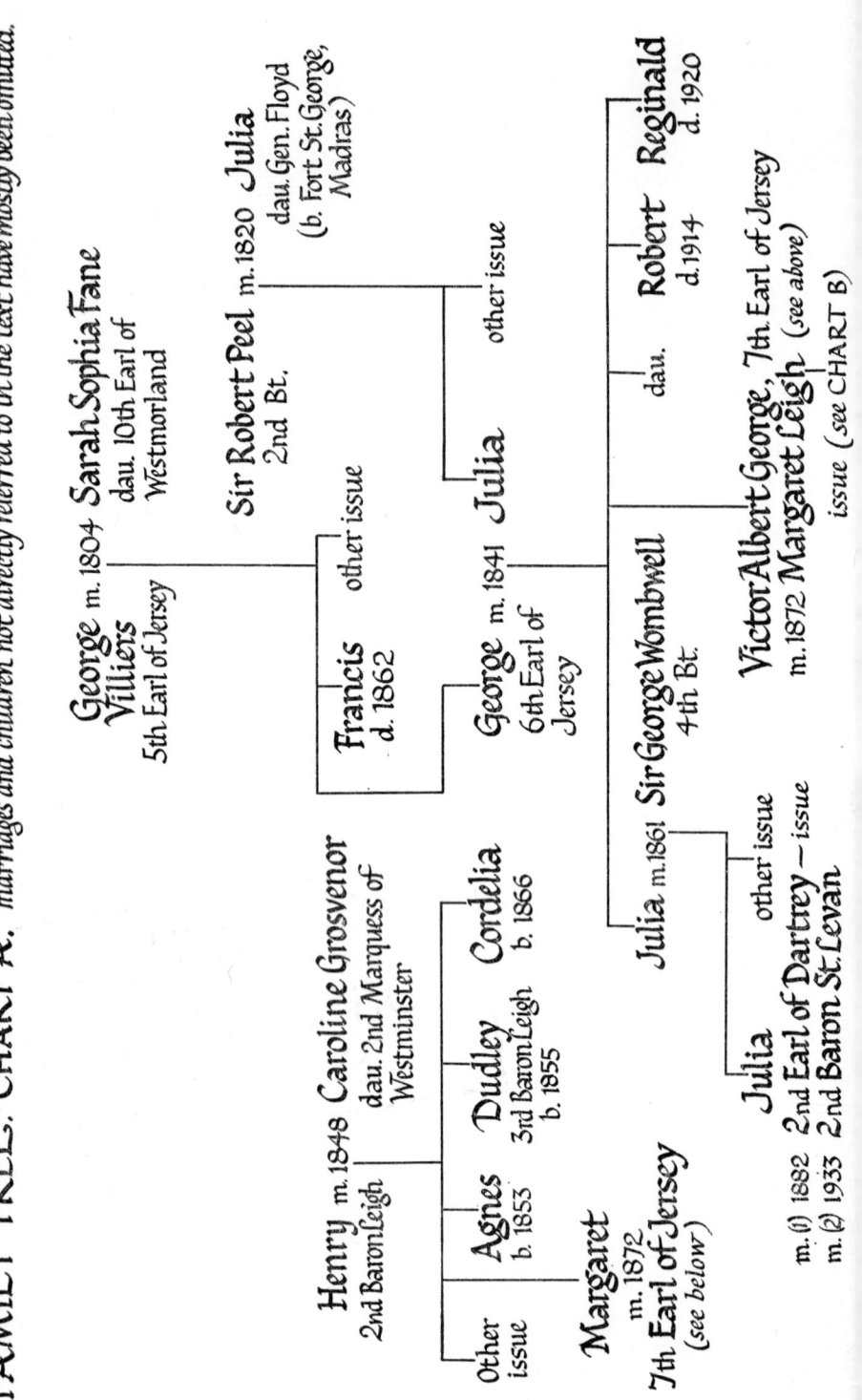

CHART B.
Issue of 7th Earl of Jersey
(see CHART A)

William Pakenham m. 1862 Selina Rice-Trevor
4th. Earl of Longford — dau. 4th. Baron Dynevor

Children:
- **George** m. 1908 **Cynthia** — 8th Earl of Jersey, dau. 3rd Earl of Kilmorey; m.(2) Rodney Slessor — further issue
- **Margaret** d. inf.
- **Arthur**
- **Beatrice** m.1904 **Edward Plunkett** 18th Baron Dunsany
  - Randal
- **Katherine** m.1904 **Hon. Lionel Vane** — issue
- **Edward** (Bingo)
- **Georgiana** m.1889 **Hugh** 2nd Viscount Gough
  - Hugo
  - other issue
  - **William** d. young
- **Mary** m. 1899 **Thomas** 5th Earl of Longford*

Issue of George (8th Earl of Jersey) and Cynthia:
- **George** (Grandy) 9th Earl of Jersey
- **Joan** m. 1933 David Colville
- **Mansel**
- **Ann**
- **Margaret** m.1898 **Walter Rhys** 7th Baron Dynevor*
  - Charles
  - Elwyn
  - Imogen
  - David

Issue of Mary and Thomas (5th Earl of Longford):
- **Edward** m.1925 Christine Trew
  - Henrietta b. 1931
- **Pansy** m. 1928 Henry Lamb
  - Felicia b. 1933
- **Frank** m. 1931 Elizabeth Harman
  - Antonia b. 1932
  - Thomas b. 1933
- **Mary**
- **Violet** m.1934 Anthony Powell
- **Julia**

* Third cousins

Author's Note

CONTINUING THE STORY TOLD IN *Five out of Six*, which carried the author from childhood to the age of eighteen, *Within the Family Circle* takes her to her marriage at the age of twenty-two. The public background of these years was one of political and economic crisis. At home, the author's mother was struggling against an illness that was to be mortal. If, in these circumstances, the author's behaviour appears frivolous or unfeeling, she can only plead that she has told the story as truthfully as she can remember it. If she has given some impression of the love and kindness she experienced within her family circle during these years, she must hope that her own failings may be, to some extent, excused.

To avoid overburdening the narrative with genealogical detail a family tree is appended, and the following summary gives additional details of the author's immediate family. She was born Violet Pakenham, her father being Thomas, 5th Earl of Longford, whose home was Pakenham Hall, Co. Westmeath, Ireland. He was killed in Gallipoli in 1915, his son Edward succeeding to the title. Thomas, Lord Longford, had married Mary Villiers, daughter of the 7th Earl of Jersey. Middleton Park, Oxfordshire, and Osterley Park, Middlesex, were the homes of the Jerseys. The Dowager Lady Longford had sold North Aston Hall, Oxfordshire, in 1929 and moved to Peverel Court, near Aylesbury. In 1925 the author's eldest brother Edward had married Christine Trew, later a novelist and playwright. In 1928 the author's eldest sister Pansy had married Henry Lamb, the painter. At the time *Within the Family Circle* begins, her brother Frank, and her sisters Mary and Julia, had not yet married.

1. The Vale of Aylesbury

WHEN I WAS EIGHTEEN IN THE YEAR 1930 the moving staircase which had carried me forward through the years of education suddenly came to a halt. The actual progress of education I have described elsewhere, together with the months of the London Summer Season. Regarding the Season as an extension of education, my mother was in the habit of saying that acquaintance with its formal pattern was as essential to her daughters as three years at a university to her sons. Although her own eldest son had married immediately after taking his degree, she still clung to the attitude of her own youth in regarding undergraduates as no more than half-fledged men of the world. In my case it happened that the end of my scholastic and worldly education coincided with a family crisis that was both sudden and long-drawn-out. The escalator had stopped. I was obliged to move of my own volition on a plateau which lacked the landmarks that the educational process gives, and on which I was to pass four years of increasing rootlessness.

Peverel Court, a new home chosen by my mother, had for her the advantage that the London & North Eastern Railway ran through Aylesbury only two miles away, whisking travellers to Marylebone Station in a bare forty minutes. From our previous home in Oxfordshire my mother had been able to join this swift service farther up the line, though in doing so she wore a rather guilty air, being conscious of the number of nearer stations and slower trains she was ignoring on her ten-mile drive to Brackley. When she reached London the benefits did not cease as she had a penchant for the Great Central Hotel at Marylebone Station, which could be reached on foot without intervention of taxi-cab, a station porter wheeling her luggage behind her. Recently I was reminded of this habit of my mother's by reading that Max Beerbohm patronized the Charing Cross Hotel for precisely the same reason.

This quick escape route to London was the principal if not the only advantage of Peverel Court as a place of residence, its majestic name giving a thoroughly false impression of grandeur. My mother was not so entirely devoid of aesthetic feeling when faced with the problems of wallpapers and chair covers as her own mother, but that would have been a difficult achievement. My grandmother had spent the first sixty years of her life in large and beautiful houses, Osterley Park being perhaps the most spectacular, but she was, nevertheless, a striking demonstration that visual education does not necessarily eradicate natural philistinism. Retreating to London as a dowager, my grandmother happily filled her house with hard and soft furnishings which ranged from the dull to the downright hideous. My mother, on the other hand, possessed the ability to choose pretty tables and chairs and to cover them in inoffensive colours, but a kind of punishing ugliness prevailed when she tackled carpets and wallpapers for the rooms to be inhabited by her children and her domestics. Living in a chronic state of overdraft, she hoped that her move to Peverel would be an economy, supported in this hope by the undeniable fact that she was exchanging a house the number of whose bedrooms was said to be about thirty for a house whose bedrooms, added up with equal vagueness, numbered about fifteen. This contraction brought a variation of Gresham's Law into operation, good furniture being increasingly driven out by bad. Somewhere buried in Peverel Court's proliferation of gables and bow-windows the outline of a snug red-brick Buckinghamshire farm-house could be observed, but this had lost its identity and exercised no influence for good.

Inside the muddled building the woodwork of the front hall was of varnished pitch-pine, and the staircase walls were scarred by the shield-shaped mounts that had supported the Small-Game trophies shot by previous residents. Allowed to choose the décor I ordained white paint, and what I hoped would be a subtle shade of misty blue for the walls. Unhappily the result was an unattractive shade of indigo, which, combined with the white woodwork, gave the staircase the air of a Victorian rectory which had become a hospital, a resemblance increased by the flowing white veil of the nurse who was caring for my mother during this first autumn in our new home.

As I write I am conscious that I am evading the moment of facing the circumstances in which I then lived. My mother was supposedly convalescent after a shattering operation, carried out for a complaint which had added another, and eventually fatal, ingredient to the burden of illness she had carried for so long. Even now, understanding much that youth and ignorance caused me, at the time, to remark without comprehending, I find it hard to disentangle the battles my mother fought against ill-health, and the battles she fought against her own highly nervous temperament. It was an added disadvantage that she regarded her intellectual gifts, which could have given her pleasure and distraction, as unimportant compared with her prowess at hockey and lawn tennis, games in which, as a girl, she had delighted. The label 'rheumatism' was used as an explanation for her lameness and the stiffness of her hands. Subsequently,

I learnt that she had fallen downstairs over a dustpan and brush left by a negligent house-maid, which accident had left her with a permanently damaged knee. When I came to read her diary I found also that a vaguely explained absence of some weeks from home in my childhood could be accounted for by an operation in which the removal of a number of gall-stones had been much resented by the patient, who had agreed to something less surgically drastic. My mother's courage in a life of constant and often excruciating pain was undefeated, but her horror of self-indulgence made her life even harder than her infirmities dictated, a situation aggravated by her distrust of open windows and sunlight. Outdoors, she considered, was the correct place for fresh air, but the faintest risk of a *coup de soleil* had to be guarded against by hats and gloves. Indoors too much heat was considered to be both a wicked waste of fuel and undesirably relaxing. This policy led, naturally, to an indoor climate of chilly fug, an ideal atmosphere for the encouragement of rheumatic demons, whose grip increased mercilessly with the years.

When my father was killed at Gallipoli my mother was only thirty-eight years old, but, as she once told me, her hands were already too badly crippled for her to have been able to play with her two youngest infants, my sister Julia and myself. I have one recollection of seeing her ride a bicycle, as I watched from the window of our Irish nursery. Otherwise I can recall no time in my life when she walked without a stick, often exchanged for crutches. Undeterred she kept goal in family games of hockey, and only abandoned striving to defeat her children at tennis when it became clear that they were embarrassed by having to conceal the ease with which they were winning. In spite of these obvious handicaps, my mother treated her infirm condition as a temporary state, not to be referred to, and towards which offers of help would be unwelcome. A passionate desire for privacy, and a phenomenal reticence about bodily functions, kept her growing family at arm's length, a distance that sometimes became so far stretched that the methods of an Oriental court had to be resorted to when an interview became essential. A suppliant's ambush on the staircase was more likely to be favourably received than an untimely appearance in the inner sanctum of 'her ladyship's sitting-room'. In extreme cases it was not unknown for a wish to be granted by a request that my mother could be quoted as refusing permission, relying on the genial side of her nature which rebelled at being publicly labelled a spoil-sport. The formidable barrier that protected her privacy was not lowered in her many dealings with the medical profession. Her advisers could get into disgrace not only if she considered them dilatory in effecting a cure, but also if they lapsed into undue facetiousness in the course of treatment.

Accustomed to my parent's reticence, her return from the London Clinic with a nurse in attendance made less impression on me than if she had not been in the habit of making frequent retreats into nursing homes for purposes never fully explained. On these occasions her lifeline for communicating with the outside world was through her maid, Annie Reason, who had come to my mother six months before my own birth. Her name gave a bizarre touch to her employer's statement of her plans. 'I am going to London with (or without) Reason.' Sometimes daughters would be invited to visit their mother, but only by appointment. Other visitors were banned, in my grandmother's case the ban including ignorance of the actual address of the nursing home. The cause of the ban was, I believe, annoyance on an occasion when my grandmother had had the temerity to leave a foot-rest, found useful by herself, at my mother's temporary residence. As I was frequently stabled with my grandmother during these periods of my mother's seclusion, I acquired a stone-walling technique in replying to sentences of some asperity which began, 'As I am not allowed to know your mother's address...'

Liking conversation in spite of her secretiveness, my mother, in the course of her experience of the medical profession, had acquired a wide range of anecdote supplied by her attendants. Fascinating details were revealed to my eager ears, as my mother took a keen interest in the financial intricacies of the establishments in which she spent so many weary weeks. She was also far from unresponsive to the emotional dramas of both the doctors and nurses with whom she was involved, and being a natural partisan heaped praise on the heroes and heroines, blame on the villains and villainesses, with a gusto that almost made up to me for all parties remaining for ever anonymous. Perhaps it was the knowledge that few secrets were left untold in the nursing world that incited my mother to keep her own nurse segregated from her family, confining this unhappy woman at mealtimes in a bleak little room inhabited by the telephone. Not unnaturally this separation was taken by its victim as a colossal social insult, nor did it achieve its object of preventing fraternization. With the first of a succession of nurses I formed a friendship, which included being given an explanation of my mother's condition. This deprives me of the excuse of ignorance in my neglectful behaviour towards my mother in the last years of her life. By this means I learnt that her condition after the operation from which she was slowly recovering had been so alarming that the doctors concerned insisted that she should give them a more accessible address of a next of kin than that of her eldest son, whose home was in an Ireland still unprovided with an air-service. Somehow I assumed that having survived this crisis there was no reason to suppose that she would not return to her previous state of courageous struggle against only too obvious crippledom. Although her nurse was uninhibited in rehearsing the details of my mother's condition, she shunned the words that might have led me to a true understanding of the struggle with which my mother was faced, a battle rendered harsher by treatment for her chronically bent knee, which, on looking back, must have been more agonizing than she should have been required to bear. I find it remarkable that I never discussed any of the aspects of my mother's last years with Annie Reason, from whom nothing was secret. Neither at the time, nor in the following four decades, when she remained within the circle of my immediate family, did we ever advert to the subject which the sufferer could not bear to discuss, posthumous loyalty operating an involuntary edict of silence.

In the old core of Peverel Court there was one cosy room which had belonged to the son of the previous residents, and still bore the name of Mr Dick's Room. This room had been allocated as a sitting-room to those of my mother's children who were still at home, one and a half in number as my younger sister was still a schoolgirl. A magnolia pushed its shiny leaves against the windows, framing a view over three flat miles of the Vale of Aylesbury to where the Chiltern Hills, rising sharply from the plain, guarded Metroland from the northward march of London. The schoolrooms of my childhood had been large, particularly the one in Co. Westmeath, where, as I have written elsewhere, it was possible for six people to live six relatively independent lives. But even in the schoolroom at North Aston Hall there had been sufficient space for three learners to have far more elbow-room than any school could have allowed, and the table in the centre was large enough to allow nine or ten players to compete at Racing Demon. There had also been room for three book cases and an upright piano. This instrument had taken a lot of punishment in its day, and appeared almost visibly startled when required occasionally to respond to a skilled hand. A considerable amount of discarding became necessary when moving into the smaller area offered by Mr Dick's Room, but two bookcases and the piano were forced into position, though the diminished floor-space obliged the inhabitants to move sideways like the Knave of Diamonds. Music was also supplied by a gramophone in a fumed-oak case, presented by my grandmother to my eldest brother Edward, ten years before. In those days gramophones depended on manual winding, so musical fanatics acquired calluses on the palms of their hands as well as aching muscles in their forearms. In the manner of large families my brother had outgrown his original choice of records which had then descended to his juniors. *Carmen, Peer Gynt* and *The Dance of the Sugar Plum Fairy* remained as mementoes when he took his bride to live in Co. Westmeath. He also left behind relics of his strongest phase of Irish Nationalism in the shape of records in which a powerful bass sang *O'Donnell Abu* and *The West's Asleep*. Perhaps he felt the less need of *O'Donnell Abu* as he was able to play it by ear, together with *Let Erin Remember the Days of Old*.

The ability to pick out tunes by ear had descended to Edward from my father's side of the family, a gift that, having passed to his firstborn, made no further impact on his children, fighting as it had to against a cosmic tone-deafness transmitted to my mother by my grandmother. Although I have referred to my grandmother's cheerful philistinism in furnishing her own home, she was a determined sight-seer, entirely prepared to admire buildings and pictures of all periods except the most *avant-garde*. Music was another matter, and, though in the course of a long and active social life lived in three continents, she must have been exposed to operas, concerts and private performances, like an unsuccessful inoculation music had not 'taken'. Only once did I hear her express any pleasure at a musical performance, which was when she described the exquisite sounds evoked by two players on the dual manual harpsichord in the library at Osterley, a pleasure unlikely to be encountered frequently.

In the curious limbo of my life at Peverel I played the piano for what must have seemed to anyone within earshot unnecessarily long periods, transferring the notes before my eyes to the notes beneath my fingers with some accuracy, but when I hit a wrong note it was my eyes rather than my ears that informed of the fact. The collection of music, except for a few numbers from such musical shows as *Show Boat* and *Follow Through*, had been amassed by chance, but I hammered away sturdily at carols, folk-songs and tunes from the back of *The Weekend Book*, which last were simply set with no pedantic complication of a bass clef. I supplied some hefty, if monotonous, chords to *Green Grow the Rushes O* and *All Through the Night*, but I never did find out how to play *Auprès de ma Blonde* in 'strict marching time'. These musical exercises would fill in the time on days when, except for brief chats with my mother, I had no occupation within doors, and no companion at my meals. I was sufficiently accustomed to this situation to be surprised when a cousin, who saw the table laid for my solitary dinner, with a napkin formally mitred and wine-glasses for which no wine was offered, burst into helpless laughter at what was to him a grotesque spectacle. Bored I may often have been, but in the process I did acquire the useful habit of being able to support my own company without undue depression.

Out of doors my life was livelier as I exercised Baalam, Frank's horse which was stabled at a neighbouring farm, where the farmer's daughters went out hunting with the three packs of hounds whose boundaries almost met at the gate of Peverel. Whenever there was an opportunity these brave girls followed hounds even if the quarry was only a drag or a carted stag.

Frank enjoyed a day's hunting, but, as his life at that date lacked a settled pattern, he found it seldom possible to spare the time for a sport which not only took place at points in the countryside difficult to reach, but was also at the mercy of frost, fog and the unsolved mystery of a fox's scent.

My father had been devoted to fox-hunting, with such a strong feeling of duty towards the Westmeath Hounds of which he was Master that he habitually rode to the kennels in order to ride on with hounds to the meet. This meant leaving home at a bleakly early hour, and leaving his new-wedded wife to fill the day as best she could in a strange Irish home. It was, I think, no comfort to my mother that her own mother had passed through precisely the same trial as a bride, transported from a lively family to a vast house and left there companionless. Self-pity was never a failing of my grandmother's, but, when she came to write her memoirs, there was a touch of sharpness as she dwelt briefly on this period of her life, mentioning hunting as a sport to which her husband was at that date 'much addicted'. When the huntsman blew his horn in the morn these folks, these bridegrooms, went hunting-ho, leaving only their fancy to dwell on their equivalent of Nancy. My mother attempted to show her wifely care by ordering a packet of sandwiches for my father, but she later discovered that these were invariably passed on to the poor man at the gate, in this case a roadmender. Consequently my mother's attitude towards the sport was marked by ambiguity. Sometimes she pressed hunting chocolate on me which I accepted gladly, being less ascetic than my father, whose hunting stocks, of a peculiarly complex design, were also handed out to me. On the other hand I was not infrequently given a talk on the theme that those women who could not afford to hunt were at least spared the embarrassment of wrecking plans for the day's sport by the onset of a menstrual period. The amount of physiological damage that might be done if this handicap should be ignored was variously estimated. Total sterility and an increase of capillary growth on the face were only two of the dooms that might be expected, though this attitude was contradicted by a doctor to whom, at the age of fifteen, I was taken for advice about monthly pains. In this medical man's opinion much less damage would be caused by a day across country than by reclining habitually on the sofa with a delicate air. Precautions to keep female functions from the notice of coarse males was a perpetual problem to my mother's generation, with the exception of birth, at which the absence of a husband was considered somewhat improper. Military manoeuvres pre-empted my father at the birth of my sister Mary, who was born in August, but when the next baby was expected, in March four years later, he was snatched back from a day with the Bicester, after his horses had already been boxed on by train. My mother owned that this had been a false alarm, but she was sufficiently unrepentant to send my father out, eighteen days after my birth, to buy a toothbrush for his fifth child. He found the object specified to be unobtainable, only realizing why when he noticed that the date was April the First.

My mother herself had never experienced the rigours of the hunting field, her nerve for riding having been broken by a savage horse she had been obliged to ride as a girl. She had, however, enjoyed following hounds by road, driving a pony carriage, and from these experiences, she had retained the taboo that no lady, particularly no young lady, could go out hunting alone. Fortunately I was able to create the impression that I hunted surrounded by a cloud of the Terry family with whom Frank's horse was boarded. It was to their farmhouse that I drove on hunting mornings, and it was in their farmyard that the pre-hunting nerves of the horses were exacerbated by an undertow of small black and white terrier bitches, any one of which seemed liable to come on heat and attract the only too welcome advances of unsuitable local *partis*. So much of the Miss Terrys' lives were spent in the saddle that they had no need of the hot baths in which lesser mortals soaked their limbs after a day in the hunting field, only choosing to have a bath the night before so as to present a well-washed appearance in hospital should accident befall them. Through this connection I made a number of acquaintances with whom I would hack home in that happy state of relaxation, when anticipation of the perils of the day had given way to anticipation of tea and poached eggs. Among my hunting companions I found the landlord of the Bell Hotel at Aylesbury the most intellectually surprising. As we jog-trotted along the cruel tarmac he began describing his travels, which had led him to Petra, and though it was obviously inevitable that he should quote Dean Burgon's lines, it was enjoyable to hear them from a Surtees style of rider, who had a face only less vivid in hue than the ginger whiskers which sprouted like ferns from under his bowler-hat.

The mornings of these hunting days would begin with a jog through the dank cold that hangs over the Vale of Aylesbury in winter, with the horses fidgeting in the knowledge that they were out for more than exercise while their breath wavered in warm streams from their nostrils. As we rode up into the foothills, a sudden splash of sunlight would break through the mist and turn the towers of Waddesdon Park into a fairy castle made from icing sugar. The actual park surrounding the house was a favourite refuge for foxes, and once among the bushes the hunted could laugh at the hunters as they jostled along the rides where statues, wrapped in sacking against the frosts of winter, stood sentinel like ghosts.

I have never regarded myself as physically stalwart, but on reflection I think I must, when young, have had unsuspected powers of endurance, demonstrated by an ability to ride on to the meet, sometimes an hour's ride, and to ride back to the haven of the Terrys' farmyard only as night began to fall. Having learnt to restrict fluid intake at breakfast to half a cup of tea, I seldom needed to get off my horse during the day, but I was useful in holding the horses of other ladies who wished to retire behind hedge or haystack. There was a gruesome legend about a girl who came out with the Whaddon Chase. She was reputed to have exercised an unwise continence, rupturing her bladder as she jumped the last fence of a run. I was prepared to risk even a fate so terrible rather than to face the problem of regaining the slippery heights of my side-saddle. Fortunately I have to be dressed with extreme inappropriateness before I suffer from embarrassment, so I was hardly abashed by a riding habit that had seen great days with the Meath Hounds when it had belonged to an aunt, and riding-boots from my mother's trousseau, which had mouldered treeless for thirty years, and now lay in concertinaed folds round my ankles.

My cheerful acceptance of an outfit with such a long pedigree may have been an example of inherited sang-froid, for my father's carelessness in matters of dress had been notorious in his lifetime. Even after his death hard-pressed gossip-writers would come up with a story that, when he was accused of a lack of harmony between his boots and his breeches, he excused it by explaining that his bootmaker was a Fenian and his tailor an Orangeman. I learnt that this story was not entirely legend when the spinster ruler of a local clan introduced her brother to me, at his request, he having been a friend of my father's. Leaning back in his saddle with a jovial air, this gentleman began to tell me his memories, 'I remember old Tom Longford very well, out hunting there was always a great gap of hairy tummy between his breeches and his waistcoat.' What political excuse for this particular sartorial lapse my father might have given I do not know, but, accustomed as I was to hearing him spoken of only as a fallen hero, I found this Rabelaisian approach daring but refreshing. My own prowess in the hunting field was still assisted by the courage of ignorance and the stout heart of Frank's horse Baalam. He seldom refused any obstacle before him, and indeed once took the law into his own hands carrying me over a five-barred gate in front of the Bicester Field at a moment when it was questionable if hounds were actually running. He also heaved me out of a brook into which we had inadvertently landed, my lack of experience preventing me from realizing that it would have been correct to cast myself from the saddle. This delay brought me, if not up with hounds, at least up with the Master and with the Huntsman, who was trying to open an LMS railway gate with a key supplied by the LNER. The Master had just blasted a member of the Field who had, with great good sense, begun to take the gate off its hinges. When this proved to be the only solution for crossing the railway line and rejoining hounds, the Master issued something like an apology, which was such a rare jewel coming from him that its recipient cherished the apology, and me as its witness, for ever and a day.

Looking at my photograph album which illustrates this period, I am not only appalled by the exquisite unfunniness of the captions written under the photographs, I am astounded by the collection of Hunt Ball programmes, preserved from a succession of Hunt Balls which appear to have filled my winter. Without this indisputable evidence I should have insisted that I was leading the life of a sequestered princess, a Lady of Shalott in whose mirror nothing was reflected except, metaphorically speaking, the fields of barley and of rye. Each of these dainty cardboard folders represented not only a ball but a stay in a country house of at least two days. (At home my mother had not exactly abandoned the idea of having a party for a Hunt Ball, but had only bent her mind to considering where the mother of some girl who must come to chaperone the party should sleep, and also where the maid of this mother and daughter should be stowed, which was far from being my own approach to a house-party.) I can only suppose that the boredom of the gaps between these parties overflowed into the days of enjoyment, and swamped them in my recollection. Or perhaps the agonies which attended some of the nights in County Hall or country mansion have left subconscious scars that I wish to forget.

Draped in an aquamarine dress, its decorous cut enlivened by a knotted string of pearls from Woolworth's, I descended to dinner in the homes of my friends in the hope that my vitality, my wit, my sex-appeal, would all be running sufficiently high to keep me supplied with partners throughout the evening. Each name scribbled in the programme represented a guard against the doom of sitting in obvious neglect, or spending a spell in the chill, moral and physical, of the cloakroom. In my own case my habit of using green face powder meant that a prolonged session before the cloakroom looking-glass would send me in search of my next partner with a countenance reminiscent of Pagliacci. In a strange country there was the additional horror of only being acquainted with one's own house party. There was not, as in London, an easy escape route, and it was a cruel fate to have to rely on four young men, perhaps never seen before, to fill a programme of twenty-four dances. Only a *coup de foudre* would have brought the sort of young men I used to meet to the point of at once writing their names against the six dances which cold arithmetic would require of them during the evening. *Dancing With Tears in my Eyes* was the hit tune of that autumn, to me a wildly inappropriate lyric. I had tears in my eyes, certainly, but only when I was not dancing. However at one County Assembly I did have the good fortune to stay in the house in which the ball was to be held, so that during a partnerless spell I was able to retreat to my bedroom and write letters. There was, however, a hazard on the way in the shape of a couple who had seated themselves on the top step of the old oak staircase that led to my bedroom. The scarlet-coated gentleman was stretched to his full length, covering half a flight, but whether he was expressing his love, or his intention to ride away, the lady beside him remained demurely upright.

On this occasion my own evasion was undetected, unlike that of a cousin of mine who, as a promising eldest son, was accustomed to preferential treatment from his hostesses. Finding the ball at the house in which he was staying to be of an intolerable boredom, he retired to his bedroom, an icy chamber in a row of attics reserved for bachelors. Putting a match to a fire that was laid but not lit, he not only filled the room with smoke, but sent black clouds billowing along the corridor to a staircase populated by sitters-out. Accidentally or by design the chimney of his bedroom's fireplace was totally obstructed. His action might be said to have drawn unkind attention not only to his hosts' unwillingness to warm their guests, but to their hypocrisy in causing a fire to be laid that could not be lit. Sainte Thérèse of Lisieux, I once read, went on record that her greatest suffering in her religious life had been from cold. She might have been more acclimatized had she spent her childhood in English country houses. Besides suffering from chilliness there were other, more personal, ways in which a guest could feel discomfort. Fortunately for myself what Doctor Johnson called 'stark insensibility' prevented me from being unduly abashed when I found I was under a cloud from putting forward my views on art too forcibly, smoking in my bedroom or indulging in High Church practices on Sunday. But even my carapace was pierced by the sharply obvious displeasure of one particular host, when I defeated him with tactless ease in a game of ping-pong to which he had challenged me.

In that winter the greatest change in my life came from circumstances concerning the pattern of my cousins' lives, and the closing of Middleton Park. This house had to my mother represented the most solid background of her childhood. Osterley Park whose blue domes emerge from a girdle of cedar trees above pink brickwork glowing free of any creeper – Henry James wrote 'like a beautiful woman scorning to wear a veil' – that house meant beauty and all the pleasures of June. Sailing to Australia, and passing through what she assured us was the worst typhoon of a generation, she had striven to keep her sufferings at bay by concentrating on summer days at Osterley. She had an equally great but different affection for the house her father owned on the hills above Briton Ferry. This house, Baglan, looked out across the Bristol Channel, while Aberavon towered in the background. Immediately below throbbed the busy industrial life of South Wales, stimulating to children coming from the flat fields of the Bicester countryside. Trains rumbled and shrieked continuously, but this did not hinder my mother from regarding Baglan as the wildest of wild Wales. When she presented the view to my father he, bred among empty hills and pastures, remarked that it was the busiest scene he had ever beheld. Besides the charm of the picturesque, the pleasure of Baglan was enhanced for the children by being sent there without their parents. Simultaneously they were relieved of the pressure imposed by their intensely active, public-spirited mother, and the ever-simmering wrath of their father, whose own unhappy childhood had not taught him tolerance towards his female offspring. If Osterley was romance, if Baglan spelt freedom, then to my mother Middleton was essentially home, beyond criticism or qualification.

2. Restlessness and Rootlessness

ONE OF THE FEW RESEMBLANCES between my own young days and those of my mother was that we each passed four years at home between growing up and marrying, but the years themselves went by in a manner totally dissimilar. In fact, one of the difficulties in persuading my mother to appreciate my point of view was her failure to grasp that the alchemy of time had dissolved the pattern of life which she regarded as correct for a well-born young lady. Additionally, she had herself developed a congenital restlessness, which had the effect of keeping me also on the move, in an existence whose shapelessness seemed to me to be surpassed only by its rootlessness. Things did not, of course, look like that to my mother, whose own peregrinations were frequently caused by her efforts to fight her ill-health, and so were regarded as exceptional. Although not infrequently required to make myself scarce, there were also moments when my absence was regarded as a desertion, showing a lack of appreciation for the home provided for me, but the rules changed with such suddenness that I developed a sympathy for Pavlov's dog confused by contradictory signs. The saying that home is a place from which one cannot be shut out lacked conviction for those seeking shelter at Peverel Court.

My mother's own roots were deeply fixed. The four years between the ages of eighteen and twenty-two had rolled by against a background as repetitious as the rotation of the seasons. A winter in Oxfordshire would be followed by a summer in London, with fortnightly garden parties at Osterley, when on Saturday afternoon the number of weekend guests would swell to a crowd of two hundred and more. In between whiles there was a constant flow of schoolchildren and groups from charitable organizations, who came to romp under the cedar trees or to be rowed on the lake by the daughters of the house. As far as the schoolchildren were concerned, my grandmother said there could be few children in the County of Middlesex who had not received a prize from her hands.

At Middleton the pressure was not so great, but there were clothing clubs and mothers' meetings to be supervised in a village that lay at the end of a mile-long drive. Down this drive some of the earliest bicycles to be seen in Oxfordshire had been ridden by the Ladies Villiers, solid contraptions with fixed wheels, which, like so much in her youth, set my mother's standard for the correct. The introduction of freewheels found her begging her own children always to pedal downhill and not risk their necks experimenting with this newfangled invention. My grandmother did not bicycle, but drove out every afternoon in a carriage and pair. If she returned early she might take a turn in the woods, but her daughters who knew all the paths that led to sudden patches of wilderness or vistas down far-flung avenues, found that their mother had no idea of the fascination of the landscape in which she lived. A traveller and sightseer from her earliest years, at home she confined her energies to intellectual pleasures and the enjoyment to be derived from entertaining. She regarded private theatricals as the most enjoyable of indoor sports, an enjoyment which did not descend to my mother nor to Arthur her younger brother.

At house parties in the Christmas holidays, neighbours would be invited as audience to productions which had been staged after long and savage arguments between the performers. Finally, my grandfather insisted that play acting should cease for ever, after the leading man had forgotten to give the schoolboy Arthur the cue for his solitary one-line speech, and instead had waved Arthur contemptuously from the stage. This ban was an acute relief to my mother personally, and all Arthur's adoring sisters felt it a just retribution for the leading man's brutality to a family pet.

More usually the stories about my grandfather showed him as an irritable Zeus, from whose hand thunderbolts were hurled out of a blue sky on to his cowering daughters. Son of a mother whose lovers' names were said to have been legion and great-grandson of a mistress of George the Fourth, he was reported to discourage his tenants from harbouring daughters pregnant with illegitimate children. His attitude towards the evils of Sunday dissipation was equally stringent, the leases he granted prohibiting Sunday opening in perpetuity. It is true, however, that there were stories in which he displayed more humane feelings. Once at Osterley he had come across two footmen staggering under the weight of a cabin trunk, the luggage of a transatlantic visitor invited for a weekend. This lady, he told my grandmother, was never to be invited again, the burden she laid on footmen's backs being greater than they should be asked to bear. If the unhappy lady did, in fact, expect a second invitation, and spent any time in agonized contemplation as to where her mistake had been made, it is sadly unlikely that she deduced that her desire to shine sartorially had been her undoing.

In her memoirs my grandmother described the distinguished people she entertained with the gusto of an indiscriminate enjoyer of any social occasion. Henry James's long story *The*

Lesson of the Master opens with an account of a Sunday under the cedar trees on the lawn at Osterley, but when he sent a copy to his hostess, admitting his debt for the background, he denied that he had made use of what he called 'the human furniture'. Making every allowance for a novelist's right to compound one character from different aspects of many, observed and transformed by creative processes, I have never been convinced that there was not an element of self-protection in James's disclaimer. The hostess of Summersoft (Osterley) who remarked that the perilously delicate wife of the Master, the literary lion, 'Really oughtn't to come to one at all,' expressed a sentiment that was not alien to my grandmother, who accepted childbirth as a permissible weakness of the flesh and allowed typhoid fever, which she had once contracted, to be a serious complaint, but regarded other physical frailties as matters to be suppressed socially.

The Cabinet ministers and generals who frequented my grandmother gave her children an education in public affairs, but the poets and novelists who were her friends did not open a window for them into the literary world. They were young children when Henry James, Augustus Hare and James Russell Lowell were growing rapidly older, and, though Lord Salisbury and Joseph Chamberlain might be replaced by Lord Curzon and Lord Kitchener, the literary tide went out never to come in again. On the other hand my mother and her sisters were ceaseless readers, but they did not, I think, share their literary tastes with their mother. Later there came a split in the family, when my mother found herself alone in buying every book she wished to read while her mother and sisters relied on lending libraries. It was never quite clear to me why my mother shunned these admirable institutions, but I suspect that she considered books that had been passed through unknown hands would convey dirt and germs. Consequently a forest of books grew up round her, overflowing from the room formally designated as the library and creeping ever higher along her sitting-room walls. Inevitably, owing to her horror of indelicacy, some of the books she bought seemed to her unsuitable for public display, and these were secluded in a bookcase with glass doors and a lock that easily yielded to a little persuasion. Known as the Obscene Bookcase, the segregation of its contents saved much time in searching for reading matter more free-spoken than that to be found on the open shelves. Finally the name slipped out in front of my mother herself, who with a touch of the geniality that made her charming at unexpected moments, showed a distinct tendency to giggle at the realization that her system of library censorship had been remarked and circumvented. When she made her move from North Aston Hall to the lesser space of Peverel Court the man who came to estimate for the move concluded with a wail of despair, 'And then there are the books. I think there's a million.'

For three years my grandmother was cut off from the delights of London Life, social and intellectual, while my grandfather was governing New South Wales. Although this period had included a delectable visit to Vailima, which her host Robert Louis Stevenson celebrated in complimentary verse, it was with thankfulness that, in the summer of 1893, she found herself back in England. At once she launched her eldest daughter Markie – the family abbreviation for Margaret – into the last balls of the London Season, with a warning that she must not expect to dance more than once or twice in an evening. On the contrary partners crowded round the newcomer, who for the next five years danced like a wave of the sea. My Aunt Markie was baffled as to why her mother had prophesied such ill-success for her eldest daughter, until she recollected that my grandmother had been responsible for chaperoning a much younger sister at many a dreary ball, when my Great-Aunt

Cordie, a shy enemy of frivolity, had remained a deeply embedded wallflower.

Different problems faced my grandmother concerning Aunt Markie. She confided to grand-daughters, in later years, that she had been obliged to point out that it would not be possible for Aunt Markie to marry more than one of the admirers who buzzed round this honey pot. Naturally some of the aspirants were more eligible than others. One even showed his awareness that he might be considered a long odds starter by quoting from the gospel he had heard in church the previous Sunday, 'Mind not high things but condescend to men of low estate,' as applicable to the girl he was courting. The eligible proposal finally to be accepted was made on the roof at Osterley against a background of Palladian domes. It was the prelude to half a century of devoted married life, in spite of being interrupted at the crucial moment by my mother. She, despairing of interesting a shy young visitor in the Gobelins tapestries and Angelica Kaufmann decorations of the state rooms, had thought that a tour of the roof might keep boredom at bay. When the emotional dust raised by the engagement had settled, my grandmother showed her feeling of relief by boasting that at Osterley chaperones were provided even on the roof.

If her elder sister was in trouble for becoming engaged too frequently, my mother was implicitly criticized for not becoming engaged at all. The tallest of the sisters, she had ash blonde hair and a slightly cat-like cast of countenance, an appearance descending from an ancestor, William Chiffinch, Keeper to the Closet to Charles II. In his portrait by Gerald Soest in the Dulwich Gallery, Chiffinch looks infinitely capable of handling such a delicate appointment and his physical resemblance to my mother's father transcends the long hair and negligent shirt front dictated by the fashions of the 1670s. Shy though she considered herself to be, my mother had no difficulty in getting on well with her partners at dances or on the tennis-court. But with a younger sister approaching the age when she would be leaving the schoolroom it seemed time, to my grandmother's circle, that Mary should be thinking seriously of her future, and the husband with whom she might hope to share it.

As the eldest in her own large family my grandmother had occupied a position of power unchallenged by parents or sisters, but that did not lead her to think that daughters should be discouraged from matrimony by undue cosseting at home. On winter evenings fires blazed in the sitting-rooms of herself, her husband and her eldest son, who lived on a pedestal high above criticism, while unmarried daughters (like Fanny Price in *Mansfield Park*) sat and sewed in front of the bright bars of an empty grate. To further the cause of matrimony my mother was given an opportunity to show her paces unhampered by rivals at a house-party which Lady Salisbury, whose husband had recently been Prime Minister, gave at Hatfield House. Possibly Lady Galloway, a dear friend of my grandmother's and a generous godmother to my mother, may have had some hand in the arrangement, she being Lord Salisbury's half-sister, but in any case my mother was the only young girl present in a house-party fielding a hand-picked team of eligible eldest sons. In a flashlight photograph that has survived of such an occasion my mother, her fringe curled in a rigid wave, is shuffling a pack of cards while two young men look on with respectful interest. According to her own account, her hostess had arranged that the young people should bicycle over to a neighbouring stately home, but feeling, most unjustifiably, that she might be an impediment to the party's speed my mother chose to stay behind and spent the afternoon sitting in a boat on the lake with a young man she described as 'Lord Salisbury's red haired Scotch secretary', as it were a joker in the pack that my mother had been shuffling.

One of the *partis* brought to meet my mother at Hatfield had already come into his inheritance. Accompanied by her parents my mother visited his house, which lay under the shadow of the Malvern Hills and was itself reflected in a moat. My mother viewed this house with considerable favour, being particularly impressed by the ingenuity with which tapestries had been hung some inches from the host's bedroom walls, so that he could lie in bed and watch the embroidered pictures swaying in the firelight. This fancy was, it should be mentioned, shown to all the guests in a tour of the house and not to my mother *tête-à-tête*. Lord Longford, a second cousin of the host, was among the house-party, and in an inspection of the home farm my mother mentally catalogued him as an aimable Lifeguardsman, principally interested in agriculture. It was a surprise to her to find that he read almost more constantly than she did herself, and indeed more widely, as his education at Winchester had given him an abiding affection for ancient literature which he continued to read in Latin and Greek. On the journey home after this visit, Lord Longford shared a railway carriage with the Jerseys and their daughter. At Swindon for some reason, connected perhaps with the remoteness of the next meal, it seemed desirable that buns should be obtained from the station buffet. Avid for exercise, my mother sprinted down the platform, and raced back again with a bag of buns perilously near to bursting. Later she learnt that her dashing turn of speed had suggested a vision of Atalanta to the man who was to be her husband.

By the summer of 1899 Lord Longford had become one of my mother's most talkative dancing partners. As he was in his middle thirties, an attendance at balls was deduced by the elder generation to have an object, one of the observers being even percipient enough to remark who the object would appear to be. My mother had not, herself, arrived at such an advanced estimation of Lord Longford's intentions, but when he appeared, uninvited, at tea-time on a Sunday in May, she realized that here was yet another crisis of romance to be staged at Osterley. My father's proposal was not offered on the roof, or even in the boat chosen by another suitor as propitious, but in principle matters were settled during a stroll round the Long Walk, a secluded path which circled a wide-skirted mead. My grandmother, whose attitude towards followers of her daughters varied from over-zealous promotion or discouragement to total unperception, found nothing surprising in the arrival of this uninvited bachelor although, according to my mother, no one else had ever so dared to intrude on the Osterley tea-table. Preoccupied by a crowd of guests, my grandmother said a hospitable if vague good-bye, adding a conventional, 'Do come again'. For this her husband reproved her. 'Why did you ask that Irish person, Lord Somebody to come again?' he grumbled, 'He'll be wanting to marry Mary next.' That evening Mary felt it correct to inform her parents that to marry her was exactly what that Irish person did want to do.

I have gone into some detail in describing my mother's background and the history of her engagement to my father because without this glance into a past now buried beneath the sands of time much of my mother's behaviour might appear bewilderingly irrational. Having enjoyed this charming story of the betrothal, I was myself bewildered when I discovered that to my mother it had ushered in a period when joy was far from unconfined. The marriage was arranged for November, to allow time for the first of the next generation, a son and heir, to be born to the pair who had become engaged on the roof at Osterley. Time was also needed for the recovery of the mother, to whom, in the practice of the day as dictated by fashionable midwives, it was forbidden to set foot to the ground for three weeks. Thus there was a period of months in which feelings of regret at the end of girlhood could build up.

In her home my mother's strongest affections had been held by her younger sister Beatrice and her younger brother Arthur, both of whom showed little enthusiasm for a marriage that would remove so devoted a sister. Beatrice was presented by the fiancés with an opal ring, she being October born and so immune from the doom opals are said to bring. Arthur, visited at school, was sufficiently magnanimous to buy a sponge cake for my mother's delectation at tea, but resignation rather than enthusiasm continued to be the attitude of both sister and brother. During this last summer holiday Arthur was smitten with German measles. While recovering himself he noticed that my mother was coming out with the same rash, but he forbore to call attention to her condition. He knew she planned to go out cub-hunting on foot at peep of day, and he did not wish to spoil her enjoyment, a reticence characteristic of himself and of his relationship with my mother. She was touched by his thoughtfulness but cherished a grudge against the unromantic attack of *roseola epidemica* which interrupted her enjoyment of her last days before she left for a new home, over the sea and unvisited before.

When I learnt that my mother had never visited Pakenham Hall until she drove there as a bride on top of the station omnibus, estate workers replacing the horses for the final stretch of road, I was astonished. To me, young and aggressive, it seemed an outrage that she should have been given no earlier sight of her future home. On reflection, I now see that she would have been unlikely to have broken off her engagement had the house not been to her taste, and it was probably sensible for her to arrive as a wife, rather than a prospective daughter-in-law. She never found this position congenial, as her husband's mother, retreating to a dowager's existence in a house in Bruton Street heavy with family associations, conducted a kind of long-range domestic fussing that my mother found irksome. Granny, my father's mother, limited her conversation to domestic servants and her own kinsfolk. She was, according to her daughter-in-law, fond of remarking that her mother had been a Fitzroy, signifying that she descended, if illegitimately, from Charles II. Granny's approach to genealogy was obviously selective, for though descendants of Charles II by way of Henrietta Maria and Marie de Medici can claim the great Florentine art patrons as their ancestors, they also have to accept Darnley, husband of Mary Queen of Scots, as a forbear. This is a corrective to any excessive pride in ancestry, for though the guilt for Darnley's murder may still be a matter for argument, the fact that he deserved his fate has rarely been disputed.¶

My mother's reluctance to leave her home was, as time went on, reduced by her increasing appreciation of the kindness of my father's character. She had grown up with a father who was generous on birthdays, giving his daughters sapphire brooches and jewelled umbrella handles, but in between whiles his barometric reading was stormy. Even when his daughters had married they found it wise to have an agreement among themselves that if advanced in pregnancy or recovering from childbirth they should protect one another from the ordeal of a game of cards with their choleric parent. My father was an equally generous present-giver, but though doubtless well able to raise his voice in anger when military necessity or the chances of the hunting field required it, he had a capacity for self-restraint that even survived the trial of a sister-in-law smashing the wing of his new pony carriage. Expecting the hurricane of displeasure that would have blown in her father's house at such an accident, the culprit experienced a stunned admiration when not a word was said to reproach her for spoiling the varnish of what had been a cherished new toy.

I have already written of the early days of my parents' marriage when my mother found how seriously my father took his duties as a master of foxhounds. She was soon to find that his career as a soldier was an even greater enemy to a settled matrimonial life. Inside a half-hoop ring of emeralds and diamonds there are engraved the dates of my father's service in the South African War, to which he sailed four months after his wedding. For the following eight months my mother led the life of neither wife nor maid, until my father, wounded and recovering from the typhoid fever that killed a quarter of that war's casualties, returned home as a convalescent. This was not a condition with which my mother was familiar, but she accepted the idea that Brighton was the correct place for recuperation. Essentially a child of the Midlands, Brighton was to her imagination a fishing village that had been made fashionable by the Prince Regent. She got a shock when the train puffed through the rows of undistinguished terrace houses which, even at that date, had begun to flood backwards into the Downs. When my father returned for a second spell of duty in South Africa my mother was in the early stages of her first pregnancy, the end of the war and the birth of my brother Edward following hard upon each other.

During the next fifteen years it seems that my parents and their children, whose number increased to six, seldom spent more than three months in any one place, and as their family grew the moves became ever more like migrations. My father was, I believe, fond of the Victorian ballad *Mrs Brown's Luggage*, which begins 'We're on the move, We're on the move, The van is at the door,' and ends 'Brown paper parcels, only just a few, The perambulator and a bath and the poor old cockatoo,' and he must have had frequent cause to sing it. Backwards and forwards across the Irish Channel the caravan would roll, returning for a vast family Christmas party at

Middleton, to London for the season and to country houses rented to be convenient for my father's military commitments. My mother, like Tristram Shandy's, was always determined to lie-in in London, on the grounds that London was a useful birthplace when it came to filling in forms. Possibly she had also a subconscious wish to erode the amount of time she was required to spend in her Irish home, towards which her attitude was, to say the least, ambivalent. Undaunted, indeed stimulated, by the political troubles that eventually erupted, she never, it seemed to me, had managed to settle herself in Pakenham Hall, which a century earlier had struck Maria Edgeworth, a neighbour and cousin, as a nest that only needed a bird. My mother's health encouraged a restlessness which increased when she became a widow, and she continued to follow a pattern in which six moves *en masse* during the year were infilled by sudden journeys on her own account. My eldest brother's marriage freed her from the need to face a twice-yearly trek to Ireland, but it did not seem that she consequently reduced the number of her comings and goings.

My mother's mobility brought into my own life a rootlessness which was in some cases an alibi, useful when I was requested to start a local company of Girl Guides, but more generally a handicap to any but short-term planning. Even immediate plans were complicated by my mother's failure to grasp not only the change of customs in the world she regarded as her own, but the change in the circumstances in which she herself was living. If Julia and I complained that the local children on their way home from school shouted mocking abuse when our paths crossed, she derided our foolishness in not asking them why, and at whom, they were shouting. The reduction of her establishment to such an undistinguished residence as Peverel Court had in no way reduced her belief that her daughters should be able to bring the force of their personalities to bear on ribald schoolchildren. She did not conceive of a situation in which there was no background of imposing houses and wide estates, no father who was both landlord and employer of the fathers of the malaperts. All recreations and pleasures that she thought suitable for a girl of my age depended on a spacious way of life which, as far as I was concerned, had evaporated like the dew of the morning. My mother's own eyes were ever fixed on the lost Paradise of Middleton, still at that date much as she had known it, every drive and avenue sacred to the bicycle rides of the past, the Heyford and Oxford Lodges having an almost mystical significance, which she could hardly believe I found difficult to appreciate.

3. Farewell to the Ghosts of Middleton

I DID, HOWEVER, REAP CONSIDERABLE benefit from my mother's attitude, she being quite unconcerned if I disappeared into the Vale of Aylesbury for hours, or even for days, provided she was assured that I was heading for Middleton, that haven of all good things. This tolerance was carried so far that entertaining Oxford undergraduates to luncheon, banned at home in my mother's absence, became by some social alchemy perfectly correct at Middleton, even in the absence of my aunt, the mother of my cousin and contemporary Joan. When I protested at this anomaly my mother rode me off with a shocking history of an unchaperoned party of young people, famed for their wildness, holding a midnight bathing party – nudity suspected though not stated. This orgy had been watched by a former dancing partner of her own, who actually had to leave the country soon after she told me this. I failed to convince her that the story reflected worse on the *voyeur* than the bathers, nor would she accept that midwinter in Buckinghamshire was unlikely to lead to moonlight bathing. No one knew better than my mother how remote the nurseries at Middleton were from the library and drawing-room, but I have an idea that she considered that the existence of a nursery, in which a nanny was tending the children of my aunt's second marriage, constituted a kind of chaperonage for the children of her first. Consequently Joan and I entertained our undergraduate acquaintances from Oxford University, only hindered by the periods when some misdemeanour or accident deprived them of their motor-cars. When Joan's eldest brother came of age he gave a large bachelor dinner party, and there was some delicacy in arranging that the two dons present should be at least technically unaware that two of the guests, having been gated by the University authorities, were, in fact, illegally present. This was, as it happened, my cousin Grandy Jersey's swan song at Middleton. His father, my mother's eldest brother, had died six years earlier, and, inheriting three estates, Grandy had decided to shorten his lines by closing Middleton and using Osterley as his home.

At Christmas my aunt assembled a last family party at Middleton, ranging in age from her two nursery children by her second marriage to her mother-in-law by her first, now in her eighty-second year. In between these extremes, ages and taste in activities overlapped. My Aunt Beatrice's husband, Lord Dunsany, for example, always preferred the company of his wife's nephews and nieces to that of his own contemporaries, and the mixture of enthusiasm with innocence in his character sometimes led him into behaviour that might have sent a psychiatrist scurrying to his note-book. On Christmas night a company of twenty or more, all connected by blood or wedlock, sat down to dinner at round tables. The fashion of the moment dictated that evening dresses should be slashed at the back to the level of the lowest vertebra that decency would allow, a pneumonia-inducing mode which in my own case necessitated stern work with safety-pins before my underclothes could be suppressed. From the crackers pulled at the end of dinner, Dunsany came into possession of a packet of beauty spots which immediately appealed to his imagination as offering an opportunity for instant art work. Turning towards the next table he found my bare back to be an ideal surface on which to experiment and began to ornament my shrinking shoulders with a pattern of *mouches*. As I proved ever more agile in scratching off the black patches, he began placing them in spots which he considered to be out of my reach. Incapable of moderating his voice in a situation that excited him, his shouts rapidly brought the conversation of the rest of the diners to a halt. Finally, when I had dislodged a beauty spot from under my right shoulder-blade with a double twist of my left arm, Dunsany let out a shattering yell. 'She must be a monkey! By Gad, she *is* a monkey!'

At the far end of the dining-room there hung a full-length portrait of my grandmother, painted when she was a bride. Her hands were clasped round her knee and her white satin gown swirled round her ankles in a foam of pleats and ruches. Her face wore an expression both interested and confident, and though her pose and her dress had been left far behind in the last century, a confident ability to cope with situations as they arose had remained with her. At this rowdy moment she turned to one of her neighbours at dinner, a baronet cousin of my aunt's, invited to spare him a lonely Christmas, and belonging in my eyes to my grandmother's generation, though he was, in fact, twenty years her junior. 'Tell me, Sir Vincent,' said Grandmama, 'You would know . . .' Whatever it was that Sir Vincent was required to know was lost in the general renewal of conversation, but my grandmother's social adroitness had undeniably brought the party back on to the rails of decorous behaviour after a perilous swerve.

My cousin Joan's talent for organization, and indeed her general enterprise, were famous in the family, ever since it had been found necessary to hold a village fête during the summer holidays in order to supply Joan with something to organize. All sporting events, an outing with the beagles, a university ice-hockey match, a meet of the drag hounds, could be sure of her enthusiastic support either as a spectator or as a participant. It was after a run with the Oxford Drag Hounds that her enthusiasm got slightly out of control when she promised the Master to give a home at Middleton to two hounds who had been found superfluous to the pack.

The matter had passed from Joan's mind when these rejects, named Sailor and Warwick, were suddenly delivered during breakfast to the front door, whose portico was ample enough to cover an entire pack. No plans having been made for their immediate future, there seemed little to be done with two hounds except to take them for a walk, and they were persuaded to follow us upstairs while we collected coats and walking shoes. The descent was less easy, for while Warwick fled down without disaster, Sailor developed acute scalaphobia. The staircase was stately, and the thick carpet gave little grip to the feet of those grappling with a reluctant full-grown hound. From the walls ancestors watched with painted calm as Joan and I wrestled with the perverse Sailor, finally abandoning him to the blandishments of a footman, while we pursued Warwick who had made a break for liberty.

We were checked by a doctor, who, as my grandmother would have said, was much addicted to hunting. He pointed out that Warwick, being an old Bicester hound, seconded to the Oxford Drag, would naturally be making for his old home, the Bicester Kennels, so we accepted that he would be unlikely to transfer his faithfulness to ourselves. The end of Warwick's story was reported by a cousin who photographed professionally for *The Field*. By coincidence he had an appointment that day to meet the Bicester Hounds, and had succeeded in grouping Master, hunt servants and hounds against a carefully chosen background when into their midst erupted Warwick, wrecking the picture and getting a savaging from his former mates.

Sailor lasted only slightly longer. He accomplished the almost impossible by making an enemy of Joan's mother Cynthia, who as a rule met the animal creation on equal terms, addressing fur and feather in tones of the warmest affection. She had been known to return from what was ostensibly a visit to a child at school with only a vague report of the child's scholastic progress, but with much delight at her afternoon's shopping at a pet shop which had lain in her path. A kitten had just seemed to her to be in need of a good home, while a pair of miniature water tortoises could hardly be said to cause much trouble, but she was most proud of two Japanese rabbits, christened by me Aldershot and Camberley on account of their upbrushed military moustaches. However, even Cynthia drew the line at Sailor, protesting that he ate ten shillings worth of food a week, and frequently bit the hand that fed him. Sailor faded out, but it would be wrong to give the impression that the dog population of Middleton was noticeably reduced.

There still remained a greyhound, and a pair of cocker spaniels, Josephine the bitch being of such an amorous disposition that, on heat and segregated at a boarding kennel, the kennel keeper had cause to write a letter beginning, 'That naughty Finey . . .' and going on to explain that her charge had crashed her way through a plate-glass window in her lust to find a mate, fortunately landing in a pen of her own breed. My aunt was also usually accompanied by what Saki called 'a ripple of Pekinese spaniel'. Frankie, the least of these, had decided to spend his life in the housekeeper's room, but, in a reversal of domestic custom, was brought each morning to the lady of the house for her to comb his inordinately long and tangled ears, the housekeeper's eyes being dim with age.

Weenie and Boydie were Cynthia's inseparable companions, bulletins concerning their digestive processes being left on the hall table among telephone messages from humans. Boydie, in particular, had a personality so impressive that a footman whom he had honoured with his favour was known ever afterwards as Boydie's William. When the news came that Boydie had been gathered to his Chinese ancestors Cynthia's children's nanny asked her employer to keep an ear open for any nursery noises, while she, the nanny, went on a mission to comfort one of Boydie's earlier handmaidens.

The closing of Middleton meant the end of the games of Slosh, a variety of snooker without the pyramid of crimson balls, of unsuccessful attempts to shoot pike with a rook rifle in the black waters of the leaf-strewn lake, and the end of days out hunting on hirelings, produced at the shortest notice by the Bonner stables at Bicester, Cecil, the son of the house, having unlimited patience with my inexperience. In the last weeks before the house was put into dust-sheets the feeling increased that past inhabitants of Middleton were still roaming its passages, along which generations of children had raced shrieking like express trains. The sad tale that a housemaid had drowned herself and her unwelcome baby in the water tank on the roof had been passed on to me in childhood, as an explanation for one ghostly presence, and I found what must have been a reference to the story in a letter of 1836 from Lady Palmerston to Princess Lieven. Lady Palmerston wrote that 'Lady Jersey talks of nothing but her wretched housemaid'. Lady Jersey, wife of the 4th Earl and famous as a hostess, could do little right in the eyes of Lady Palmerston. Lord Byron, on the other hand, enjoyed her hospitality, writing of Middleton as 'the pleasantest of all possible houses', and adding 'I prefer that where I am to all visiting residences'. This hostess was singular in remaining loyal to the poet, when he had been transformed by evil-tongued Rumour from Apollo the Sun God into Apollyon the Destroyer from the bottomless pit.

Ghosts began to quicken as if they knew they would soon be playing to an empty house. My cousin Mansel, sleeping in the room that had been his late father's dressing-room, saw the door open, and was aware that someone had entered and left the room without speaking. Joan, attended by Rob the greyhound, was passing through the billiard-room on her way to the telephone, when suddenly the balls on the darkened billiard-table took a life of their own and ran clicking against each other, Rob rushing from the room in canine panic. On my last evening in the house, three of us sat on a sofa in the library. This long room had recently been the background of bridge players, backgammon players and the whirr and rattle of a game in which a spinning top rotated among an array of skittles poised under arches composed of the straddled legs of goblins. Now, in silence, we watched the door at the far end of the room, for it seemed to us that many people were waiting in the drawing-room beyond. Spirits, as Hotspur remarked to Owen Glendower, are not always willing to come when summoned from the vasty deep, but had I known at the time how frequently Byron had been entertained at Middleton, I think I would have had listened especially for the uneven footstep of the poet, lingering after more than a century in the 'pleasantest of all possible houses'.

4. Two Dianas in the Irish Midlands

ALTHOUGH, AT MOMENTS, I WAS still capable of relapsing into the childish state of not knowing what to do with myself, situations more frequently arose when my mother found it difficult to know what to do with me. When her sixth child, my sister Julia, had been born, my mother wrote in her diary of her disappointment at having produced four daughters, three of them in sequence. She gloomily noted that four girls were a formidable tribe to be coped with if they did not marry, adding that she did not approve of women working. In this case she meant by 'women' females of private means, who would not be justified in taking the bread out of the mouths of those who needed to earn it. As she was also deeply suspicious of any life devoted to good works, it never became clear how she expected unmarried women of means to fill their days and retain, as it were, their amateur status. Paradoxically the daughter, whose birth had caused her to grumble at the prospect of an eternity of bringing up young girls with the fear that they might develop into old maids, became one of her more favourite children. Their relationship was not, however, without its stormy passages, when argument degenerated into cross words and eyes filled with tears of rage. In the earlier months of 1931 Julia did not, as it happened, present a problem, she being disposed of at school, where she was studying for the Oxford Entrance Examination. I, on the other hand, was in the position of a character in a play, stranded on an empty stage, while the dramatist, in this case my mother, was obliged to invent some business with which I could be occupied. Much the same problem faced Joan's mother, so between our parents a scheme for exporting us among our Irish kindred was put into operation. At the end of this tour it was expected that my mother would have emerged from the nursing home to which she had currently retired and that Joan's mother would have accomplished a house-moving of which the disposal of assorted animals was even more of a problem than the re-housing of assorted children.

After a visit to Pakenham our journey was to take us to Dunsany Castle, where the Meath Hunt Ball was to be held and where our kind aunt had promised us hirelings for the after-the-ball meet. Although her maternal uncle's home was in Ireland, Joan had not had such an extensive battering by the Irish Channel as had been my lot. I was impressed when I met her in the cruel light of a winter's dawn at Euston Station to find that she had taken precautions, unknown in my experience, to mitigate the rigours of the journey. She was escorted to the train by her family's chauffeur. He bore the charming name of Piggin, and carried a rug and a cushion, adjuncts of travel which I had imagined to have disappeared with the Edwardian era. In addition Joan had been given a flask of brandy and twenty pounds for travelling expenses. I, on the other hand, had only ten pounds with which to finance the emergencies of the journey, and nothing to keep me warm within or without. The rug and cushion certainly came in useful when their owner decided that the least sea-sick inducing spot in which to weather the crossing was in the shelter of a smoke stack on the top deck.

Ineffective in its purpose this situation also threatened us with acute chills from exposure, and Joan's state came close to collapse. A tot from the brandy flask gave her enough strength to seek shelter, but she was still frail and empty when we disembarked at Dun Laoghaire. Even when we reached Broadstone, where in those days the train for Mullingar – so evocatively labelled Galway and the West – had its starting-point, Joan's wan face made me feel nervously responsible. By a miracle the station refreshment room offered sponge cakes for sale. These cakes were a delicacy for which there appeared to be an hereditary fancy in the Villiers family, my mother, abnormally ascetic about eating, finding sponge cake irresistible. At the sight of the crisp, sugary husks above the rich yellow sponge Joan revived, while the train pounded across the flat levels of the Irish Midlands.

There is a poem celebrating the horror of the town of Kinnegad which begins:

> 'Longford is a dirty hole,
> On Boyle I leave my curse,
> Athlone is the devil's place
> And Mullingar is worse.'

In spite of this sweeping objurgation I have always been happy to arrive at Mullingar, and never was I more glad than on this February evening. Joan had no means of judging the town's aspect for when we had left the station, which being extensively tiled in white resembled the approach to a public lavatory, the few dim lamps slipped quickly away and the dark of an empty countryside lay beside us for fifteen miles. At the wheel was my family's chauffeur, White, who had been with my mother before he had settled with Edward and Christine on their marriage. By his domestic colleagues he was considered to give too much enthusiasm to his role of faithful retainer as he was, relatively speaking, a newcomer among them. It was as a newcomer that he had fetched Julia and me from some children's party, when heavy rain had necessitated him carrying us from doorstep to motor-car, an exploit to which he often referred, on this occasion bringing it up as part of his credentials for Joan's benefit. Actually, while in my mother's service, his most famous exploit had been to appear on the Fourth of June to drive my mother to Eton, wearing an Old Etonian tie, whether intentionally or not, no one had the nerve to inquire. Travelling backwards and forwards from Mullingar, White enjoyed an audience, captive and, owing to his habit of turning round to convey his choicest comments, highly nervous. Visitors, other than members of the family, were further confused when declarations of feudal devotion alternated with inquiries as to the possibility of a change of job for which he might be recommended.

In the days before the labour force that supplied large establishments had dried to a trickle, and the establishments themselves became greatly reduced in number, this form of restlessness was much more prevalent than might now be supposed. Even Andrews, who had graduated from being a footman in the household of an uncle to becoming butler to the young Lord and Lady Longford, showed occasional desire for change, which was however manifested in such a roundabout way that by the time his employers became aware of it he had decided to go about on another tack. In his earlier situation he had contracted a friendship with a ladies' maid, and in conversation with the younger members of my family he would sometimes dangle the possibility that she might lure him elsewhere, though in what capacity it was never quite clear. These bubbles of fancy soon dispersed, Andrews remaining a well-known local figure for thirty years. Indirectly he expressed contentment with his lot, by speaking with disdain of the work pattern at Buckingham Palace, where a former footman whom he had trained happened later to be employed.

In the kitchen the head of department was also a bequest from my mother. She ruled jointly with Andrews, until her brother, gardener at Dunsany Castle, retired and needed her as his housekeeper. Mrs Cruickshank reigned over a kitchen whose windows had been built to a near Venetian design, with a tall rounded centre flanked by two lesser arches. Through these the morning sun streamed on to burnished copper pots and pans, engraved with a coroneted initial, and seemed to be reflected in the wonderfully deep grey-blue eyes that looked out from under Mrs Cruickshank's helmet of iron-grey hair. In my mother's day Mrs Cruickshank had been the housekeeper. Had she been my mother's cook she would not have been encouraged to turn out meringues, pale golden paragons of deliciousness, nor would she have been enabled to send up eel pie and stuffed pike, only added to her repertoire when Edward took to fishing in Lough Derravaragh.

Not since time before my memory had I spent mid-winter days in the home of my ancestors, and I rather doubt that I had spent much time there at all in the winters of my infancy, my mother at my birth having established an English base. After he came of age Edward had put in electricity, replacing candles, lamps and the gas-jets which lit in the passages and for which the gas was supplied by a small gasometer lurking behind the saw-mill in the farmyard. Home-made in its turn, the electricity only lit patches of the hall, and far too high for blind or shutter its windows framed the inky night outside. Richard Lovell Edgeworth, father of Maria, had directed the installation of hot-water pipes to warm the library, when he had been a neighbour of my father's grandfather. The idea had not been applied to the higher floors of the house, beyond allowing a somewhat chilly pipe to run along the corridors, but, by putting on a turn of speed, the haven of a bedroom, where a log fire roared up the chimney, could be reached before the warmth gathered from the fires downstairs had evaporated.

My mother had impressed on Julia and me that, though Pakenham might seem to be our home, it would pass to Edward on his coming-of-age, an event followed by his marriage eighteen months later. She then made it clear to us that we must now ask Christine, our hostess, for permission for activities previously taken for granted, such as helping ourselves to nectarines and peaches in the line of glass-houses, cleverly slanted to catch the capricious Irish sun. Having given us this admirable code, my mother dispatched us annually across the sea, without, it appeared, reflecting that we had advanced in age or sophistication. She had left us stuck in the amber of past summer holidays, when her chief concern with her youngest children had been that the period in theory dedicated to hearing their prayers should not become too hopelessly eroded, outdoors by the last games of a tennis tournament, and indoors by the need to dress for dinner. Probably she did not realize that, housed in the best bedrooms, we had access to an uncensored collection of novels. It is true that guilt did sometimes hamper my enjoyment, as on the occasion when I embarked on a work of Max Nordau's, my father's name on the title-page being, I considered, a certificate of propriety.

With excitement, I read about a lady, a baroness, who was recounting the story of her life to a gentleman guest at her Parisian tea-table. In earlier days she had been seduced and abandoned. As she cast herself and her unborn child into the Seine her second last thought was a revulsion at the prospect of her naked body being stretched on a slab in the morgue, and her last thought of all a vision of her father in all the splendour of his bemedalled uniform. I was not, at that age, clear in my mind as to the possible interruptions of a pregnancy, but I did manage to gather that the plunge into the Seine had at least settled this part of the baroness's troubles. Guilt now took over, and so I never discovered how she had acquired a baron and a social position. I turned to reading the novels of Rose Macaulay, varying this literary diet with a novel about a priest who lost his vocation and returned to secular life, where his first difficulty was that he had forgotten how to tie his tie. Over forty years later I was amazed to learn that this author, Gerald O'Donovan, had been romantically involved with Rose Macaulay. Having read their works simultaneously, such a live conjunction would have seemed the wildest improbability.

Looking back, I seem to have become fossilized at Pakenham in an adolescent shell, partly because while Julia was still a schoolgirl I continued to be paired with her in the eyes of those not so many years older than myself, and partly because the life which my brother and sister-in-law led was curiously mysterious to me. I would consult their photograph album which did not provide much enlightenment, for, as neither of them were photographers, its pages depended on chance. Both the Dublin Horse Show and the local Castlepollard Show would produce an annual contribution of pictures taken by press photographers, giving a somewhat unbalanced view of their social life. To practise the Irish language Edward and Christine would talk to each other in this tongue, its incomprehensibility increasing to me the mystery of their life of which I saw so small a fragment. On the other hand when I once tried to explain to Edward the system by which enough dancing partners for young ladies were recruited at London balls, he, having married too young to have been exposed to such entertainments, expressed an almost scandalized disbelief at a process by which a brother might dine out nightly, while a sister might rest in the limbo of the uninvited. My life may also have had its mysteries, when I was living it in England, but in

Co. Westmeath I was eager to take part in all goings-on. This was in contrast to Julia who, taking advantage of her status as a schoolgirl, would spend the daylight hours between meals drawing self-portraits from her own reflection in her bedroom looking-glass.

Recovered from the rigours of the journey, Joan raised the question of finding horses for us to ride, and such was the strength of her personality that White was summoned to drive us through the evening murk to Coolure, a neighbouring mansion which had once belonged to the Pakenham family, but had now drifted into the particularly helpless semi-decay that overcomes Irish country houses. This quality of mildewed despair is also apt to overtake the inhabitants, but the then owner of Coolure was thought to do some horse-coping and so might have some horses to hire. The gloom of Coolure's frontage was so complete that it seemed only natural that the door should at length be opened by a crone obviously escaped from a fairy-tale. Surprisingly she was prepared to accept a message of inquiry about the availability of horses for hire, and even more surprisingly the following morning breakfast was interrupted by the news that horses were actually at the door. Never since the days when I had sat on the back of the Shetland pony Countess, led by an ancient groom and escorted on foot by the rest of the nursery party, had I mounted a horse from the mounting block outside the front porch, an object more generally used for photographic grouping. Habitually Joan and I hunted side-saddle, so riding astride, our clothes were eccentric, particularly my boots which, concertinaed round my ankles, came barely half-way up my calves. Guided by me, we trotted gingerly down to a grassy road beside Lough Derravaragh where the horses' stable at Coolure loomed ominously across the grey lake water. Here Joan urged her mount into a canter, but I judged it wiser to stick to a jog-trot, though Joan subsequently put about the story that my horse had swum back to its stable with me on its back.

As it happened our visit coincided with a local campaign for Edward to take on the joint-mastership of the Westmeath Hounds. This was an appeal to his social rather than his sporting instincts, as he had never much cared for riding and early in life had put on an amount of weight that would have made finding a mount difficult, even in a country famed for its production of weight-carrying hunters. The search for a Master, a recurrent problem in many hunting countries, was so permanent as to be practically perennial in Co. Westmeath. Frequent interregnums had been presided over by a vice-master of immense charm, who to me in my childhood seemed the rightful ruler of the hounds, and other masters to be merely superfluous characters brought in to provide necessary financial backing. There had been a period when the current Master had been a dashing figure with the habit of greeting my sisters with the inquiry, 'Are you the little girl I blooded?' He was probably unaware that such an initiation was anathema to my mother, who had never recovered from her rage and horror when she had failed to prevent Edward's 'little pink face' from being bedaubed. A fox had been killed on the front lawn, and he had had a ringside seat in his perambulator. This gruesome early experience had been less off-putting to Edward than my mother might have expected, for after some Machiavellian work by a go-between the prospective master came to luncheon, and Edward agreed to take on the joint-mastership. It should perhaps be explained that the local attitude towards the hounds saw them as a barometer of behaviour as well as a sporting opportunity. Many years later Edward pointed out to me a house considered to be occupied by a family of inexplicable mystery, of whom it was remarked, 'They don't go to Church (meaning Church of Ireland). They don't go to Chapel (meaning Roman Catholic). They don't go to Meeting (meaning the Kirk of Scotland). They don't even subscribe to the Hunt.'

This new commitment on my brother's part offered an opportunity to Joan and myself to have a day with the Westmeath on the horses hired from Coolure. To me this prospect was more than the offer of a day with the hounds. It was emancipation of a special kind, dating back to the days of my childhood when for a spell in the summer holidays my mother had summoned a riding-master, complete with horses, to give lessons to my elder brothers and sisters. The riding-master existed on a social level all his own, and although the hierarchy of the household required that at five o'clock in the afternoon a minimum of eight separate teas should be simultaneously in progress, the riding-master's refreshment meant a ninth tea-pot to be filled. In spite of this segregation, I heard long afterwards that there had been doubts in the neighbourhood as to the propriety of my widowed mother sheltering an equestrian tutor under her roof. Julia and I were not included in the riding lessons, though our morning ritual visit, carrots in hand, to the Shetland pony Countess, was now expanded to include the temporary visitors. When the cubbing season arrived my envy grew in intensity, for my elders were now mounted, and following the huntsman and whip in their gallops through the labyrinth of rhododendron walks, while I among the followers on foot had to dodge into the bushes. In the meantime the midges made more of a meal than hounds usually achieved. Indeed the more inept hounds were apt to be captured as hostages when unable to find their way out of bog drains in the woods. Held prisoner until their fellows had returned to kennel, they would then be brought to my brother's front door for ransom. But now, all glorious, it was I who cantered along the rhododendron walks, and, though the reluctance of the local foxes to leave the security of the woods for the risks of the open country limited the day's sport to this kind of progress, I felt that I had advanced along the path of an independent life. My exhilaration was hardly affected when the strap that passed round the girth of my borrowed saddle became detached and began to trail on the ground. Keeping well up with hounds on their own feet was a posse of estate workers, to whom I appealed for the gift of a piece of string. With exquisite politeness one of this group offered me string which he untied from below his knee where it performed the vital service of keeping his trouser end out of the dirt. Further he opened the neck of his shirt and from a bag hung round his neck, repository, I imagine, of a scapular and agnus dei, drew forth a knife of the type I recognized as having been awarded by my mother as a prize at the annual school treat sports. With this string and this knife he effected a repair to my saddle, the whole operation taking place in an intensely chivalrous silence.

Besides enlivening life outdoors by bringing horses into my orbit, my cousin Joan galvanized my life indoors by introducing Slosh, which had not been previously played in the billiard-room at Pakenham. If his brother-in-law Henry Lamb, or his cousin and contemporary David Talbot Rice, should be staying in the house, Edward would retire with one of them for a game of billiards after dinner, but the rest of his family were apt to use the billiard-room as a refuge from polite society. The billiard-table was only three-quarter size, so there was room for a writing-table banished as too vast from a study used by my grandfather. Ping-pong was played on its leather top, the wrinkles of age adding some interesting hazards to the game. Along one wall a bookcase loomed in which the more sporting of my father's books had come to rest, the most sporting title being, perhaps, *Two Dianas in Alaska*, though what the Dianas did is still unknown to me. To warm us, Two Dianas in the

Irish Midlands, while we played Slosh a log fire was lit in the rather gothic steel grate, adding that touch of luxury that only a log fire gives. Edward was drawn in to join us, and, although he retained some loyalty to the purity of classical billiards, he at once appreciated the opportunity Slosh offered for bigger breaks and higher scores. His technique had always been to hit every stroke with the full force of his hefty arm, so that in his company Slosh could become a game of some peril to the bystanders, for with seven balls spinning round the table it was not unusual for one to bounce over the cushions. In fact a house by-law was needed to cope with this situation. In extreme contrast to his usual forceful manner of play, Edward also had a fancy for using the long cue, which he never omitted to chalk, remarking that many a match had been lost by such an oversight. These games were watched from the walls by the miniature portraits of my grandfather, a general, and his six brothers. The eldest was known to his great nephews and nieces as Fluffy on account of his golden hair and handsomely frivolous air. There were also the two clerical brothers, one of whom was ordained in the Established Church, while the other left the army to become a monk of the Passionist Order (which he introduced into Ireland) changing from Charles Reginald to Father Paul Mary. The naval brother became the father of a famous admiral, who, besides his reputation for pithy remarks, passed into literature, and even into films, as the seducer of the Japanese admiral's wife in *La Bataille* by Claude Farrère. This cousin for some reason objected to the dolphins that ornamented his admiral's barge and, when he found they had not been removed, remarked, 'I told you to take those fucking fish away.' To return to the seven brothers there was, besides the two clerics, a hermit, who, when he abandoned his military career, retired to a hideaway in the Wicklow Mountains, where against a suspected domestic background of a housekeeper-mistress and a stiff consumption of whisky, he concealed his identity under the name of Parker. He had been celebrated by Dunsany in a not entirely accurate quatrain,

> 'We've an Uncle called Mark
> But we keep that dark,
> His *real* name is Parker,
> But we keep that darker.'

Finally there was the seventh son who became an Ambassador, but leaving no issue, bequeathed his Sussex estate to his widow, who in the course of time – much time, for she lived to be ninety-six – left it to her godson, my brother Frank. It is remarkable that of such a plethora of sons only two left descendants. My own grandfather owed his inheritance to the death as a bachelor of his handsome eldest brother, as my father, in his turn, owed it to the death of his elder twin brother at the age of eleven. The only relics of this little boy's brief and invalid existence were some yellowing photographs of a curly headed cherub, and a hooded bath-chair which lurked for years in the coach-house. His outings must have been of an arduous slowness for the efforts of his nieces to move his cumbersome carriage were always unsuccessful.

To arrive or to leave the house that sheltered these ancestral relics had always some element of arriving or departing from an island, the slopes of the park and the clumps of trees keeping the house curiously well concealed until one had, as it were, made one's landfall, and on sailing away the figures in the porch would recede as though waving from a dockside. Should the host and hostess be absent, Andrews in his black butler's apparel would be the first and last inhabitant to be seen. As I have said he was an adept at concealing his thoughts, but he never looked more enigmatic than when standing under the coat of arms that ornamented the grey granite arch.

At the end of this winter visit Joan and I sailed away to Dunsany Castle, which bore no resemblance to an island, callers being continuous, and the gossip of the countryside ebbing and flowing over the drawing-room hearthrug. It was a remark by a lady who had called on the day of our arrival that caused Dunsany to greet me with, 'I say, Violet, I've just written a poem'. This was no unusual greeting, for no poet was ever more eager to try out his productions when hot from the oven, but on this occasion he had the excuse that he wished to emphasize that he was alive, and proposed to continue in that state.

It was in the course of discussing the question, perennial if less immediately acute than in Co. Westmeath, as to who might be prepared to take on the Meath hounds, that the caller had made the remark which had inspired Dunsany's poem. 'We are waiting for several young men to come into their own in this country,' she had said, 'Randal, of course, would be quite splendid, not that I mean anything by that, but you know what I mean.' Randal, it should be explained, was my uncle's only son, at that moment far away with the Guides Cavalry on the North-West Frontier of India. Seizing a goose-feather quill, with which he invariably wrote, Randal's father moved in to counter-attack by establishing that he was not only alive, but prepared to kick. The poem was built round the Grange, which was the name of the neighbour's house, and the name of her son, which was Denis. With a voice growing ever more vibrant Dunsany declaimed,

> 'There'll be a change at the Grange,
> And a fine mausoleum of stone,
> And Hounds will range without mange
> When Denis comes into his own.'

The poet's voice became louder as he described the fine sport and the great runs that would follow the 'change', ending in a triumphant shout

> '... with a line from Dunsany to Naas
> When DENIS COMES INTO HIS OWN!'

When Denis's mother arrived for the dinner party before the Hunt Ball the poem was recited to her crescendo, as evidence that the Meath Hounds must for the present look elsewhere for a new master.

The owner of Dunsany Castle regarded electricity as an outrage on the human eyeball. He carried this feeling to such extremes that, dining in London with his mother-in-law, my grandmother, he would sit after dinner in her drawing-room with his hand shielding his eyes from the glare of the cut-glass electric fitting which depended from the centre of the ceiling. Although the rest of her family made no active demonstration, his feelings were shared sufficiently for a scheme to be set on foot for presenting an alabaster bowl to my grandmother on her birthday, so that the glare might be mitigated. Unhappily, with what appeared to be clairvoyance, my grandmother sabotaged this plan by announcing shortly before the festival that she had a particular dislike for electric fittings quarried from alabaster, so Dunsany continued to sit as if in a brown study. No electric light had been installed in the castle over which he had control, and he was not prepared to accept that a late appearance at the dinner-table might be due to finding the stairs and passages in darkness. Undeniably the dancers at the Hunt Ball, ladies in ball gowns and gentlemen in scarlet, looked at their most romantic by candlelight. The only moment of horrid truth came when a flashlight blazed out to photograph a group assembled in the hall. The flashlight may have been overpowerful, for the picture that appeared next day in the *Irish Times* had needed heavy touching-up by an over-confident hand, my uncle's white tie and waistcoat being drawn in with more attention to symmetry than to the slap-dash nature of his evening-dress. The same pencil had remorselessly drawn in the company's eyebrows, and in my case adding eyelashes that would have been the envy of any authentic colleen. This looked all the more eccentric as the hall at Dunsany was plastered with the trophies of Dunsany's safaris, so that in the photograph a pair of diabolical horns appeared to spring from my head. Another trophy, a small curved horn, had been mounted as a tie-pin, and when, a few hours after the ball the company reassembled to meet hounds outside the castle, I observed that my uncle's solution of the tricky business of tying a hunting stock was practical rather than elegant. The result was as if he had carelessly twisted a towel round his neck, effected a bumpy knot somewhere in the region of the sternum, and transfixed the knot with the curved horn tie-pin, which on a smaller breast would have stretched from ear to ear.

Before she saw us off on our hirelings, my aunt warned us that we should find the Meath obstacles a contrast to the stone walls and hedges by which the Oxfordshire fields were fenced. Coming to Ireland as a bride, she had had to adapt herself to what a follower of the Bicester might have considered to be a small hill rather than a bank, and she warned us that we must not attempt to take a line of our own. Of the first double bank we came to when hounds went away Ion Villiers-Stuart, a fellow guest, remarked that there were always some empty saddles after this one, and, as I saw that the bank seemed to tower above my head, I realized the importance of my aunt's advice. Accustomed to cantering into fences before taking off it was a surprise to find that horses were required to spring from a trot up these green mounds, creep along the top, and then leap clear into the field below. Boggy ditches at take-off and landing added to the excitement of jumping the banks of

Meath. In my aunt's hunting days her horse had once landed himself and his rider in a ditch on the Hill of Tara, where the ancient Kings of Ireland had been crowned. The claim to have 'helped her ladyship out of that ditch on Tara' had become part of the appeal for alms from every beggar to approach Dunsany Castle. When I saw that far more experienced riders than I were struggling, with attendant beggars, to retrieve their mounts from bog drains, I realized that one aspect of Diana, Goddess of Hunting, must have been her willingness to protect the ignorant.

The beasts that my uncle had shot on his African safaris were confined to the outer and inner halls, where assorted heads lined the walls, and a lion snarled from a small jungle of pampas grass at the foot of the stairs. From there civilization took over, the shallow steps rising elegantly beneath a collection of paintings. The largest, attributed to Opie, showed an obviously ailing young lady, a reclining figure in a high-waisted white dress, the state of whose pulse was baffling her medical adviser, portentous in a red robe and with a frowning countenance. As my aunt had pointed out to me on my first visit to the house, a comment on the young lady's condition came from a lascivious little cupid, who lurked in a darkly varnished corner of the picture, challenging the world with a roll of his eyes, though it was uncertain whether he was proclaiming himself to be responsible for the malady or suggesting that he might be the cure. The drawing-room was in consequence on the *piano nobile*, a room whose Adam ceiling was the only surface on which my uncle had been unable to deposit objects inherited or bought by himself on the frequent occasions when something caught his fancy. Armchairs in much the same cabbage rose chintz that I later found in Rosa Lewis's sitting-room at the Cavendish Hotel, jostled each other like animals of different sizes at a fair, the one pre-empted by the host being easily distinguished by its gargantuan size, and by the fact that a teapot of handsome china with a cup and milk jug stood almost perpetually on a stool beside it. After hunting, poached eggs would appear at the tea-table, while in my mother's house these would be banished to the dining-room. Even less would she have told me to disregard the top-dressing of horse's hair, as my aunt did when, my hand shaking from the day's sport, I allowed a poached egg to slip on to my habit skirt. As tea proceeded it became apparent that my cousin Joan and Ion Villiers-Stuart were lost in the February night. No sound of horses' hoofs on the gravel below came to reassure the listeners, and Ion's wife Elspeth, with the face of Venus and the build of Juno, agitated herself into a state where a search party, headed by herself, seemed the only means of averting hysteria. My aunt hardly attempted to conceal her opinion of the uselessness of this proceeding. She had become inured to delayed hunters when in troubled times either her husband or her son were invariably late in returning through a countryside where there were dangers to apprehend that were not only sporting. This evening's particular delay turned out to have been caused by hounds having been taken on to draw one last covert as a farewell to a member of the field who was due to return next day to India, and to five years' exile from the plump green double banks of Meath.

5. West Waterford

STILL FLOATING ON WAVES OF hospitality, Joan and I separated, and while she went to stay with friends of her mother's on the Curragh of Kildare, I moved south-west to Co. Waterford where Ion and Elspeth Villiers-Stuart had promised me a day with a neighbouring hunt called the United, though I remained ignorant as to what union had given it that name. Pleased as I was with this opportunity, I had a hankering to have seen the Curragh, for when my father was stationed there my mother had enjoyed an unrepeated experience of actually being obliged to go out and buy a leg of mutton. Surrounded as she had always been by cooks who ordered supplies, and butchers who delivered, this remained ever afterwards to her a romantic memory of her life as a soldier's wife. Meanwhile my father was training the Irish Horse whose activities were recorded in an album of photographs which came to rest in the library at Pakenham. When the Irish Horse sailed from Cork on their way to Table Bay, my mother was the last person to board the tender, resisting the temptation to stow away in my father's commodious cabin as bad for discipline. Her disembarkment was dramatic, the commanding officer's bride falling on her hands and knees as she reached the deck of the tender. As it pulled away from the troopship the yeomen lining the railing raised a delighted cheer. Indeed one of them cherished such an affectionate memory of my mother that, when he had emigrated and prospered in the fur trade in Canada, he sent her big bundles of sable and mink. These became the collar and lining of the coat in which she travelled in winter, a garment almost ceremonial in weight and size, the wearer herself far removed from the carefree days when she could tumble off troopships onto tenders. After this farewell, my mother had gone to stay at Dromana, to be comforted by her friend Mrs Villiers-Stuart, and in due course to become the godmother of Ion. My mother's visit had been in 1900, but when I arrived thirty-one years later I was given the treatment of a most cherished guest by the same housemaid who had greeted my mother on the morning after my father's sailing with an encouraging 'It is a fine day,' as she pulled up the blinds.

To travel from Dunsany to Dromana had been a journey to tax even the stamina of someone as addicted to railway trains as myself. Without my mother's truly passionate love for timetables, my Aunt Beatrice was sufficiently an adept to discover that, by driving to Sallins station, it was possible to cut off a train which had started from Dublin, and was scheduled to stop at every station across the countryside until, at a point half-way towards the roaring Atlantic, the junction of Mallow was reached. Driving to Sallins my only recognition of a familiar sight was when the motor-car happened to pass through the Meath Hounds and I suddenly saw Joan's red-gold hair under her bowler-hat among the followers. Subsequently I learnt that I had unawares gone past Clongowes, where Stephen Daedalus wrote in his books his name and the ubiquitous rhyme '. . . Ireland is my nation, Clongowes is my dwelling place, And Heaven's my destination', and where his soul was wrung by the Hell-Fire sermon, which described in harrowing detail what would happen to those whose destination turned out to be the reverse of heaven.

Although my mother had ultimately grasped that it was possible for her daughters to travel alone by what was then called Third Class without being violated or murdered, indeed being gratified by this economy, she was prepared to finance travel by First Class if a long Irish journey was in question. In consequence I settled down to a day of solitary confinement on the generously broad cushions of the Great Southern Railway, a solitude occasionally broken by a few words with the ticket-collector, who could not conceal that he regarded my route as eccentric, not to say masochistic. The Slieve Bloom Mountains jogged slowly by, after being a purple-blue backdrop to a long pause at Port Laoise. This halt gave time for reflection on the changes of political weather which, after the establishment of the Irish Free State, had led to the reversion of Maryborough to Port Laoise and Kingstown to Dun Laoghaire. In the nursery passage at Pakenham there hung a set of maps which could be released by strings, like venetian blinds. I wished I had paid more attention to them as I looked out on the darkening countryside. The map of Ireland, in particular, might have been helpful, for it must have dated before George IV's visit to Ireland on his succession, the port known to me throughout my childhood as Kingstown, renamed in honour of that monarch, appearing in the spelling of the period as Dunleary.

Night came down over the countryside, obliterating mountains, stone walls and the architecture of Limerick Junction. It seemed likely that I should spend the rest of my life in a dimly lit padded cell, decorated with photographs of Glendalough and Killarney, which time had faded to the colour of *crème garbure*. But even the Southern Railway of Ireland had not achieved the extension of time to infinity, and I eventually found myself on the platform at Mallow. Later I learnt that the Rakes of Mallow had been famous hell-raisers,

> 'Beauing, belling, dancing, drinking,
> Breaking windows, damning, sinking,
> Ever raking, never thinking
> Live the Rakes of Mallow.'

On that dark February evening nothing would have seemed more improbable than such goings-on. I waited for the express, called locally the Old Rosslare, which carried the Irish of the south-west to Saint George's Channel and the mail-boat that would carry them to Fishguard, doomed to face the sort of sea described only too often in weather reports as 'moderate to rather rough'. The only traces of rakes of Mallow behaviour that came to my notice occurred when I had left the Old Rosslare boat train at Lismore. As I followed Ion to his motor-car, and the train pulled out of the station, another car surged into the yard. This came from Lismore Castle, the Irish home of the Duke of Devonshire, and marked the failure of Charlie Cavendish, his younger son, to achieve the first step of a journey to England. 'He won't catch up with the train at Dungarvan, but he might at Waterford,' said Ion, speaking with expert knowledge of form in races between road and rail.

Although there had never been a year of my life that I could remember without at least one visit to Ireland, my experience had been limited to the home of my paternal ancestors and the home of my mother's sister. Pakenham Hall stood roughly fifty miles from Dublin, while Dunsany Castle was only eighteen miles from the capital city. Dublin itself I had begun to know after Edward's marriage when he and Christine bought a pretty urban home in Rathmines, but the rest of the island was a land of mystery. I knew that the train that deposited me at

Mullingar would in due course reach Galway, Sligo and the last rocks of western Europe. North-east I had seen from a local eminence the Mountains of Mourne frosted with snow under a turquoise sky, but the south-west was even more of an unknown territory. My mother's reminiscences of Dromana had been on the personal rather than the scenic side, and even my sisters, more recent visitors, had never thought fit to mention that the entry to the demesne was along a road hewn through the living rock, which passed through a gateway pillared and domed in the style of Brighton Pavilion.

In the morning a new world of beauty lay before me, a landscape which forty years, and travels west to California and east to Calcutta, have never displaced in my inward eye as a view constantly to fill my heart with pleasure. Along the banks of the river Blackwater castle and mansion stood in the happiest relation to the broad river, shining silver bright as its own salmon as it ran towards Youghal Bay and the open sea. From the lip of its own cliff Dromana's windows gazed down river towards woods and rich green fields, while upstream the view was closed by the infinitely subtle sweep of the Knockmealdown Mountains, as Pepys said of the view from the terrace of Windsor Castle, 'the fairest prospect in the world quite'. There was a softness in the air which made it seem far away from the lake-washed chill of the Westmeath climate. This I managed to appreciate, even in the high drama attending any expedition in which Elspeth, my hostess, was either organizer or participant. Drama rose to its most acute on a hunting morning, which, in any case, offers every opportunity for agonizing loss of essential equipment for those facing a day's sport. I have said that Elspeth had the physique of Juno, and, in her bowler-hat and side-saddle habit, she combined Juno with Diana. Ion, on the other hand, wore a velvet cap, as acting master of the West Waterford, and looked totally professional. My ignorance of hunting was still so great that I had not even learnt that apprehension was supposed to be felt at the prospect of going out on a strange horse over a strange country, my only sensation being one of pleasure that I was moving in such impeccably sporting circles. Elspeth had lent me a side-saddle and one of her horses, so I had for once the confidence that a strange horse would be up to my weight.

A confused delay at starting for the meet of the United, as the neighbouring hunt was called, and a puncture on the way meant that hounds were moving off as we arrived, but, by the time I got my breath, I found that the obstacles in Co. Waterford were less acutely mountainous than the Meath banks. Indeed the banks were of a height that allowed the clever horses to change feet and spring clear into the field beyond. My self-congratulation at the quickness with which I had acquired this technique was, however, shattered by an accident that took place as I was scrambling through a gap under a well-grown tree. Squeezed to one side by one of my few acquaintances in the field, a girl who was considered to be making too much of a recent visit to Leicestershire, I managed to get through the reduced space only to find that the lower pommel of my borrowed side-saddle had been snapped off by catching the trunk of the tree. Probably the breakage averted a multiple spill, but as I rode away I was conscious that part of the machinery by which a rider adheres to a side-saddle had rolled to the ground. Earlier, when we had been delayed by a puncture, which in those days necessitated a great deal of crawling under the wheels to get the non-hydraulic jack in position, Elspeth had remarked that she was going to write a book about their hunts with the United. My accident would certainly have qualified for inclusion. Hounds, as Elspeth phrased it, were running like stink. With attractive generosity, and the plea that she was recovering from influenza so had no business to be out hunting, Elspeth changed horses with me, herself riding on the mutilated saddle in the direction she hoped the car might be found. The exchange of horses found me mounted on a horse whose powers were untried, and I realized that, did I not follow on the heels of Ion's gallant grey, I should be lost forever in a strange country. Concealing from him that I could see little difference between the places he announced to be jumpable, those that were not, and those that he knew his horse could jump but was uncertain if mine would have the power to o'erleap, I panted at his heels. Under Ion's protection I was at least shielded from my usual experience out hunting in Ireland, which was to be accosted by strangers, who, regarding the hireling I was riding, would either remark that the horse had come a long way, or had already been out twice in the last ten days. Remarks made in the friendliest spirit in the world, but distinctly undermining for someone as ignorant of equine capabilities as myself. At the end of the day by what to me was a miracle, Ion's driver appeared, having followed the chase through a complication of bohireens. In addition he crowned his day's good deeds by bringing the car to a halt at a cross-roads having seen that Elspeth was emerging from one of the establishments which in Ireland combine bar and general shop. Her adventures had included a crippling ride, for, as she complained, not only had she only one pommel but, far less tall, I naturally rode with a shorter stirrup than she did. She had also amused herself the day before, while nursing influenza in bed, by painting her nails a particularly virulent shade of scarlet, and her consciousness that this might seem inappropriate had caused her to try to keep her hands concealed from the publican and his wife while accepting refreshment.

 Among the romantic associations of Dromana was a connection with that Countess of Desmond whose life had straddled the sixteenth and seventeenth centuries, having, according to Thomas More, 'lived to much more than a hundred and ten, and died from a fall from a cherry tree then'. *The Complete Peerage* deals rather coolly with these claims to a centenarian's arboricultural interest, although it cannot be denied that there are cherry trees in the neighbourhood, said to descend from those imported by Sir Walter Raleigh in the days when he governed Waterford. On the other hand *The Complete Peerage* looks more sympathetically on Lord Stuart de Decies, a Villiers-Stuart forbear, who had supposedly married a Viennese lady in an Austrian and an English ceremony. His heir, claiming his father's barony, was required as routine to produce evidence of his parents' marriage, but 'experienced the painful shock of being unable to do so', doubts having arisen as to whether the late Lady Stuart de Decies had been free to marry. This châtelaine had died and been buried in the name and style in which she had lived before a question of bigamy arose, and her position became mysterious and unresolved. In the round drawing-room at Dromana reflections from the Blackwater danced on the portraits of ancestors, and even cast light on an earlier mystery, the small dark portrait of the Countess of Desmond, formidable enough in old age to make it credible that she had cast her teeth and grown a third set when past her century.

It was in the round room that, occasionally, Elspeth played the piano with tremendous attack, having been trained, I believe, to concert level. The relics of a concussion that afflicted her husband prevented him from listening to his wife's playing with anything except pain, so it was only when he was out of earshot that Elspeth's virtuoso rendering of 'I'll see you again' from Noël Coward's *Bitter Sweet* could set the wild echoes flying. My mother had a great affection for her godson Ion, and showed pleasure on finding that she was still remembered at Dromana from the days when she had gone there as a bride whose husband had left her to go to the wars. I did, however, think it wiser to edit my account of my adventures, emphasizing that Elspeth and I had attended afternoon service at Villierstown's church, with its reassuring ring of family association in public worship, while suppressing the fact that Sunday morning had been passed in a round of inspection of horses for sale. This was more in the nature of keeping an eye on which horses might be expected to change hands rather than with an actual idea of purchase. Incidentally, this was one of the neighbourhoods from which the Knox family of Somerville and Ross's *Some Experiences of an Irish R.M.* supposedly sprung ('all were prepared at any moment of the day or night to sell a horse'). Horses visited on the Sunday morning round belonged sometimes to Palladian mansions and sometimes to farm-houses or country public houses, but at each stopping-place a ritual glass of port was on offer. The cheerful hospitality of these horse-dealing expeditions must, I think, have left a visible mark on me at an impressionable age. Ten years later in the English Midlands, I told a chance acquaintance from the south-west of Ireland that I had friends in Co. Waterford. Taking one look at me he stated rather than inquired, 'They're called Villiers-Stuart, aren't they?' complete understanding being at once established.

6. Julia Spreads her Wings

IN IRELAND IN THOSE DAYS it was a habit to link pairs of goats by a yoke round their necks. Based on a knowledge of goat psychology, this restraint effectively prevented the pair from straying too far from their owners, for, as no two goats ever wish to proceed in the same direction, the weaker acted as a brake on the stronger. Sometimes, as we were growing up, it seemed to me that my relationship with my younger sister Julia was analogous to a pair of yoked goats, eternally linked but for ever pulling in opposite directions. The twenty months between our ages was a gap artificially widened by Julia's nostalgia for her nursery days and my own wish to get out into the world. Paradoxically, separation brought us into far greater sympathy with each other than we had known in the days when we lived in compulsory twinhood.

When Julia came to shed her chrysalis she grew eager to warm her new butterfly wings in the sunshine. The hatching process began gradually, and was hardly perceptible when she passed into Oxford. She had risen to be second Head Girl of St Margaret's, Bushey, though her uncompromisingly Low Church attitude had probably prevented the High Church authorities of the school from appointing her to be a Chapel

Monitress, an honour usually given to head girls. Summoned to Somerville College for an interview, to judge if she would be worthy of a prized place at the university, Julia paused at my grandmother's house, ever a family railway junction, which gave an opportunity for some modifications in her essentially schoolgirl appearance. Our object was to make her appear unfrivolous but not immature, a matter of difficulty, for the youthfulness of her appearance was so persistent that at the age of thirty she was questioned by a barman as to her eligibility to order an alcoholic drink. Her golden hair still straggling under the brim of a respectable black hat on loan from me, she went up to Somerville where she handled the interviewing tutor with awesome dexterity. Deducing the interviewer's tastes from the reproductions of Italian paintings that decorated the study walls, Julia edged the conversation round to a recent Italian tour, and played a final, unexpected trump by claiming that the writer she most admired was Turgenev. She reported that the professor's pleasure had been so obvious that it was hardly a surprise that, although she was only seventeen, Somerville College expressed its wish to receive her.

When term began they received a young lady who had blossomed spectacularly. Her natural colouring was so brilliant that she glowed against the grey walls of Oxford, standing out among her paler contemporaries like a coloured capital in a missal. The effect was particularly dazzling against the background of her own college. It was said that a pair of anxious parents, interviewing the Principal before trusting their cherished prodigy of a daughter to her care, had said that their only hesitation concerned a girl they had seen whose hair, complexion and air of frivolity struck them as boding ill for industry and sobriety. The Principal was understood to have allayed these fears by mentioning Julia's well-sounding social antecedents, so the college gained a student who later soared to the dizziest academic heights in political economy.

Julia's French was considered by her examiners to need some native polish, as she planned to read modern languages at the university. Accordingly Miss Rawlins, our governess in earlier days, was resurrected, as happened periodically when a crisis of chaperonage arose, and under her care Julia was dispatched to Tours. Offered a share in the expedition I refused, as I wished to keep an eye on the social and sentimental pots that were simmering in my own life. I had no regrets when I heard Julia's history of her stay in the Touraine, for efforts to improve her French had been overshadowed by the awkwardnesses originated by her chaperone. Miss Rawlins had always regarded French conversation lessons given to her pupils by extraneous *demoiselles* as a reflection on her own ability to teach the language. To this sensitiveness she had now added an exaggerated suspicion that sexual irregularity might occur whenever a former pupil chanced to be left alone with a man, any man, age or close kinship being, in her eyes, no barrier. In my own case she had expressed horror when she discovered that I had spent the day alone with a male friend at the Heythrop point-to-point, a function famous for the bitter cold of its *locale*, and more likely to be the scene of a collapse from exposure than a collapse of morals. On the banks of the Loire she made even stronger protests when a fellow guest in the *pension* invited Julia to assist him in the development of some high art photographs of the château de Chenonceau, sailing dramatically white against billows of dark cloud. Necessarily this operation took place in a dark-room, a cellar below the *pension*, whose door could only be secured from interruption, liable to ruin the process, by being locked on the inside. According to Julia, Miss Rawlins pursued her charge to the cellar and, baffled by the locked door, was even more agitated by hearing an equivocal dialogue from inside the dark-room. 'No, don't put it in like that . . . let me show you. You put it in like this.'

Whether her French had acquired polish or not, Julia returned with a determination to apply some English polish to herself. Her hair was soon swept up into a riot of golden curls, her beautiful big mouth took on a rosier hue, and she began to experiment with eye-black and eyelash curlers. This eye make-up was a joint stock affair between us, as one owned the curlers and the other owned the eye-black, cross words passing on the subject of spitting into the eye-black by its non-owner. Otherwise cross words were far fewer than in our schoolroom days, and in the greatest amity we went shopping for clothes in which Julia was to face the London Season. Once when we had been bathing among the rushes of Lough Derravaragh I had had a glimpse of Julia emerging as a Renoir girl from the lake, but it was only when she tried on a pink net *robe de bal* decked with rose petals that I realized how clothes such as these could transform her appearance.

In her memoirs my grandmother ended the story of the first fifty-one years of her own life with the death of Queen Victoria, and a meeting to found the Victoria League. This was to commemorate the Queen by keeping the links of Empire strongly knit, its object being that visitors from overseas should find a welcome as members of an Imperial family. Having been the first president, my grandmother had never let her interest in the Victoria League slacken, and when, in this summer of 1931, there was a question of raising funds by means of a ball, she mobilized her grandchildren in matriarchal style. The latest hotel to be opened in Park Lane had been built on the site of Dorchester House, an upstart replacement, gleaming yellow, where once through a porte cochère in high blank walls it had been possible to see a smoke-darkened mansion, heavy with the histories of past lives. In the new Dorchester the Victoria

League was to hold its ball, the organizers ordaining a cabaret to be recruited from young ladies of fashion, stiffened by a sprinkling of professionals. The latter were due to arrive late after the end of whatever shows they happened to be in, so that the amateurs were required to fill in the early part of the evening. My cousin Joan and I were chosen to dance in a quadrille, my grandmother agreeing to pay for the wide crinolines which were to be our costumes. To my grandmother the crinoline was a fashion that had begun to lose its popularity when she was a child, though she told a story of a governess who continued to wear a hoop on account of the buoyancy it gave her when taking long walks with her charges. At the age of twelve I had inherited three dress boxes of black and white lace from my godmother, and at last this bequest, too valuable to throw away, and too fragile to be of everyday use, came into its own.

My crinoline was of a width that caused a disobliging gossip writer to comment at my difficulties in getting through a doorway, but it made a handsome foundation for three deep lace flounces. A pink rose ornamented the flounce that covered my shoulders and more roses concealed the elastic that held in place the long curls that had been bobbed from my head seven years before, but were now restored to their original situation. The hoop from my crinoline was lost in a series of moves in which it had always been an unpackable problem, but the gown itself and the curls survived forty years of war and peace, the former earning its keep as an evening dress, a fancy dress 'copied from Longhi', in the words of W. B. Yeats, and finally as the queen's dress in a production of Maurice Baring's sketch *Catherine Parr or Alexander's Horse*. The dress had been dyed and the dye had faded but the curls remained undimmed in their pristine colour which, to my pleased surprise, I realized in later days it would have been barely an exaggeration to call red gold.

Much as Joan and I appreciated our grandmother's generosity, our feelings were mixed owing to the necessity of finding partners, not only free to rehearse, but prepared to stick on whiskers for the dress rehearsal. My own partner had the sensible idea that champagne cocktails at the Ritz would mitigate the agony of rehearsing, but the luxuriance of the whiskers which Clarkson's the theatrical costumiers had stuck to his cheeks caused waiters and guests to gape in amazement while I collapsed, most ungratefully, into laughter that re-echoed through the gilded hall of the hotel.

At the ball itself the quadrille passed off without a major disaster, but the polka to be danced by professionals had an unexpected development. The lights were dimmed for this number, but Nelson Keys, a hobgoblin of a comedian, was seen to be wearing a boat-shaped hat and a fur boa that whirled round above his flying coat tails. He had met my mother's maid, Annie Reason, in the hotel corridor as she was on her way to help me into my crinoline, and, spotting the value of her hat and fur as properties, had bluffed her into agreeing to the loan. Long after the notes of 'See me dance the polka See me cover the ground' had died away Miss Reason pursued her belongings round the edge of the ballroom, being naturally unwilling to return without them to the house in Upper Berkeley Street that was our temporary home.

When Julia and I reached our beds in the cold grey London dawn, the sedate emptiness of the street was rhythmically broken by the clash and jingle of the horse-drawn carts which passed on their way from Paddington Station to Covent Garden Market. Laden with vegetables from the West Country, these leviathans could be heard gathering speed as they turned out of the Edgware Road and, in a crescendo of hoof beats and rumbling wheels, came clattering through Upper Berkeley Street. Coming singly, the surge and thunder of each vehicle would die away to be followed at what seemed to be a regular interval by the next van to have been loaded. At the time these waves of sound, rising, breaking and dying away, seemed only to be murderers of sleep for those who had not come home till morning, but now I recall them tenderly as the last relics of an age of horse-drawn economy. Nearly thirty years later, standing on the roof of the colonnade of Saint Peter's, I waited among a crowd of thousands for Pope John XXIII to receive the bones of two newly canonized saints into the Basilica. Silence hung like a fog over the multitude, who waited while the horse-drawn hearses halted and the coffins were carried up the steps to where Pope John waited to speak, in his voice of velvet, the prayers of reception and blessing. Decorously the empty hearses went away at a walk until, out of sight but not out of earshot, the coachman whipped up the plumed and draped horses. In the hush the clattering of the hearses over the paving-stones of Rome brought back to me the memory of Covent Garden vans, thundering below my bedroom windows with a cargo more lively than the bones of saints.

Our temporary home, unlike most of the houses we rented, belonged to a young married couple, beds and sofas being less penitential than in houses furnished at an earlier date. My mother's state of health confined her to an upper floor, so the ground-floor library was occupied by Julia and myself without the constant threat that we would be caught reading books judged unsuitable. In this particular house unsuitability might be said to include illegality, for in a bookcase whose edge was shielded by a window curtain the owner of the house had concealed a copy of *Lady Chatterley's Lover*, presumably smuggled in from abroad, and not to be published, unexpurgated, in England for another thirty-five years.

Apart from inciting us to boast to our friends of the sophistication we had acquired by reading D. H. Lawrence's most heavily banned production, I do not think that the book had a depraving or corrupting effect on the minds and behaviour of my sister and myself. It certainly did not affect Julia's attitude of extreme reserve where matters of nakedness were concerned. Her modesty caused her to refuse to allow any assistance when getting into her evening dress before a ball, a restriction not even relaxed when she was preparing to put on the white net gown and green lined train in which she was to be presented at Buckingham Palace. This bashfulness was, however, something that stopped in her own territory, for she did not hesitate to send Annie Reason on a foray into the bathroom, whence a petticoat, judged by Julia superior to her own, was snatched, in a rape that I, soapy in the bath, was powerless to prevent.

The Court for which Julia was dressing required ladies both presenting and presented to wear three white feathers, from which regulations dictated that three feet of tulle should depend. All of these trimmings, along with the Courts themselves, have passed into the social discard as an early casualty of the Second World War, but at that date the five Courts held in the summer provided fruity material for copy-hungry journalists. Excitement, the readers were given to understand, built up from the moment when it was permissible for cars to line up in the Mall. Only the earliest comers had a chance of seats in the throne room in which the presentations took place, so those determined to extract the maximum from their royal occasion would set out in their fine feathers and cause their chauffeur, with footman beside him, to circle Belgravia and Westminster in the late afternoon sunshine until police signalled that the long, stationary wait might begin. Press photographers snapped their way up and down the line, until in due course, the motor-cars rolled on into the Palace court-yard towards the great moment when the name of presenter and presentee were shouted in the Royal Presence, and curtsys were made first to the King and then to the Queen. This was the newspapers' rendering of events. In reality matters arranged themselves in a different fashion. Every Court was followed by tales of preceding crisis, spots appearing on previously clear complexions, blinding headaches smiting the healthiest, nightmare disasters disrupting Court apparel. The mother of a friend suddenly found that the weight of the medals she was required to wear had stripped her of her chiffon gown down to the waist, but this was a matter which stern work with needle and thread could repair. Far worse was the fate of a client of my dressmaker's who, in a sudden panic, confused the eighteen inches which was the required length of a Court train with the three foot stipulated for the veil. The tearful dressmaker was forced to truncate the veil, and the unhappy wearer was barred from the Royal Presence as too grotesque a spectacle. But even more melodramatic was the experience of the bride who celebrated her presentation on her marriage by commencing a miscarriage, while watching the procession into the Royal supper room. The ambulance summoned to fetch her away must have added to the confusion of Court traffic, but times had certainly changed since the incident recorded by Samuel Pepys, when an embryo was slipped during a dance at the Court of Saint James, responsibility for its origin never being traced.

In a conspiracy with my sister Mary, a party at which I was to be hostess was arranged in her studio in Jubilee Place. With her friend and co-tenant Mary herself had entertained friends in Ascot week, when the grey top hats parked on the staircase had much impressed the caretaker, but this was my first party given away from my mother's house. Mistrusting my friends' ability to find their way along four hundred yards of the King's Road, Chelsea, I took the precaution of drawing a map on the back of each invitation card. It was also necessary to put down a smoke screen for the benefit of my mother, for, although my social life had become to resemble only remotely the edited version presented to my parent, to give a party without her knowledge was yet another step on the steep downward path of deception. Unlike her sister, my Aunt Markie Dynevor, who had actively campaigned in the cause of temperance, my mother admitted that there was nothing inherently wicked in the drinking of wine, regarding it, however, as an extravagance, particularly for young females. Her own mother had always drunk wine, and continued to do so until her death at the age of ninety-six, but my mother had never herself downed a single glass. She regarded the custom of some mothers, who gave their daughters a glass of wine during their monthly periods, as calling undue attention publicly in the dining-room to a delicate matter. Gin was also known to be a palliative for period pains, but its association with the gin-palaces of the nineteenth century made it a commodity that, to avoid placing temptation in the way of employees, could only be purchased by their employers. This principle was carried to extremes when my Aunt Beatrice found herself obliged to drive her own pony-carriage down from her Irish castle to the nearest public-house to buy gin for a writhing guest, the errand being judged dangerously corrupting for a groom.

At that date students of social goings-on were fed on a rich diet of three shiny periodicals, appearing weekly, but displaying subtle differences in their handling of news and personalities. One had a leaning towards photographs of Irish occasions, both in Ireland itself, and among such exiled groups in London as the ball given by the London Irish Medical Golfers. However, the photographer went North for the Twelfth, and remained there long enough to send back a harvest culled from Highland Games on Deeside and Highland Balls on Skye. The second of these magazines had an interest in the Theatre, sometimes devoting a whole page of photographs to a current play, obviating the need actually to buy a ticket for the show. The third paper specialized in what might be called insinuation by lay-out. Photographs of a couple linked by adulterous romance might appear in the same issue, but the captions would be strictly biographical, and the photographs separated by several decorous pages. Hints to the already well-informed could also be conveyed by inserting the consecutive names of an estranged husband and wife, in a paragraph otherwise innocuous.

The technique had not made much advance since Jane Austen described how Fanny Price learnt of the elopement of her cousin Mrs Rushworth with her suitor Mr Crawford from a paragraph of gossip read aloud by her ramshackle father. Befuddled with rum and water, Mr Price was still spry enough to spot that there was an excellent occasion for moral strictures in this scandal among his wife's rich relations, but he had, of course, a personal reason for enjoying the disaster. More detached readers in the 1930s must have been baffled by such sentences as 'How could she help him falling in love with her?' a puzzle to which the reader was expected to supply the identification. Then, of course, there were engagement photographs, some carefully posed and lighted so that the subjects were barely recognizable in a kindly fog, others snapped in the street and often equally unrecognizable from the unhappy angle.

Apart from the engagements of my friends, celebrated by one with a photograph in which she and her saluki were each collared by one half of a jewelled Egyptian belt, prospective marriages began to be announced in my immediate family. Among my grandmother's fifteen grandchildren only two, my eldest brother and sister, had married by this summer of 1931, but now the balance began to shift, and, though the fifteenth and final wedding was some years ahead, the four years of which I write were punctuated by eight matches. Calling to announce her son's engagement, the mother of one of these bridegrooms was so delighted that she seized my hands and whirled me round in a dance. Had my mother been mobile enough to whirl I am sure she would have done so when my brother Frank became engaged to Elizabeth Harman, already a confidante of the lives and loves of her future sisters-in-law.

My mother had given up sending her children with any regularity to be photographed, when the number rose to more than four, though new photographs of her schoolboy sons continued to appear in frames dotted about her drawing-room. Perhaps because they were, for a while, more constantly before her eyes, her daughters' growth went mostly unrecorded. She did, however, make an attempt to take a group of her six children with her own camera, posing them beside a bridge at Pakenham, a bridge that she herself had caused to be flung across the dry moat that surrounded the house, so that the prams of her children could be wheeled forth without offending the grown-ups by passing before their eyes. My mother had never herself set a good example by smiling into the eye of any camera, and her influence was apparent in the group of her children, Edward and Mary in particular presenting countenances of grim rigidity. Indeed the impression achieved was that of a group of total strangers, obliged by unfortunate circumstances to huddle together. In fairness it must be said that Mary could present a more genial aspect of herself, and did so when she was photographed standing at her easel with her palette on her thumb and her brush in her hand. The actual photograph had been taken in Rome but appeared in the *Tatler* above the caption 'Lady Mary Pakenham in her Chelsea Studio'. With a brilliant display of detective efficiency the Post Office, given no more than this as an address, delivered to my sister a letter from an admirer who had been struck by the photograph, and wrote proposing marriage, asking also for a prompt reply as he wished to settle his plans for the summer. To avoid an accusation of wasting my money in vulgar seeking after publicity I had neglected to mention to my mother that I had accepted the offer of a free sitting from a Mayfair photographer, which meant in practice that the results were far from free. I had a shock when, browsing on the bookstall at Mullingar, county town of Westmeath and our local station, I was confronted with seven portraits of myself, reproduced on the front page of the *Bystander*. Luckily the *Bystander* did not often come my mother's way, and she did not object to photographs which appeared haphazard.

In consequence I was not obliged to conceal a photograph that appeared of myself in Regency costume at a charity ball given approximately on the anniversary of the Battle of Waterloo, and in aid of good works in the neighbourhood of Waterloo Road. My dress had been made to measure by a theatrical costumier, with the understanding that it should then pass into his own wardrobe to be hired out. The dress, sky blue satin, was far more lavishly embroidered with imitation gems than any that I might have bought, and the fittings were weirdly romantic compared to the depression of trying-on at a more mundane establishment. As she pinned me into my high-waisted gown, the fitter ducked to avoid the jewel-studded shields, the silver-laced doublets and the plumed helmets which dangled from the walls, and appeared to have been designed for one of Mr Crummles' less *avant-garde* productions. Lack of foresight had led me to believe that I could adapt my Victorian curls to the hair style of an earlier age, but when I was dressing it became clear that the effect would be too uncouth to be displayed in public. My mother's way of wearing her hair had remained virtually unaltered for thirty-five years, a style requiring the use of curling tongs when dressing for an evening occasion. Annie Reason saved the situation. Heating the tongs she twisted my own hair into a riot of ringlets, which looked far more convincingly Empire than the painstaking efforts of professional coiffeurs. Posing with a friend to be photographed, I took up what I hoped was the sort of attitude that Sir Thomas Lawrence expected from his sitters, but my companion was less thorough-going, and had not even made the compromise of removing an obviously twentieth-century wrist-watch.

Apart from food and dancing the entertainment offered was the chance to feast the eye on Jack Buchanan and C. B. Cochran, while J. C. Squire read aloud 'There was a sound of revelry by night'. This evocation of Byron's thoughts on the Battle of Waterloo was hampered by the un-Byronic spectacles worn by the reader, though he had done his best by putting on a plum-coloured tail-coat. Other gentlemen present had hired every variety of contemporary uniform, complaints abounding that Wellington's soldiers fought their campaigns with no pockets in their trousers. Given a latch key and small change by a friend in this predicament, I reached home with these still in my possession, while the owner marched through Mayfair in full fig as a Fusilier.

This London Season came to an end with unexpected éclat, when the King and Queen decided to give a ball at Buckingham Palace, with the rather charming wish, it was said on good authority, of seeing some young people around them; young people dancing rather than in a continuous stream of pink faces bobbing curtsys beneath white plumes. The category of young guests was somewhat elastic, and included my cousin Hugo Gough in his capacity as officer commanding the 1st Battalion of the Irish Guards. Losing an arm in the First World War, Hugo had overcome his disability, continuing to hunt and ride in point-to-points. He was also famous for swift repartee, among the stories attributed to him being that of the defeat of a general, who complained that he failed, on manoeuvres, to see Lord Gough's scouts. Having failed to post scouts, Hugo replied that he certainly hoped the general could not see them as he had given particular orders that they should keep below the skyline. To Julia and me he belonged to an older, remote, generation, and the arrangement that he should escort us to Buckingham Palace had been cooked up between his mother and my mother. It was an evening when Hugo was struggling to suppress the suffering that his war wounds continued to inflict on him, and it was only afterwards that I appreciated that our party must have had a romantic appearance to those who had gathered to see a free show. Hugo, heroic in his bemedalled full dress, his bearskin nursed in his remaining arm, was the centre-piece in the Daimler landaulette, flanked by houris, in orange and and sea-green.

In my mother's girlhood Court balls had not been for dancing, to take the floor for a few turns being the most that was expected, after the assembled royalties had marched their decorous way through a state quadrille. Afterwards I heard that one of my partners had, most unworthily, purloined some writing-paper from a blotter at Buckingham Palace. On this he was said to have written to the ex-German Emperor, who was sufficiently impressed to grant the interview thus requested. Paying my mother the call in the small hours on which she always insisted, I was able to reply to her inquiry if I had taken the floor with the boast that I had danced for most of the night, and that a cousin who was Comptroller of the Household had signalled for the band to play God Save the King, our host, far too soon for my taste.

7. Bavarian Rhapsody

Julia had been required by the authorities of Somerville College to perfect her German, as well as her French, before she went up to Oxford. This intellectual sharpening up was to take place in the family of Count H. whose house stood in a romantic grove of chestnut trees at the extreme edge of the Schwabing district of Munich. In the United Kingdom the economic situation was moving towards crisis. In Germany there was a rumbling of sinister forces on the move, but when it was suggested to my mother that her plans for Julia might turn out to be perilous, she reacted with the same contempt for danger that she had shown ten years before, when warned that Ireland was no place in which to risk a family of young children. Immediately she arranged that I should accompany my sister, a separate lodging being conveniently to hand in the *Pension* run by the sister of my mother's own German governess, to whom she had given an exemption from the distaste she felt for every other German. This governess had, in fact, been my mother's confidante, and the dear friend of all the family, her wedding being celebrated in Middleton Church, with her pupils as bridesmaids and my grandfather to give the bride away. On this occasion Madlon Witzell had also been a bridesmaid, so my mother associated her with the sunlit days of her girlhood. The H.'s, on the other hand, who were to be Julia's hosts for six weeks, had only been seen briefly by me the previous autumn, when in the dark of the evening my chief impression had been of the imposing appearance of Halva, their old English sheepdog.

These plans had to be made at long range, for Julia and I had been dispatched on a round of visits to Dunsany and Pakenham. The object was to keep us away from home while my mother's domestic staff took their annual holidays, a problem always taking her by surprise, and, paradoxically, becoming no easier as the size of her staff decreased. Our visits were punctuated by telegrams from my mother, giving contradictory instructions as to how we were to return and start for Germany. After attending the Dublin Horse Show, where my uncle's generosity in giving us luncheon at the Kildare Street Club was vitiated by his objection to the table salt, which he regarded as a poisonous powder, we moved on to Pakenham.

Edward was now an eager fisher after pike, and I, catching two fish in one morning, set up a record for some weeks, until the catch of a pike over twenty pounds in weight eclipsed my feat. Even smallish pike can give a nasty bite long after they have been considered to be dead, and Edward's letter describing the gaffing of this Leviathan gave me to understand that the scuppers had been awash with the blood of the fish and the fishermen.

Finally a telegram arrived from my mother in which her determination to spend no more than the lowest statutory charge had overcome her ability to condense her meaning, and we smugly replied telegraphically asking for clarification.

When Julia and I set out on the long haul which started from Liverpool Street, and after twenty-four hours brought us to München (Hauptbahnhof), the journey was already familiar to me from an expedition I had made at even shorter notice the year before. So little time had I had to prepare for the journey that was to take me to the Passionsspiel at Oberammergau that I neglected to notice that the soles of my shoes were worn through. When pebbles began to irritate the soles of my feet I sought to protect them by buying a pair of half-galoshes, bright yellow in colour. These unglamorous adjuncts had made my appearance so Teutonic that an English couple had asked me if they might take my photograph, to give a human touch to a view of the house of Alois Lang, the Christ in the Passionsspiel. In slow, loud English they thought to reassure this supposedly Bavarian belle, by telling her that they came from a little place called Worthing.

Even to those like Julia and myself, who had been exposed since earliest childhood to the stern embrace of the Irish Channel, this particular crossing to the Hook of Holland was a stomach-shaker. It needed little imagination, even to queasy eyes, for Cuyp's red-cloaked horseman to appear through the golden morning mists, but it was not until we staggered to the Speisewagen at midday that I began to set up as a German expert. Julia, who retained some of her childhood's mistrust of any advance into sophistication on my part, refused to accept a glass of Mosel from the half bottle I had ordered in imitation of the lady with whom I had travelled the year before, and which certainly helped to wash down the gelatinous Kalbskopf, speciality of the Mitropa menu.

The journey from the Hook of Holland to Munich had the quality of a haphazard travel film, excellent visually, interesting historically, but assembled without a coherent plan. Leaving Cuyp and Holland behind us, Julia and I found ourselves recognizing in the Rhine Valley a scene made familiar to us by Richard Doyle's illustrations to that nineteenth-century masterpiece *The Travels of Brown, Jones and Robinson*. The flow of the

River Rhine between its rocky crags, each summit bearing a ruined castle, had been drawn by Doyle with such faithful feeling that his record remained a perfect representation. The tower where Bishop Hatto was deservedly eaten by the avenging ten thousand rats (commemorated by Southey with more enthusiasm than historical accuracy) and the rock on to which the unhappy boatman was lured to shipwreck by the Lorelei's song (celebrated by Heine), added a fairy-tale element to this part of the journey. Then we passed through the water-meadows of a lesser river, where autumn crocus grew prodigally among the deep grass. Yet another change of landscape came in view, in a breath stopping moment when the train ran out on to a high plateau, where the onion domes of the village churches brought the realization that, scenically speaking, central Europe had taken over. Evening came on apace, and with it an exhausted lack of belief that the journey would ever end, but finally at the Munich terminus we were winkled out of the train by our respective hostesses, waving letters of identification to avert the risk of white-slavers intervening. The letters were written in my mother's illegible but unmistakable handwriting, and so we separated to destinations which turned out to be in many ways the social antithesis of each other.

Madlon, with whom I was to stay, had reason to show her forbearance almost immediately. My first night under her roof was disrupted by a telephone call from a group of friends who, sitting convivially in a café, had happened to recall that I was due in Munich on that date, their cheerful inquiries being rebuffed by Madlon's niece with the tart information that young ladies were not to be disturbed at one in the morning. Later I found that the telephone was the hub of the varied clientele that boarded at Ainmiller Strasse 21. At home it had only been with reluctance that my mother had allowed the telephone to be installed in her country house, regarding it as an instrument of destructive extravagance, suffered as a necessity in London, but in the country to be discouraged, its very existence to be concealed from outsiders by keeping the number off the writing-paper. I was surprised that the midnight telephone call was not held against me, until I discovered that I was living among compulsive telephoners, the number of whose calls were jotted down in strokes like the score of a parlour game, linked together when they reached double figures.

Suffering from traveller's disorientation, I found the first midday meal far from reassuring. Probably it was a Friday, as in memory I associate a bony fish, covered in a skin of knobbly black macintosh, with a flow of conversation, to me incomprehensible, between the other pensionnaires. At my arrival the rest of the lodgers were male, including an Englishman who had been romantically involved with one of my friends in London, but had now become attached to a Bavarian lady, with whom he presumably ate all his meals, as he did not patronize Madlon's table. More convivial were two brothers from Swabia, and a professor from Italy, who was occupied at the University of Munich in a capacity that remained mysterious to me. When he had returned to his own country one of the Swabian brothers revealed that the poor Italian, far from glamorous in person, had fallen in love, and finding his passion unreturned had left Munich wailing 'Mein Gott, mein Gott, warum hast Du mich verlassen?' Heaviest in hand was a young American, who incensed Madlon by continuing to sit with his feet on the table when she entered his room. Never, Madlon said, when she had been governess to the Ladies Acheson at Gosford Castle, had their father failed to rise to his feet when she entered the room, nor to open the door for her when she left it. I knew the appearance of the Ladies Acheson after they had left the schoolroom, the Tate Gallery displaying a picture of them by Sargent, posed round an orange tree in a garlanded urn, with as much grace as their rigid corsetting allowed. Grown-up, they seemed remote from the study of German irregular verbs; which Saki suggested might lead an elephant to murder his teacher. I should have enjoyed hearing more tales about these carefree girls, but Madlon shunned any reminiscence which might lead to a contemplation of the agonizing blow which, in 1914, had sundered pupils and governess.

Madlon did not herself give me German lessons, which I took with a teacher in a neighbouring flat, where dark brown and black were also the colours favoured for decoration. In the intervals of translating Oscar Wilde's fairy stories into German, I would ponder on the taste that seemed to choose the dullest colours to fill apartments constructed on generous lines with high ceilings and big windows. I had been warned by my grandmother, who considered rightly that my mother would be unlikely to pass on such worldly wisdom, that in Germany the sofa was a seat of honour on which one must never sit without invitation, and I observed that a table on which lay a mat invariably stood in front of every sofa. This was even the case in the H.s' drawing-room, though they were a family both cosmopolitan and cultivated, but any air of subscribing to a national convention was, in this instance, physically dispersed by the frequency with which the coffee-making machine exploded, covering sofa and table in splinters of glass and coffee grounds.

While Julia studied her grammar and improved her conversation among the H.'s, I led a life both less intellectual and more sedate. I had so much of the evenings to myself at the beginning of my stay that I began to write a novel, an enterprise which foundered, partly because I found myself unable to create any characters who were not female and sunburnt blondes (the fashion of that year), and partly because my friends the F.'s, who had telephoned on my first night in Munich, now returned from the Salzburg Festival. The food at Madlon's *PENSION* had never again struck quite such a low level as on my first day, and sometimes the suppers, not attended by the male guests, were savoury with Frankfurters, but taken by the F.'s to dinner at the Vierjahreszeiten, I suddenly realized how long it was since I had eaten a delicious meal. In fact Julia and I had been in the habit of filling in the gaps with Eiskaffee at the Kaffee Hag, where we found the platinum blonde manageress a reassuring symbol that the planet was not only inhabited by women with shining faces and sleeked down hair. Seeking more smart blondes, we had developed a taste for the films of Brigitte Helm, though our sense of history was outraged by a spy picture in which Germany appeared to have won the war. Additionally cheering to those accustomed, as we were, to unrestricted raiding of kitchen gardens, was the bountiful vintage which had brought barrows piled with surplus grapes to every street corner, a small coin buying as many as even I could eat.

With the vintage had come the Oktoberfest, on which the F. family advanced *en masse*, though for some reason their first attempt to reach it ended instead in the Löwenbräu. The vastness of this beer-hall could not absorb the thunder of the Schuhplattler as they twined the ribbons of the maypole with infinite cunning. I had retained enough primness to prefer an English friend as a partner when asked to dance by a Bavarian in all the trimmings, coloured braces, hat with chamois beard, and footless stockings. Additionally I felt that, having just presented me with a large chocolate heart bearing on its curves the legend 'Wie ich Dich lieb', so liebt Dich keiner', my countryman deserved to be rewarded. Our next attempt to reach the Oktoberfest was successful. We had with us the music-master with whom one of the F. sisters had been studying, who knew the moment when a change of tune indicated that the table should link arms and sway in time to the shouted chorus. The music-master was only one of the friends who the F.s amassed in the manner of a snowball rolling down hill. Pausing to buy a motor-bicycle and abandon the tedium of the train, they had, earlier in the season, collected a golden-haired Rhine maiden with an English chaperone, who had followed her charge from beer-hall to restaurant, until she rebelled at being required to enter a night-club at four in the morning. So, after singing at the Oktoberfest, it was no surprise that in the Café Luitpold the manager appeared to be a close friend of the family, encouraging us to play billiards in a room officially closed for the night.

While we were trying to subdue our English technique to a pocketless table, billiard-balls the size of grapefruit, and cues like toothpicks, one of the F. brothers told us about an experience he had had the night before. Walking home along the Brienner Strasse he had been harried by what he called 'little leather men', who had emerged from the bushes surrounding a large mansion. Consulting a near-by policeman, he was asked in a quaking voice, 'Meinen Sie das Braune Haus Hitlers?' with the implication that bad had better be left alone. It was now 2 a.m., and as the Brienner Strasse was close at hand we agreed on some field-work, to see if this scuffling round harmless passers-by was a nightly occurrence.

Passing through Munich the year before, I had eavesdropped at the desk of the Regina Palast Hotel, when a guest had been arguing with the concierge over the expense of a telegram he had sent to the then Lord Rothermere. Seventy pounds was, I overheard, the sum involved, and well it might be, for I learnt later that this telegram had been the basis of an article in which the *Daily Mail* had assessed the future of Adolf Hitler. The goings-on of this political newcomer were responsible, I also understood, for the squads of police marching below my hotel window in the early morning. Twelve months later Hitler was less of a political newcomer, but he was still only the leader of one of a number of warring parties. The shop that sold the uniforms and insignia of his party had a window display of such stodginess that, passing by on the step of a tram, I was convulsed at the idea that a movement of such a drab outward appearance could win recruits among a people who delighted in gold braid and bright local costumes. My own German teacher had treated me to a tirade beginning, 'Ich bin eine Dame . . .' and going on to explain that there was no appeal for her in being led by dreary chaps who, instead of gorgeous uniforms, wore black overcoats and carried umbrellas. Wrongly, I assumed that brown shirts would rank as low among my teacher's compatriots as black overcoats.

For our approach to Hitler's stronghold on the Brienner Strasse we split into couples. Julia was carrying a bunch of flowers, bought in the Café Luitpold as a birthday offering for one of the H. sisters. From the same source I had acquired a copy of the *Tatler*, which brought with it a breath of another world by containing a picture of my cousins Joan and Ann at a local horse show. With these objects we signalled across the street to each other, and sure enough from among the bushes 'leather men', their hands indubitably on their revolvers emerged by ones and twos. Possibly the frivolity of our behaviour may have conveyed an idea that they were being ragged, for they stayed behind their railings, like animals suspicious but not prepared to attack. Fifty yards further on, the street converged with others in a circle dominated by a monumental fountain. On its steps, forlorn in an empty townscape, a woman sat crouched, her head bowed over her knees. Suddenly in the pale lamplight a man approached her, and she sprang up stiffly, seizing him by the hand in a welcome jerky as a marionette's.

Without pondering on the juxtaposition of the sinister figures lurking in Hitler's shrubbery with the dejected prostitute at last finding a client, the two pictures remained in my memory. Immediately I was preoccupied by the need to regain my lodging, where empty milk-bottles were a trap for night birds, without calling attention to my late homecoming. Next day I thought to enliven the midday meal with an account of the night's prowl round the Braune Haus, in the manner to which, as a child, I had been accustomed to hearing reports of a night's adventures during the Irish troubles. Insensitive and insouciant as I was, it did strike me that the story was not a success. I was even conscious of a real tremor of fear among the Germans at the table, preventing any justifiable criticism of behaviour which had been both irresponsible and potentially dangerous.

Two English governesses prospecting for an establishment of their own had arrived in Madlon's *PENSION*, and took it upon themselves to resent my evening games of ping-pong with Doctor Louis, the younger of the Swabian brothers. I suppose attaining some academic standard had allowed him to be called doctor, but it had not softened a strong Swabian accent. After accompanying me to *The Love Parade*, then showing in Munich, the English governesses picked up the point that Maurice Chevalier's French accent was explained by association with a French doctor's wife, and suggested that I had better be careful about my accent and Swabian doctors. In fact Louis' brother, Doctor Eugen, was much more polished in speech and manner. A lecturer at the University of Munich his formidably erudite subject, Old Church Law, was no barrier to an active social life, he being the most animated of the *Pension* telephoners. Finally he gave a party himself, to which I was charmed to be invited, for, to tell the truth, I found him more attractive than poor Doctor Louis, who played ping-pong with me for two hours each evening, and took elaborate photographs in which he assured me I looked like a Madonna.

To my surprise Madlon, who had cheerfully tolerated earlier escapades, including returns home in the side-car of the F.s' motor-bicycle which could be heard three streets away, showed signs of fuss at the idea of an English girl being a guest at such an aboriginal party, begging me to remember that I need stay no longer than politeness dictated. In fact I still remember it as one of the parties of my girlhood at which I was an unqualified success. The punch provided was somewhat mysterious to the taste, the company drinking it to ritual 'Prosts' round the table big enough for ping-pong. Doctor Eugen's room next door had been cleared for dancing to a gramophone, his library on Altes Kirchenrecht giving richness to the background.

In the course of the evening I laboured to explain the reason which made it correct to introduce me as 'Lady Violet' rather than as 'Miss'. I may mention, in passing, that although myself a born busybody and an ace contradictor, in Bavaria I was hopelessly outclassed, it seemed, by every male I met, from Madlon's nephew who told me I smoked too much, to Madlon's landlord who, on a rent-collecting call, told me I was leaving no turnings on the shirt I was cutting out on that so useful dining-room table. Another guest opened the conversation by asking if I was called 'Buckingham' because I lived in Buckingham Palace, but it was with the non-speakers of English that I got on best. My partners chasséed and side-stepped over the bumpy linoleum with a delicious ease rarely encountered on the polished floors of London town. I glowed with gratification when complimented on my own proficiency, one partner showing a flattering regret that I was so soon to return to England, while another suggested that I should come to a meeting of the Pan-Europa movement of which he was the local organizer. As I did not attend the meeting I only learnt at second hand that the movement proposed to include all Europe except the British Isles, nor do I know what line was taken about the persistent low rumble of anti-Semitism, which had first come to my notice in connection with the local attitude towards Richard Tauber. In London he was immensely popular, singing in 'The Land of Smiles', where demands for encores of 'You are my heart's delight' sometimes reached double figures. I had assumed that the deprecatory attitude taken towards Tauber in Bavaria was based on jealousy of a German doing well abroad, when so many Germans were enduring hard times at home, but after a while it dawned on me that it was antipathy to his ancestry more than envy at the adulation he received that sharpened the disobliging stories in circulation.

Contrary to what has often been said on the subject of the film *Im Westen nichts Neues* never having been shown in Germany, it was running in Munich that September. I did, however, refuse Doctor Louis' suggestion that he might take me to see it, explaining, with either great fortitude of mind or stark insensibility, that as a war orphan I did not care for war films. But I did agree to go with Doctor Louis and a friend to the Oktoberfest, an evening of a very different social category than the one spent there with the F. family. Both my escorts wore broad brimmed furry felt hats, which gave me the feeling that I was sitting between two animals escaped from Kenneth Grahame's *Wind In the Willows*. Knowing only by hearsay that my sister was staying in Munich, Doctor Louis had suggested that Julia might join us and square the party, but she refused, having a justified suspicion that the evening would bear no resemblance to the cultivated life of the H.s' circle.

The H.s had the erroneous impression that my fellow-lodgers in Ainmiller Strasse were elderly, passion-spent professors, though Count H. thought that I needed a caution even from these supposed greybeards on the subject of a serial in the *Münchner Neueste Nachrichten* which they, he and I were all following. The dialogue was in an old-fashioned Bavarian *patois*, and the story concerned the difficulties of a girl called Senta (presumably after the heroine of *The Flying Dutchman*) in bringing her preferred suitor, of the two young men who were courting her, to the point of proposing marriage. Success seemed in sight at a well-planned picnic, the young man being enchanted by the felicity with which cheese followed varieties of sausage, at the exact moment when his taste-buds demanded a change. But poor Senta had undone herself by planning too perfect a meal, the sleep of satiety preventing the proposal of marriage from materializing. She had to content herself with marrying an unattractive second string. Better acquainted than he with the rules of popular serials, I assured Count H. that Senta would marry her first love in the end, explaining that, when defeated by the Bavarian dialect, I was in the habit of applying to my fellow lodgers for a translation. Warning me that the coarseness of the dialect might lead to embarrassment, Count H. also refused to accept my prediction of a happy ending. However, weeks later in England I received the last instalment of Senta's adventures with Count H.'s greetings. It was a generous gesture, for Senta did indeed marry her first love in a second marriage at the Frauenkirche, fulfilling, I suppose, the dream of every Münchner Mädchen.

It had already come to my attention that natives got far shorter shrift in the night-life of Munich than free-spending foreigners, when Madlon and I, with some of her family, had been refused admission to a beer-hall because the management had set up an 'American Evening', prices presumably doubled. I had the same experience of natives being treated with contempt when touring the side-shows of the Oktoberfest, in the company of Doctor Louis and his friend, invited so that I should not be left unescorted when drinking necessitated one or other of the chaps retiring to the lavatory. Prospecting into some show on the point of closing for the night, Doctor Louis was ejected through the turnstile as if by catapult.

One of the few live exhibitions still open on a slack evening was a booth which advertised a Sensational Electric Maiden. She wore a black velvet dinner-jacket with trousers, and the showman explained that by passing an electric current through her body not only would she become insensible to pain, but a source of heat of an intensity to ignite a newspaper. The lighting on the grubby little stage was of the fiercest green and the colour of the Electric Maiden's face was scarcely less ghastly. Undeniably when a battery was attached to her leg she did appear to pass into a cataleptic trance. She was cast to the floor and bounced as rigidly as a doll made from rubber, and a newspaper drawn across her trousers flared up into instant flame. After this gruesome demonstration, the victim was given a glass of water, before addressing the Herrschaften with the assurance that she felt no pain. Into the collecting-plate, which she passed round the exiguous audience, most people dropped with reluctance the smallest coins in circulation. Shaken by the demonstration, I myself contributed an obtrusively large piece of money, which caused Doctor Louis, realizing perhaps that this show had been an unhappy choice, to look at my distressed face and remark, 'Das arme Mädchen', an expression which could have as well served for me as for the Electric Maiden.

It was not only the adventures of Senta (an essentially un-electric maiden) which was fixing my attention on the *Münchner Neueste Nachrichten*, a paper taken at my mother's suggestion that its daily perusal might improve my command of German. As it happened the economic crisis which exploded in England in the month of September would have encouraged the most monoglot tourist to study the local papers. In later years I have never read the history of the 1931 crisis without recalling its progress as set out in black gothic print. The report of the naval mutiny at Invergordon was so startling to me, to whom the navy was represented by infinitely reliable grey silhouettes seen in Portsmouth Harbour on visits to Admiralty House, that I appealed to Madlon for corroboration. Madlon attempted to soften the bad news by assuring me that at the end of the argument officers and men had given three cheers for the King, but I knew enough to realize it would be better in future to puzzle out the reports from London for myself. With the announcement of the formation of a National Government in England, the paper was laudatory, and even envious at such a display of patriotic purpose, publishing a cartoon of men from different levels of British society, top-hats, bowler-hats, cloth-caps, marching arm-in-arm with cheerful amity. Below the drawing was the wistful caption, 'Wenn es so bei uns möchte sein!'

Letters from England were, of course, concerned with the financial upheaval and its effects, momentarily obliterating details of the preparations for the wedding of Elizabeth and Frank, or such a sensation as the fight between two of our acquaintances in the Forty-Three night-club. The occasion had been a supposed insult to a girl with whom one of the belligerents had been sitting. My sister Mary and my future sister-in-law had celebrated the fight by a parody of Tennyson's Revenge – The One and the Forty-Three – which, it will be remembered, begins 'At Flores in the Azores . . .' The parody, neatly called 'The Two in the Forty-Three', began 'With Whorès on the Floorès'. When Julia and I received this letter our shouts of laughter rocked the *Pension* to such a degree that, although seldom aware that I was making an undue amount of noise, I did later feel that an apology was necessary. Madlon assured me that she, and her niece who was her partner, had rejoiced to hear evidence of young girls being so innocently merry.

With a national crisis to get her teeth into, my mother's letters were of sterner stuff. She relished a challenge to her patriotism, and a ten-per-cent cut in the salaries of public employees, together with a rise in the rate of income tax, seemed to her to call for a reduction across the board on the domestic front. Her daughters' dress allowances were thus reduced from £130 (a curious sum, but hallowed by having been that given to her by my mother's own father) to an annual £120. This was not a full ten per cent cut, and some months later the original allowance was restored to Julia, but unhappily by then my mother and I had embarked on a system of financial give and take which made the nation's effort to balance its budget appear to be a simple exercise. A more immediate problem was by what means Julia and I, representatives of a rocky off-the-gold-standard economy, were to pay our debts and regain our devalued homeland. Julia's debt to the H.s was only finally liquidated by means of a banker's draft sent from England, a means of paying for board and lodging which sounded romantically archaic.

In the English-speaking cinemas of the 1930s a ten-minute gap in the programme was apt to be filled by a coloured travel film, the commentary spoken by The Voice of The Globe, whose name was, I think, something like Patrick Fitzpatrick. The Voice of The Globe invariably sailed as a particularly blood-red sunset was throwing the city of, perhaps, Lima into silhouette, and his exit line 'And so we say farewell to this jewel of the Pacific (as the case might be)' was a welcome signal that the big picture might now be expected to unroll its credits. And so I said farewell to Munich, to the chestnut trees round the Damenbad, whose leaves fell on women bathers, models worthy of Maillol but becoming increasingly unbeautiful as they covered their starched white underclothes with sad coloured outer garments. Gone with the chestnut trees are the turquoise blue onion domes of the Frauenkirche, said to have been a piece of architectural improvisation, when the Münchners, finding they lacked money for the proposed twin spires, started a new style of church architecture. And it was good-bye to the coffee and honey sent home by Madlon's kin in Guatemala, which made every breakfast a feast. Madlon's own stormy crossing of the ocean had, she told me, been cheered by hearing the voice of a sailor on deck singing the song that celebrates the Münchner's love of his city, 'So lang der alte Peter am Petersbergl steht'.

It was also farewell to the Alte Pinakothek, where I had enjoyed that sense of ownership in being a solitary in an empty picture gallery. Possessing Dürers and El Grecos, Rubens and Goyas, I had particularly valued a Flemish Danaë, whose robe was of blue more cerulean than the domes of the Frauenkirche, as she sat, eyes raised in expectation, under Zeus' impregnating shower of gold. I still possess more ephemeral outdoor effects, and an impression of the inky clouds rushing over the arch of the Leopold's Thur after a storm comes back to me when I read the beginning of the *Waste Land*.

> 'Summer surprised us, coming over the Starnbergersee
> With a shower of rain; we stopped in the colonnade,
> And went on in sunlight, into the Hofgarten.'

Paris, Rome, Venice, Lisbon, New York, cities that I knew before 1939, have come up again like numbers on a roulette wheel, and so have taken on a new meaning, but Munich lies, crystallized as I once knew it, on the far side of a chasm filled with the wreckage of war.

The first snow of autumn had fallen on the roofs of Munich

when Julia and I pointed our noses for home. In the very chill early morning Madlon saw us off on the coach labelled Hoek v. Holland. Beside our train stood another bearing the infinitely more seductive legend Venedig-Rom, and had I known that it would be twenty-five years before I would once again enjoy the delights of Italy that lay beyond the Alps, the pang travelling northwards would have been even more acute.

At an early stage of our journey we were joined in our carriage by an English woman, elderly to our young eyes, and determined to extract from us the details of whence we came and whither we were going. Undeniably lacking in drama, the information was also unsatisfactory in that it gave her little excuse to embark on the saga of her own life and times. A Swiss businessman, who joined us as the day wore on, proved to be more worthy of her mettle. Forced to reveal that he was a jeweller by profession, he was next driven to admit that he had heard of the Gulbenkian family, the tallest social feather in our travelling companion's cap. Held in a reverse situation of the Ancient Mariner's wedding guest, he was obliged to listen to a summary of the rare jewels and fine fare, which had adorned the bride and regaled the guests, at Miss Gulbenkian's wedding.

At this point Julia passed to me rhymed lines celebrating these nuptials, and by the time we reached the Hook we had exchanged seven sheets of verse on the theme of our fellow traveller's life story. Material was not wanting. Her name, she said, was splashed all over the evening papers when detected smuggling dresses from Paris, the dresses themselves being described in detail by their smuggler.

'Chiffon and Chantilly lace
And over all that bloody face,' wrote Julia.

Crossing the United States from coast to coast this frenetic traveller had missed the train at Salt Lake City, which enabled lines about her adventures as Brigham Young's head wife to be added to the saga.

If our behaviour might seem coarsely critical, we were punished at the Dutch frontier where the Swiss jeweller gave way to a young Dutchman, on his way to London for a cheap holiday, in a country that had abandoned the gold standard. As, besides Dutch, he spoke only German, this information was extracted from him in a cross-examination in which I was the interpreter. Julia only came to my aid when I floundered in forming German sentences, for, though her German was more grammatical and fluent than mine, she was equally more determined not to be bullied into conversation with strangers. After a series of questions beginning, 'Die Dame würde gern wissen . . .' my relationship with the Dutchman became so close that he kept in touch throughout the rigours of the rest of the journey. He remains unique in my experience in being the only person who chose Liverpool Street Station at seven o'clock on a bleak October morning as a propitious moment to invite a new female acquaintance out for an evening at the theatre. I heard a voice, supposedly my own, explaining that residence in Ireland made this an impossibility. An Irish habitat was hardly a true excuse, but we did at least have to travel on to Buckinghamshire, where my mother for a moment forgot her horror of war-guilty Germany to welcome us with 'Wie geht's? Wie geht's?' This was a memory of the days when she and her sisters had formed a garland of girls to walk up the aisle with Madlon behind Madlon's own sister, dressed as was the fashion for bridesmaids at that date in white dresses and big hats trimmed with ostrich feathers.

8. The Family Circle Widens

BRIDESMAIDS WERE, IN FACT, WHAT Julia and I had returned to be, an experience of which I had, in earlier years, felt unduly cheated. At the children's parties of my childhood I had taken an envious interest in a child with a halo of golden curls, who bore the name of Nefertari, her father having assisted the expedition which revealed Tutankhamen's tomb to the amazement of succeeding generations. Although remote in appearance from the Egyptian princess who had given her such a tintinnabulary name, Nefertari was so much in demand as a seraphic bridal attendant that she possessed a wardrobe of period dresses for which she was duly pitied by grown-ups, who thought an Elizabethan gown in cloth of gold with a ruff absurd on a child of six. Personally I could imagine nothing more enjoyable, but since opulent Edwardian days, when Pansy had been a bridesmaid to my Aunt Cynthia in a Kate Greenaway frock and blue sash, there had been no demand for child bridesmaids among my mother's little daughters. I had early realized that this was inevitable, as the divisions between the age groups in my family were unusually clear-cut, but with a brother and a sister nine and eight years older than myself I did envisage that there might later be a chance to come into possession of a dress which, if not of historical picturesqueness, had not been chosen to measure up to my mother's unadventurous taste in *robes de demoiselles*. Disappointment came with my brother's wedding, whose simplicity was such that even a best man was dispensed with, while my sister was married in a Registrar's office, where bridesmaids do not, as a rule, attend the bride.

The wedding of Elizabeth and Frank was postponed by the forces of history, which had picked the same date for a general election. The national unity, so much admired by the Bavarian newspaper, now carried the country through a general election, when support for a National Government swept Conservatives into the House of Commons, some to their astonishment finding themselves representing such Labour preserves as constituencies encompassing docks and coal-mines. Still too young to vote, I was myself swept into the election campaign of a friend of Frank's, who was standing as a Conservative for a constituency where Liberal roots were thought to be too deep to be disturbed by a national crisis.

I was summoned from addressing envelopes, to attend a meeting that was to be addressed by Lord Beaverbrook. This was a welcome relief, though the envelope addressing had been brightened by coming on an addressee with the name of Daisy Two, which suggested a contraction of the refrain of 'A Bicycle made for Two'. At the meeting I had a seat on the platform, to the concern of the mother of a friend who, seated in the body of the hall, thought that I was bound to display an improper amount of underclothing to those at ground level. My underclothes, however, remained severely concealed, which was fortunate as, half-way through his powerful speech on behalf of the candidate, Lord Beaverbrook muddled his notes and had to quote statistics from memory. Of the figures for such foreign imports as fruit, shoes and ladies' underwear which, he urged, might well have their duties increased in the interest of protecting the pound sterling, the only statistic he could recall was that for ladies' underwear, but unabashed he brandished this verbally before his audience as a strong argument for voting for the Conservative nominee.

At the end of this stimulating evening Frank and I spent the night in the house of the chairman of the local Conservative party, a house haunted by what appeared to be an uncounted number of footmen, but lacking in electric light. Consequently the party-workers trudged up the grand staircase to bed, candlesticks in hand, like the followers in procession at a Breton pardon. Outdoors a private zoo added exoticism to the unremarkable landscape of Bedfordshire, a llama being brought round for an after-breakfast ride. As the candidate left to put in his nomination he was pursued by me, sedately trotting on the llama's long-haired back.

Weddings notoriously cause ripples of disorder which spread far beyond the central figures, even without the additional confusion brought about by times of public crisis. My mother had given tickets for Noël Coward's *Cavalcade* to a party of daughters and nieces, and something of her own incapacity to arrive before the rise of any curtain seemed to have infected the operation of this pre-wedding treat. After an agony of mistiming, we reached Drury Lane to find that, as the opening of the show was played in darkness with a single spotlight on the actors, late-comers were penned in the foyer to avoid spoiling the effect. We were co-operative, but beside us was a theatre-goer, certainly infuriated and probably intoxicated, who called the curses of Heaven and Hell on the unhappy programme-seller and on C. B. Cochran, whose orders she was struggling to obey with the force of her girlish arm. *Cavalcade* is a show that is now apt to be remembered for a child's remark, 'She must have been a very little lady', when

Queen Victoria's funeral cortège passed off-stage. Down the years this line has been quoted in derision for its arch sentiment. Long forgotten is the dazzling previous scene, in which the two families, whose fortunes formed the rather tenuous plot, met and greeted each other in dumb-show, black figures mourning their Sovereign against blue-white snow, scored by the black lines of the park railings. Even more unremembered is the sequence of the First World War. Against a dimly seen background of soldiers bowed under their packs and forever marching to the muted sound of 'Tipperary', women painted and bedizened were suddenly spotlighted, each year growing more haggard, as they sang, 'We don't want to lose you . . .' or 'I'll make a man of every one of you'. Thirty-five years later when *Oh! What a Lovely War* was acclaimed for the brilliant use of songs from the First World War, it passed apparently unremarked that the brilliance of the idea belonged to Noël Coward and its original execution to *Cavalcade*, a production conceived in a spirit that might be called diametrically opposed to that of *Oh! What a Lovely War*.

Too young to have done more than receive impressions of sadness at my father's death, the emotional disturbance around me had left a bare nerve that quivered in response to any recapitulation of the agonies of the First World War. The last curtain of *Cavalcade* found me in a pool of tears, induced by the harrowing scene where the leading lady, Mary Clare, receiving the news of her only surviving son's death in action, by grisly coincidence just as the sirens heralded the Armistice, rushed out to join the rejoicing crowds. So shaken was I that a voice beside me, which calmly remarked, 'You know, I quite liked that woman in the end', seemed speaking from a remote planet, inhabited by monsters of insensitivity.

In addition to their families, whose numbers were only equalled by the complexity of internal links by blood and marriage, Frank and Elizabeth had invited a myriad friends to their wedding. The guests covered an area stretching from Downing Street, where Elizabeth's cousin Neville Chamberlain was moving into No. 11 as Chancellor of the Exchequer to Stoke-on-Trent, where both bride and bridegroom had taught for the Workers' Educational Association. No church smaller than St Margaret's, Westminster, could have contained the number of guests, though a principal one was missing, my mother having decided against attempting the struggle it would have been for her to achieve the front pew on the bridegroom's side. This sacrifice did not spoil her enjoyment in sorting out the degrees of kinship among the senders of presents, many of his kindred being previously unheard of by the bridegroom. Always drastic in her classifications, my mother spoke with some disfavour of a distant cousin, whom she deemed purse-proud, but praised another, a widow, who, although the daughter of the vastest of Irish country houses, had been, we were told in the idiom of my mother's period, 'always rather hard up'. There was a feeling that the rich, if not sent empty away, should at least be relegated to a back pew, while the chronically poverty-stricken widow should go up higher; though identifying the latter, as Frank pointed out, was going to be difficult for the ushers, unless the wind was actually whistling through her rags. He also suggested that it would be a problem to give her due place to another cousin, loved by all, but certain, from congenital vagueness, to be found seated by the font.

In order to be on the spot, my mother had established her base at the hotel in Park Lane where the wedding reception was to be held. Knowing her enjoyment of hotels de luxe when travelling abroad, I suspected that she did not object to having an excuse for staying in an hotel where a private bathroom was not an eccentric demand, in comparison with the terrible

London hostelries, in which guilty feelings of economy only too often drove her to pitch her tent. Edward and Christine joined her there, without Edward appreciating the scale of charges to be expected. 'Preposterous. Never again,' he wrote under 'Price,' in the book in which he recorded merits and demerits of the hotels he patronized. This was a valuable record, particularly for those travelling the roads of the west of Ireland, as it was a home-made Guide-Michelin, unhampered by commercial inhibitions, local delicacies being recommended under the heading 'Food', though this, on one occasion, was simply described as 'Odd'.

Preposterous though the hotel charges may have been, it was under its roof that my mother and her six children were assembled for the last time, and as it happened it was also the last time that the six children were themselves to be gathered together. My mother's pleasure in her new daughter-in-law was unconcealed, but she was more reticent, though equally delighted, about Pansy's expectation of giving birth to her first child in a month's time. Four months before Pansy's own birth she herself had remained hidden in Ireland, rather than appear at the wedding of her husband's sister, but she did admit to me that Pansy's own appearance was eminently discreet. This opinion did not allow my mother to relax her guard towards an acquaintance, who received the setting-down reply, 'Rather fat', having had the hardihood to remark how well Pansy was looking.

For her bridal cortège Elizabeth had mustered twelve bridesmaids, six from the Harmans, and six playing for the Pakenhams. She had decided that their velvet jackets should be in twelve different colours which had the advantage that no bridesmaid could complain, as they were known to do, that the colour chosen became everyone except themselves. On the other hand, the size of the wedding order came near by overwhelming my dressmaker, who had been given it, with all her workgirls. As the morning of the wedding wore on, the emotion engendered by *Cavalcade* the night before disappeared in the acute anxiety that two at least of the bridesmaids might either have to resign their position or appear like the Emperor in Hans Andersen's story. Far too near the time for leaving for St Margaret's, two cardboard dress boxes were upstairs, where Julia and I were waiting in petticoats and panic. In that pre-zipper age hooks and eyes made dressing a more haste less speed affair, but as we struggled with the fastenings it seemed that these dresses were not only belated but a vile fit into the bargain. The agony was only relieved when it was discovered that they had been packed in the wrong boxes, for, though the feet that peeped out beneath our petticoats were of identical size, Julia and I had individual measurements with a variation of inches.

Tall enough to be posted near the back of any bridal procession, I was thus at some distance behind the bridal pair as they paced towards the west door of St Margaret's, but I hoped that Frank was not too preoccupied to observe that his prophecy, that the cousin who suffered from poor orientation would have found a place by the font, was totally fulfilled. The paved walk running from the church door to Parliament Square takes a right-angled turn, so that while the bride and bridegroom face the cameras the tail end of their procession are also under fire. Bridesmaids are unaware of this, and are apt to be caught tweaking a wreath, scratching a nose or, as in my own case on this occasion, stooping to examine the hem of a skirt. Grouping for photographs at the reception was more formal, gaining in decorum what it lost in spontaneity, though there was a lack of uniformity in the position in which the bridesmaids held their posies, some clutching them to their bosoms and some holding them in the position more usually associated with fig leaves.

Her enthusiasm for family parties unabated, my grandmother had invited all her children and grandchildren on whom she could lay her hands to dinner at the Metropole Hotel, now defunct, but then occupying a large site in Northumberland Avenue. This choice of rendezvous was dictated by the situation of my cousin David Rhys, who was passing through a training period in hotel management, which he was to make his profession. Later he moved on to be banqueting manager at the Dorchester and at Claridges, to which my grandmother faithfully followed him in celebrating family weddings and engagements by luncheons and dinners. Recapitulating these events her only complaint was about a charge on the bill for cocktails, supplied, she was sure, by the wicked hotel, without David, her grandson's, knowledge. She was unappreciative of the fact that these parties were regarded by some of the guests as a stiff social hurdle, which David had rightly judged would need a strong apéritif in the interest of the guests surviving the course.

In spite of fleeing from home three years earlier, my sister Mary had remained much involved with the life of her family, although no longer under its roof, but hardly had the dust of Frank's wedding settled than she sailed on a tour that was to circle the globe. Her programme of travel sounded austere, her final destination being a sheep station in the North Island of New Zealand, with a halt on the way at a ranch in British Columbia. There was, however, some reassurance when her first postcards were dispatched from the Château Frontenac, Quebec, a hotel of formidable magnificence. My mother's good-bye to Mary, the daughter who had the largest share of her love and admiration, was a much warmer demonstration than she usually offered her children on occasions of farewell. At the time I attributed this to apprehensions about the perils facing the traveller, though later I came to realize that my mother might have feared that the parting would be final from her own dissolution before Mary's return.

Julia had been obliged to return to Oxford on the evening of the wedding. She had reported that the assembled freshmen and women in *sub fusc*, as they bowed to the Vice-Chancellor, looked like nothing so much as a school of respectful penguins. She also mentioned in passing that, on discovering that V S on her German prose stood for *Vix Satis* rather than Very Satisfactory, she had decided to throw the language lessons of Munich into the discard, and change to reading a school which would not exact weekly torture by German prose. The parting with my mother was softened by its temporary nature, and by the fact that Julia needed to be given her fare back to the University, a heartwarming sign that one of my mother's children still needed her support.

This mood of unquestioning maternal benevolence was transitory. With one of the sudden changes of direction that made dealings with my mother an operation in zigzag, she laid before me a financial plan which would increase both my allowance and my obligations towards herself. For motives too deep to explain, she was not herself prepared to undertake to pay the £25 which would entitle me to a day a week with the Bicester Hounds. On the other hand she was prepared to accept that in the season of the year a day's hunting was my delight. Her suggestion was that she should increase my allowance, and that, as well as my sporting *menus plaisirs*, I should accept responsibility for the upkeep of the Morris motor-car, which, though it was an unglamorous model also used by the local constabulary, was still my life-line to the outer world. In addition, I would be required to pay my mother a fixed sum for my board, though the weight of this exaction was modified by being postponed until I had found my feet under the new arrangement. Always anxious to keep my money matters concealed, particularly wishing to hide how much of my dress allowance was spent on meals at the Berkeley Hotel, I agreed to the scheme as presented to me with an enthusiasm that I later realized was ill-judged, not to say idiotic. For safety's sake, my mother insisted that I should pay a daily wage to the proprietor of the village garage for an inspection that was to keep my car roadworthy. Unfortunately so inept were his methods that I was later obliged so spend a stiff sum repairing the damage he had caused. As far as paying for my board was concerned, the initial delay caused a debt to pile up which remained uncancelled and unliquidated. Occasionally a cheque would pass from me to my mother, but never of an amount large enough to prevent me from being stuck forever in the red.

Pondering on the confusion that attended my mother's financial arrangements, I have sometimes wondered if it was not an hereditary strain that led her to fancy herself as a shrewd operator. Her great-grandmother, Sarah, Countess of Jersey, had inherited Osterley Park from her grandfather, Robert Child, the banker, and a commensurate fortune, which included Child's Bank. It may have been the same atavistic need to manipulate sums of money which earned her brother Arthur immense respect in the City, but in my mother's case the banking blood had run a trifle wild. I doubt if, in the course of her life, she had ever played cards for money or backed a horse, but, as I shall explain later, she had a different approach to the Stock Market, which was to her a Tom Tiddler's ground, on which the adroit might hope to pick up gold and silver.

Shocked as she could be at the broad-minded realism with which her own mother faced life, my mother interpreted the fourth commandment as an obligation laid on children to entertain parents with special hospitality. Domestic standards were raised when Grandmama came to stay, fires being lit at an hour earlier than usual, and such delicacies as a savoury mousse appearing at luncheon. Rude plenty – described by the writer Saki as plenty about which one is rude – was the more normal fare at my mother's table, and I was surprised that the cook and my mother could arrive at an agreement to make such an excursion into *haute cuisine*. If my mother was unable to leave her bedroom, Grandmama's entertainment would be provided for by a fellow guest in the shape of one of her sisters, a presence which was apt to lead to a relapse into the schoolroom attitudes of sixty years before. Although constantly in my grandmother's company, my Great-Aunt Aggie never showed signs of rebelling against the domination of her elder sister, nor did she appear to resent impatience at any slowness of wit she might herself display. Accustomed as I was to the taunts exchanged in my own family, I felt that to hear one octogenarian say to another, 'Aggie, you're too stupid to understand even if I did explain', was lowering the age barrier to an alarming extent.

Religious speculation was another subject which Aunt Aggie could not listen to without protest. She found herself fighting on two fronts when one of my grandmother's dinner guests put forward some vaguely Hegelian proposition concerning a thought behind the Visible Universe, while on the same evening my grandmother spoke with approbation of those who, unconvinced by any creed, adopted Buddhism in order to be provided with a set of ethical standards. As my grandmother's maid remarked tolerantly, Miss Leigh – which was Aunt Aggie – believed you could do good to people by talking to them. Another of my grandmother's themes, which her sister obviously regarded as unsuitable for discussion before girls of my age, was the question of the parentage of the grandmother from whom she and Aunt Aggie descended. This lady had been the daughter of the Duchess/Countess of Sutherland, whose husband was created duke of the title of which his wife was a countess in her own right. According to my grandmother this tremendous heiress, after giving birth to an heir, had taken up with someone described as a 'French lover' (presumably his nationality rather than his tastes was meant to be conveyed) who was the father of her younger children. If this story was true, my grandmother pointed out with considerable relish to her embarrassed sister, they would themselves be one-eight French by blood. My grandmother could certainly not be accused of undue pride in her lineage, for by lopping off this particular branch of her family tree she sacrificed a descent from four separate dukes in favour of a murky if romantic French ancestry, showing a theoretical abandon worthy of the lady who ran off with the Raggle-Taggle Gypsies-O.

To my eyes there was nothing improbable in this tale of illicit passion in the past, for Grandmama and her brothers and sisters had the dark eyes and sallow skins that belonged to the old-fashioned English idea of a typically French appearance. Indeed the portrait I have mentioned of my grandmother as a bride had been painted by a French artist, who had obviously found no difficulty in handling his sitter in the manner of Ingres. However when I suggested that appearances supported the theory of French blood to my Aunt Markie, herself possessed by a romantic enthusiasm which bathed all things French in a golden light, she replied that she did not see much French *espièglerie* about Grandmama's youngest sister Aunt Cordie. She spoke with some authority, as it was Aunt Cordie's lack of success on the ballroom floor that, as I have written earlier, led my grandmother to warn Aunt Markie that balls might not be pure delight. On the other hand there is no reason to suppose that French families of the last century did not produce as many maiden aunts devoted to works of charity and piety as English ones, so Aunt Cordie's busy life dedicated to Sunday Schools and missions would not necessarily have disqualified her for having a 'French lover' among her forbears.

Aunt Cordie had been brought up in Stoneleigh Abbey, and, when her brother had remarried after a long widowhood, she had retreated to live a few miles away, still continuing to occupy herself with the spiritual welfare of the families she had known from her infancy. Her other preoccupation, foreign missions, resulted in the arrival of a pair of Himalayan black sheep, the gift of a grateful missionary, for whom her brother Dudley, Lord Leigh, granted her a sheep run in the park at Stoneleigh. Aunt Cordie's great-nieces were in the habit of insisting that she was uncomprehending of the means by which this pair multiplied into a flock, whose grazing required an ever-increasing slice of the park, but these mockers never despised the lengths of sepia-coloured tweed, water-proof from its natural oils uncontaminated by dye, which were woven annually from the wool shorn from Aunt Cordie's black pets. When Aunt Cordie arrived to meet my grandmother on one of the latter's visits to Peverel, I realized that her life was lived in an intense local activity, which it must have been difficult to lay down for a sisterly visit. A stack of postcards were put out to be posted on the hall table, which I unashamedly read, having always regarded postcards as fair game. From these I learnt that Aunt Cordie was still directing her good works at long range, including, astounding ability in the sister of my tone-deaf grandmother, commands to organist and choirmaster as to what music was to be attempted the following Sunday.

These postcards made it easy for me to believe that, as one of her sisters-in-law told me, in Aunt Cordie's house there was a feeling that could only be described as the beauty of holiness, but away from her home she wore the air of a mouse who had strayed into Vanity Fair. She was known to have left an hotel because a female guest appeared in trousers, and her shy reserve made Aunt Aggie's cheerful manners seem positively rollicking by comparison. Aunt Cordie must have needed all her inner strength to tolerate the worldly, and sometimes Rabelaisian, conversation of her eldest sister, particularly on an afternoon drive when I was an unwilling third passenger. So deeply ingrained in my grandmother's generation was the habit of driving out between luncheon and tea, that the ritual had not altered with the invention of the motor-car, which merely increased the distance that could be covered. My grandmother's Rolls-Royce had been acquired by her son, Arthur, from the estate of Lord Revelstoke, a partner with Arthur in the firm of Baring Brothers. The size of a small caravan, this Rolls-Royce had the peculiarity that there was a speedometer between the two little seats to which grandchildren usually found themselves relegated. Presumably this had been installed to allow the previous owner to check his chauffeur's speed, and, if necessary, to command that this should be reduced by means of a speaking tube connected with the driver's right ear. My grandmother held the theory that her own chauffeur proceeded at a sedate fifteen miles an hour, the speed which she could see registered on the internal speedometer. To those seated on the little seats the speedometer on the dashboard was visible which told a different and faster story. This adjustment must have been designed to deceive Lord Revelstoke into thinking that he was being habitually driven at a speed which would barely have allowed his chauffeur to achieve top gear.

Usually an adept at evading the afternoon drive I had, on the day of which I write, been cornered without my best excuse that I was going out with the hounds. Seated on one of the little seats, I had fallen into the trance which a drive to nowhere and back always induced in me, when I was roused by the realization that my grandmother was talking about kilts.

It was *de rigueur*, she instructed her youngest sister and her granddaughter, that no underclothes should be worn beneath these Highland petticoats. There was even a story, she continued, of a man from some city, who knew this to be the rule, but who had only acquired a kilt when he had bought a house in Scotland. In the days of which Grandmama was talking tailcoats were habitually worn by businessmen, and the hero had the habit, not unusual, of standing before the fire with his coat tails tucked under his arms so that he could enjoy warming his backside. 'One day he forgot he was wearing a kilt,' said Grandmama, 'and turned his back to the company.' Mistaking the appalled look on Aunt Cordie's face for misapprehension, Grandmama impatiently stressed that this pseudo-Scotsman was wearing nothing under his kilt, and so, it was to be understood, would be presenting his bare bottom to those assembled in his drawing-room. My great-aunt's frigid silence and my own efforts to fight down hysteria prevented this story from having the success its *raconteuse* expected.

It would be unfair, however, to give the impression that my grandmother did not have her own strict code as to what was unsuitable to be said or acted in public. In private she would repeat with enjoyment the tale of a French lady who had expressed distress at some aspect of male nudity. To the suggestion that, as a married woman, she might have been supposed to have seen her husband in this state, she insisted, 'Toujours dans sa chemise'. For theatrical performances my grandmother had different rules, which became apparent when Julia and I mistakenly allowed her to learn that we wished to see *Helen!*, C. B. Cochran's production of *La Belle Hélène*, adapted from the *opera bouffe* of Meilhac and Halévy. We knew from experience that so far as enjoying music was concerned my grandmother might have been born without ears, and we knew enough of *Helen!* to suspect that boredom would not be her only or most painful reaction. Appeals to my mother to sabotage this ill-advised evening jaunt were unavailing, and in the centre of the front row of the stalls we sat, one each side of our ancestress, while before us the seduction of Helen by Paris, Prince of Troy, moved to its climax. As the curtain fell on the pair, lying embraced in a white rococo four-poster, presided over by a painting of Helen's parents, Zeus and Leda, also in an amorous embrace, there was a moment's pause before the audience began to clap their hands. Into this silence Grandmama projected her sense of outrage in a voice that seemed to reverberate through stalls and pit. 'I wonder,' she exclaimed, 'that the Lord Chamberlain gave his consent!'

9. The Practice of Deception

AT THE GATE OF PEVEREL Court there stood a pair of cottages belonging to my mother, one of which had briefly housed a chauffeur. He had been interviewed for the post, partly by me, all too easily impressed by a demonstration of how to clean a sparking-plug, and partly by Aunt Beatrice, an enthusiastic rather than a reliable judge of character. Consequently when my mother was well enough to be driven out, she found that her driver had not only a manner lacking in basic respect, but wore a pair of wings on his cap to indicate that he had once been a test driver at the Bentley works. Far from keen on dogs, my mother also disapproved of the chauffeur's Alsatian bitch, who disconcerted unsuspecting strollers in the garden by approaching silently from behind in order to run a wet nose up the victim's calves. To my relief a policy of retrenchment on my mother's part led to the chauffeur giving notice, my own drives with him having been made embarrassing by his habit of getting as close to me as the gear-lever between us permitted. At an early age it had been impressed on me that undesired male advances were likely to be either my own fault, or the work of a conceited imagination, neither hypothesis being an encouragement for the laying of a complaint. The chauffeur's cottage now being empty my mother arranged for it, and its neighbour, to be converted into a messuage in which Frank and Elizabeth began their married life.

The two cottages made a snug house, once the problem of curing wood fires laid on brick hearths from smoking had been solved. This was very much a problem of the period for junkyards were stacked with the black grates of the previous century, thrown out by those who had uncovered the wider fireplaces of the past in their cherished country cottages. Only too often the desire to have a glowing heap of logs was defeated by a lack of draught from below, and the smoke could only be coaxed up the chimney by keeping open a window through which the bracing air of a winter's night would send a chill down the backs of the company. I could give no aid to Elizabeth, when she telephoned for help from a room full of log smoke. It was not till ten years later that I learnt the firemaker's secret of leaving spaces between bricks, and cementing them only to the floor, Elizabeth's suggestion that my mother might know of a cure, seemed to me so fantastic that I did not even trouble to refer the matter to one who considered that fires should be confined behind bars. With the installation of copper hoods, the flames were drawn up the chimneys to warm the impressive number of Elizabeth's admirers from her Oxford days, who came to call with a touch of auld lang syne in their manner. Sitting round what Roy Campbell called the 'hearth's reviving pyre' soul-searing games were played, marks being given to those absent for such qualities as cleanliness, or those present being required to state what two qualities lacking in themselves mitigated against their success in life. Maurice Bowra, then Dean of Wadham College, agreed that Evelyn Waugh deserved a high mark for cleanliness, but showed most untypical hesitation when declaring the two qualities he himself lacked, finally settling for only one, the want of a thick skin, which he seemed to think should count as a double handicap.

The birth of Henrietta, Pansy's eldest child, took place soon after the wedding of Frank and Elizabeth. My mother was proud to write in a Christmas letter to Madame de Rosée, a former refugee guest from Belgium, 'Enfin je suis grandmère'. The actual visit of the de Rosée family had been marked by acute domestic tensions, but the wounds had been healed by friendly correspondence over the next seventeen years. This baby was also the first great-granddaughter for my grandmother, her son-in-law Dunsany remarking that he was glad the stigma of no fourth generation had been removed from Lady Jersey. In fact the fourth generation increased with such rapidity that, less than four years later, Grandmama was able to drive down to Osterley to be photographed in that Gallery, which Henry James had called 'a cheerful upholstered avenue into the 18th Century', among a cluster of five mothers and seven infants. Two of the great-grandchildren belonged to Elizabeth and had only 352 days between their births, but on this historic occasion they were not prominent among the children who ran wild or created a hullabaloo, to such an extent that at no moment was every one of the sitters quiescent. The defeated photographer had to resort to scissors and paste to achieve a publishable picture.

Across the road from Peverel Court stood Hartwell House, an infinitely melancholy Jacobean pile surrounded by noble trees, and looking out at traces of formal ponds, of which seventeenth-century painted records survive. In this house those Bourbons who had escaped from the Terror had lived in exile, notoriously learning nothing and forgetting nothing, but finally commemorated by Bourbon Street in Aylesbury. In the house itself these tenants had reduced the splendour of the grand staircase, on whose balustrade statues had, previously, been poised. The bibulous habits of one of the ladies of the family had caused the statues to topple from their plinths when she was helping her uneven feet upstairs to bed. Perched like a bird on a knoll in the garden stood Hartwell Church, a mid-eighteenth-century copy of part of York Minster, its walls set with memorials to a family whose chief virtue would appear to have been their urbanity, though this might be considered less than perfect in the mention of a wife curtly described as the daughter of '——O'Grady of the Kingdom of Ireland'. This church was to me a favourite place of worship, owing to the custom of holding an early service there at the relaxed hour of nine-fifteen. My predilection was not shared by other parishioners, and on one occasion, arriving late at a gallop, I found the server and celebrant in conference in the porch as to whether they might expect any congregation. It may have been in defiance of the rubric in the Book of Common Prayer, but the celebration was then held for me alone, in the blue-washed interior under the monuments to the urbane dead.

This incident could hardly be called typical of my habit of life, nor did the grace of the sacrament give me strength to follow the admonition of the Church Catechism to be true and just in all my dealings. My sisters had solved the problem of conforming to my mother's prohibitions and taboos by leaving these behind them when they left home. On my part, I decided that it was better to bend the truth to my purpose than to live in a permanent state of frustration from a veto being exercised on my dearest plans. I had, of course, certain natural alibis, which included driving my brother and sister-in-law on visits to neighbours, at a period when neither happened to have learnt to drive a motor-car, but there were many occasions when covering-up operations required considerable forward planning. In these matters Taylor, our butler, was an ally, both sympathetic and intelligent, so that when, early in 1932, my mother told me that Taylor had decided to leave domestic service and set up in business on his own, my reaction was to declare that I could imagine no one whose death would make so much difference as would the departure of this member of the household, established in it long before I had myself been born. My mother was surprised that I seemed so deeply affected. I was astonished at her nonchalance in the face of this domestic revolution, only afterwards coming to realize that she was aware of complications in Taylor's private life which obliged him to plot a new course.

Taylor had graduated from first footman in my father's time. According to my mother, he had had an adverse effect on my father's military career at a period when my parents were living in Putney, neighbours, but not acquaintances, of Swinburne and Watts-Dunton. To their hired house my father invited his Brigade Commander and staff for refreshment, after a hot and thirsty day of field manoeuvres. Unluckily, Taylor, with the keys of sideboard and cellar in his pocket, had vanished to that famous public-house, The Green Man, at the summit of Putney Hill, where he was engaged in supervising a jollification ordered by my father to revive his troopers after the rigours of sham fighting. When the general put in his report the disastrously dry situation was reflected in the comment that Lord Longford showed no talent for organization.

Taylor's ordinary household preoccupations included the now derided but, in fact, sensible duty of ironing the newspapers, so that the printer's ink dried on the page rather than on the reader's fingers. He had also particular opportunity to develop his own talent for organization. It was his responsibility to arrange for the transport of fifteen or sixteen souls across the Irish Channel, in some years as often as four times, the drama of the journey being increased by the possibility of being torpedoed on the way over, a peril which, with the end of the First World War, was replaced by the chance of being picked off on arrival. In my nursery days, while our nanny staggered up the gangway with Julia in her arms, as a larger child I was carried on board by Taylor, thereby rendering him useless for helping any other of the struggling family party, as an unfeeling sister did not hesitate to point out.

At Peverel, Taylor had been a rock of reliability in the stormy domestic sea, imperturbable when it came to reconciling his duty towards his employer with his sympathy for the undercover activities of her children. Ever willing to cash a cheque, or even unasked to leave money available in his own absence, he also supplied glimpses of a rougher side of life. When the climax of a story in the *Strand Magazine* turned on the breaking of a bottle of vitriol in the villain's face, Taylor was appealed to as one qualified by his occupation to judge the plausibility of such a situation. He professed ignorance about bottles of vitriol, but he assured us that in Ireland he had seen fights in which the combatants cracked bottles of porter on each other's skulls.

Taylor also made sartorial comments on the young men who were the guests of my cousin Joan and myself. My father's clothes were notoriously haphazard, and this trait seemed to have descended to my brothers, so perhaps it was thirty years of attempting to valet the ungroomable that led Taylor to place at the top of the list of my friends one whom he described as 'a bit of a dandy'. On the other hand he took such exception to the hat worn by one of Joan's admirers that he arranged for it to be squashed under the wheels of its owner's Bentley. Keen on all sports, Taylor was prepared to discuss the comparative gifts of the local huntsmen, contrasting one who was so eager to get hounds away that he would lift them out of the bottoms along the River Cherwell, while their quarry lay snugly in a drain, with another who, though no great shakes across country, was, in Taylor's words, 'a lovely hounds man'. With such a gifted oracle on whom to rely, it will be understood that, when my mother fell down a flight of stairs with a terrible clatter of crutches, Taylor's panic-stricken summons of 'Lady Violet' was to me the most frightening moment of the accident.

In the past my mother's Christmas house party at North Aston, if not of the splendour of the pre-1914 parties at Middleton, had been a cheerful feast, but at Peverel both the house and the circumstances were reduced. There was no longer a library large enough to house a billiard-table, and leave room for my Uncle Walter to smoke a cigar in the comfort of a green leather arm-chair. The billiard-room at Peverel did, it is true, accommodate the billiard-table we had brought with us, but the floor space had been cut down by a line of protruding bookcases, which in themselves made some shots near the cushion a test for a contortionist. Ever considerate, Uncle Walter insisted on retiring from the drawing-room, with his cigar, to the room where my mother's nurses had been fed in segregated fury. Here he sat, his feet stretched out on the bleak linoleum of the floor, and, as the room contained only one arm-chair, no one bore him company except the telephone. Shortly afterwards this instrument was moved into a cupboard under the stairs, a devastating change from my point of view as the cupboard conveyed a false sense of privacy, every word spoken ringing out across the hall. While Uncle Walter smoked in solitude, the rest of the party were employed with bridge and conversation, my family never having conceded that playing bridge was any reason for stopping talking. An old friend of Frank's, who was among us, particularly enjoyed the remorselessness with which my mother contested any remark of her elder sister, Aunt Markie, if she felt the slightest disagreement on any point. It was not that the habits of the schoolroom died hard; in my mother's case they continued in the best of health.

'Nonsense, Markie', she would exclaim, at any sentence that offended her by a suggestion that every old friend might not always behave with the utmost propriety, or act from the highest motives.

A temporary replacement for Taylor immediately began a flirtation with Annie Reason, my mother's maid, who had been trained in an Edwardian household, famous for fast living and for visits from King Edward. In the circle almost devoid of male companions in which she now lived she must, I feel, have sometimes yearned for the old days when, so she told me, she had been courted by menservants impeccably dressed in clothes handed on by their employers. On one occasion she had been taken to the zoo on Sunday by a valet wearing a morning-coat and top-hat; Sunday at the zoo being only accessible to those given tickets by Fellows of the Zoological Society and formal dress implying that a church service had already been attended. My mother first noticed that the temporary butler was having a success when she became aware that her maid was absent from my mother's room at moments when she was customarily in attendance, this lapse being emphasized by the peals of laughter which came echoing from the servant's hall up to the bedroom floor. From her vantage-post at Stairways, Elizabeth reported that the couple could be seen bicycling together through the gloaming, but when the butler suggested that he should abandon his permanent situation from which he was, as it were, on loan, and settle with us, my mother refused to consider the matter. Servant poaching was high on her list of social crimes, particularly heinous when one employer had trusted another with a reliable retainer for a stated period. By such scrupulousness she lost a butler, but she did retain Reason, who might otherwise have been reft from her by marriage.

Perhaps this butler, though forward in love, would have found, in the long run, that the place did not suit him. He failed, for example, to realize that it was on occasion necessary to ignore some of the rules laid down by my mother, on such matters as when the drawing-room fire could be lit without undue extravagance over fuel. Herself a late riser, even in her days of comparative health, my mother would have agreed with the cheese-paring character in one of I. Compton-Burnett's novels, who thought that to heap 'a great showy pile in the grate' was a 'coarse and common thing to do'. Taylor would have seen to it that this happy warmth would have greeted guests who might not expect to see their hostess till luncheon time, but the temporary butler and I lacked the courage to bring this matter to my mother's notice when her cousin Julia, a distinguished lady of seventy years, came to stay. Cousin Julia had the reputation of being a hardy and resourceful character. At a primitive South American inn she was reported to have refused to resort to a peon-haunted latrine and, finding that no chamber-pot was available, had undauntedly requested that a tumbler should be brought to her. Hardy traveller she may have been, but in the flow of healthy, fresh air between the open window and the grate where the unlighted fire lay in chilly smugness, she turned perceptibly blue as she sat reading the morning paper with shaking hands.

With Taylor's departure I had also lost a sympathetic sharer of discussions on the form of the runners in the Grand National, to which sporting fixture a party of my friends had booked a coach on an excursion train. I had suggested to my mother that I might take my sister Julia with me on this a jaunt, a splendid bargain, first-class return to Liverpool with four very square meals (five courses for luncheon and dinner) included at £2 17s. 6d. My mother, however, used her veto, on the grounds that she did not wish her youngest child 'to get accustomed to that kind of thing', presumably meaning the wicked world of the racecourse. Subsequent events proved her prohibition to have been futile, Julia choosing a husband who might often be seen first past the post in point-to-point races, and herself becoming part-owner of a steeplechaser. Not unnaturally, Julia was irritated at being prohibited from joining a party of pleasure likely to give her new friends. When on the evening of the day of the big race my mother was unwise enough to remark that she supposed I would be getting back from the Grand National at about half past nine Julia retorted, 'I wonder you dare mention the subject to me'. Although she could object to remarks made with no wish to be anything but agreeable, my mother usually relished a show of spirit, and even, I think, made some monetary compensation for Julia's disappointment. On my birthday, 13 March, she had also refused my suggestion that I should be given the fare to Liverpool as a birthday present, finally compromising by handing over three pounds on the understanding that I would, at my own convenience, buy myself a new tennis-racket. Presumably her conscience did not then plague her with accusations of financing a daughter on the road to ruin, on which she obviously regarded Aintree Race Course as one of the principal starting-points.

The first time I went to the Grand National our party, as I have said, was large enough to occupy an entire coach on the excursion train that the London, Midland & Scottish ran from Euston to the Liverpool meeting. To while away the journey others brought packs of cards and even a gramophone with records of what was then known as Hot Jazz, but I chose to bring the first volume of *Du Côté de Chez Swann*. Consequently the chapter *Un Amour de Swann* has ever since brought back to me the heavy aroma of mock turtle soup, brewing for luncheon in the kitchen of the train, together with a tang of coal-dust, lost reek of the age of steam. It was at a moment when the train was running through the billowing fields and fly fences of the Pytchley country that I laughed aloud at Swann's surrealist nightmare of jealousy which culminates in the tortured lover being told that Napoleon III (long since in his tomb at Farnborough) is the lover of Odette. I was detached from the study of Swann's Amour by Hamish Erskine at the far end of the coach calling to me to open my mouth. When I obliged, he threw a lump of sugar with such a deadly aim that I was able to clamp my jaws on it, as if in an act rehearsed to perfection.

On the racecourse it was apparent that the LMS had also transported from London the two pillars of the tipster world, Prince Monolulu and the Old Harrovian. Both of these styles were, one might say, given to themselves by the men who bore them, and the bearers' approach to business was a model as to how an area of commercial exploitation could be amicably worked by two operators whose methods did not overlap. Prince Monolulu added to his considerable height by a nodding headdress of three tail feathers, usually red, white and blue, but occasionally purple or pink. His billowing white bloomers and shirt inadequately concealed that, under an approximation of the clothes worn by his African forbears, he wore garments designed to keep the chill airs of the English racecourse in winter at bay, and I never saw him without a sensibly large umbrella in his hand. His magnificent appearance and his cry, 'I got a horse! I got a horse!' was famous far beyond the racing world, but his origins were only revealed by chance when – perhaps from celebrating a win or softening the blow of a loss – he was fined for being drunk and disorderly. In court he gave his nationality as Danish, a puzzle only solved when it is remembered that Denmark had owned two of the Virgin Islands until these were sold to the United States.

The Old Harrovian's appearance and line of patter was in direct contrast to that of Monolulu, the Black Prince of Denmark. Owning a face whose complexion was an interesting *mélange* of strawberry and aubergine the former's clothes, in the 1930s, had already become a trifle out-moded; navy-blue overcoat, bowler-hat and the Old Harrovian tie standing out among the check suits and macintoshes of more up-to-date race-goers. His appeal, more personal and less ritualistic than Monolulu's, culminated, on one occasion, with a pledge that he did not see his way to fulfilling. Addressing the circle gathered round him, he cast his bowler-hat on the ground with the wild cry, 'If Golden Miller wins this race I shall give up racing!' At that moment Miss Dorothy Paget, owner of that steeple-chasing champion, Golden Miller, happened to pass, as ever a sombre figure dressed in muted shades of brown, her clothes in style as old-fashioned as the Old Harrovian's. No one, among my friends, had the prescience to take this as an omen. When Euston was regained, the layer of smuts induced by steam travel covered a sad party who had failed to back the victorious Golden Miller.

Among other signs of the contraction of social life at Peverel was the diminution of the number of names inscribed in the visitors' book. This volume, bound in green morocco and stamped in gold with the ambiguous couplet, 'We should a guest love when he loves to stay, And when he loves not give him loving way', was the pivot of one of my mother's most successful domestic booby traps, ensnaring both the guests who were being given loving way, and her daughters who had the responsibility of seeing that they did not go unregistered. Being bound to a spine as strong as a steel spring, force was necessary to keep the book open while the guests signed their names. My mother insisted also that the signatures should dry naturally, without benefit of blotting-paper, so that the book spent much time splayed open on the hall table, its rebellious pages pinned down by ponderous glass match-holders. These rites attendant on her guests' departure were operated by remote control, but although the diaries of my mother's youth showed that her own handwriting had always resembled a pine forest shattered by a hurricane, she nevertheless expected that her daughters should encourage visitors to write neat names and accurate dates. Distracted by train fever, many failed in both neatness and accuracy, but total defeat came at the end of a visit from her nephew, the son of her sister, Beatrice Dunsany. A boy of eight or nine years old, he found it impossible to decide on the number of l's and t's with which his names, Randal Plunkett, should terminate, achieving a black beetle effect, duplicated on the opposite page and soaking down the book's edge into the years ahead. Even at Peverel, years later, the book tended to spring open at this splendid smudge, when the moment came for my cousin, Joan Child Villiers, to record the curlicues of her signature. A frequent, indeed as the visitors' book showed, almost our only visitor, Joan's continuous presence may have suggested to my mother that, in the month of May, I might be disposed of under the roof of Joan's mother.

My Aunt Cynthia's house stood at a point where the river of traffic from Oxford and Cambridge Terrace flowed into the delta of Sussex Gardens. Its immediate neighbour was a house whose tenants were said to be of a disreputability that caused anxiety to the Church Commissioners as the ground landlords. Judging by the saturnine countenance of the man who appeared to manage the establishment, and the number of girls who arrived there at strange hours of the night, the Church Commissioners were probably right to suspect that their property was being used as an assembly point for what was then known as the White Slave Trade. This sinister house was the only black spot in an area where several neighbours happened to be close friends, Cynthia's own house being, in particular, a port where many chose to call. Accustomed as I was to the rigid privacy of my mother's house, where butler and footman had almost permanent orders to say 'not at home' and callers who left cards found that this traffic was one way, the social turnover in Sussex Gardens was immensely exhilarating. My enjoyment began on my first night in the house, when it happened that I would be alone for dinner. Cynthia at once suggested that I might like to ask some young man to share my meal. My pleasure at her thoughtfulness was only equalled by my surprise that for me to be eating a solitary dinner was a matter that anyone should think needed to be put right.

Before I left the light airs of Sussex for the twilight shades of Norfolk Street, Park Lane, where I was to rejoin my mother in the house rented from my Uncle Bingo, a party was organized by Joan. Her mother joined eagerly in the arrangements, although concerned that sitters-out on the balcony might be a threat to the window-boxes which she had filled with yellow pansies. Almost as devoted to flowers as she was to animals, Cynthia took the precaution of nailing notices to the window-boxes on which she wrote, 'Please respect the pansies'. The music came throbbing forth from a panatrope as we danced to 'Hello, Beautiful' (so firmly appropriated to a friend of mine that the Embassy Club band once switched to it when she appeared on the floor) followed by 'Ooh that kiss', and 'She didn't say "Yes", She didn't say "No" '. Outside on the balcony Cynthia's window-boxes glowed golden against the inky curtain of the London midnight sky.

It was not only to me that residence in Norfolk Street seemed to have a jail-like quality. Julia, home for her first long vacation from Oxford, found that London had lost the interest of novelty which had carried her through her first Season the previous summer. Pleasure had evaporated, leaving a void, which the reading expected of her during the vacation was powerless to fill. Before he had moved to a fairly recently built house in

Norfolk Street, my father's brother had lived a life of seclusion in the Bruton Street house which had been the London home of the Longford family for nearly a century. There were long years when it was a Dowager's residence, in the days when widows wore weeds for a year and caps for life.

A letter survives from the 1st Duke of Wellington to my great-grandmother, his sister-in-law, addressed to 24 Bruton Street. Dated 1851, the letter explains that while the Duke would be present at the wedding of his wife's niece at St George's, Hanover Square, he must excuse himself from attending the breakfast, as he 'was obliged to go into the country'. The interior of 24 Bruton Street included some imposing features, a fine staircase with ornamental plasterwork, and a gallery for the display of furniture and china, and at the date of that wedding the furniture must have belonged to the period covered by the term Regency. I suppose some dispersal of graceful and charming objects must have taken place, for by the time I remember the house in Bruton Street the furniture belonged mostly to a later date, having been installed by my father's parents. When he moved to Norfolk Street Uncle Bingo had furnished the back-drawing, where he usually sat, with the most unlovely of the *meubles* he had inherited. The light was harshly reflected from the yellow oak curves of a roll-top desk, while odd corners were filled by those mysterious narrow chests of drawers, bought, it seemed, in bulk by my grandparents, their inelegance presumably redeemed by the security of the hinged flap that locked the drawers. On the walls hung photographs, faded to ochre, of my uncle's parents and his elder twin brothers, all deceased. But the vast photograph of Pakenham Hall, Co. Westmeath, had been printed by a process of an excellence that time was powerless to fade. It hung above the bookcase, and under it my uncle sat, reading books that might have been thought more suitable for his nieces than for himself. Was it loyalty to his former neighbour in Bruton Street that accounted for his possession of the entire works of Ian Hay? Irish affiliations made his purchase of the works of George A. Birmingham more comprehensible, though I doubt if the book in which the West of Ireland landowner obliged his little son to swear undying enmity to the Act of Union with England, an oath taken on the Sacrament, would have won Uncle Bingo's sympathy. *Jock o' the Bushveldt* may have recalled his fighting days in South Africa, though I have, myself, always had difficulty in recalling if Jock was a man, a horse or a dog.

The only touch of prettiness in the room came from the crimson chintzes, of that Victorian pattern in which birds perch on bamboos. Besides armchairs, this chintz covered a large sofa, comfortable in aspect but furnished with rock-hard bolsters, bruising to those who incautiously cast themselves down upon it. On this sofa Julia reclined, in an outfit whose crimson blended into that of the upholstery, while she turned the leaves of gramophone record catalogues in search of titles that appealed to her. She lacked the restlessness which drove me to circulate through parties to which I was asked, and parties to which I was taken by friends. Consequently Julia had less need to practise the deception which my period of liberty in Sussex Gardens had made ever more necessary in my dealings with my mother, her unadjusted rules for the behaviour of her daughters becoming increasingly archaic with the passage of time. This fabric of concealment grew ever more monstrous, in the manner of that game when a precarious structure is created on the foundation of a single match laid across the neck of a bottle.

On evenings when I was invited to a ball I had no problems, for my mother did not regard staying out until dawn as reprehensible if the entertainment was policed by chaperones. More care was needed if Julia and I were supposedly dancing at the same party but had gone our separate ways, whichever got home first leaving a note in the hall so that our stories could be synchronized. This co-operation was particularly necessary on a night when I had pooled invitations with an escort to see how many parties we could jointly attend in the course of one evening, an evening that ended when the score was eleven and the sun was rising over Battersea Bridge. This round of parties was, however, sedate compared to the jollification into which I was swept by some friends, on an evening when my mother was under the impression that I was spending a few days in Wiltshire as the admiring aunt of Pansy's six-month-old daughter, Henrietta.

The owner of a house in Hertford Street had been persuaded to lend her home for the sort of bottle party to which most of the guests neglected to bring bottles. Her neighbours must have passed a restless night, not least because one of the guests in a moment of depression jumped from a balcony into the street below, though, the drop being a short one, the personal damage was slight. Depression was excusable after two cabaret acts, each in its own way an embarrassing disaster. The first was an attempt at an all-in wrestling bout, which began with a man dressed in an exiguous leopard skin bounding on to the floor with a girl partner whose nakedness was protected by a few strategically placed vine leaves. Hardly had these performers struck a pose which promised a jungle dance routine, when they were interrupted by a chap in the audience who shouted, 'My God, that's my wife!' and tearing off his tail-coat went into a clinch with the male dancer, while the girl cringed behind her vine leaves. The spoof wrestling bout came to a swift and bloody end when the bare-footed Tarzan trod on a broken glass. A singer with a corncrake's voice also failed to get a grip of her audience with a rendering of 'You used to sign your letters with all my love and kisses, But its only Yours

Sincerely now'. As the company refused to stop talking the first lines of the lyric, 'I've done the best I could, All that a lover should, But it wasn't enough for you', seemed only too applicable. The anarchy of the evening may have been redeemed for the hostess in the midsummer dawn when the party had rolled away. An opposite neighbour happened to glance out of his window, and saw her on the doorstep in her nightdress, welcoming a returning young man.

Strolling back in the same grey dawn to Half Moon Street where I was hoping to doss down for an hour or two in the flat of some friends, I was aware that a small crowd of police and revellers had collected across the street. I had just become aware that the revellers included my host, when his wife burst out of the house in floods of tears, exclaiming that a squad of policemen were arresting her husband. There had been a misunderstanding over a supposedly stolen motor-car, in which the inspector and his men were not taking much interest, being engaged in arresting an extraneous character. Among those pursuing the question of the stolen car was the son of a retired Chief Constable of Metropolitan Police. Like a gamekeeper turned poacher, he had become concerned with the running of night-clubs, but he possessed a knowledge of the varying tempers of West End police inspectors comparable to the Irish ability to assess the relative 'crossness' of local bulls. The particular inspector involved in this street scene, famous we were told for a choleric temper, brought a charge for assaulting the police which even the magistrate agreed was unserious.

The defendant was advised to describe himself as Master of Foxhounds, as likely to create a better impression than if he was labelled as an idler of independent means. When the case was reported no mention was made of the original transgressor whose arrest had been interrupted, the evening papers offering only a poster which declared 'MFH In London Street Scene'.

The country which this MFH hunted lay across the Irish Channel, where evening papers were unlikely to be delivered, so he had some security that he would not appear as one who found the summer months to lie so idly on his hands that he had to go to London to see sport. I was equally thankful that my mother was in the country, as I suspected that the story would not be to her taste.

That I had been only too right about my mother's reaction to tangles with the police was revealed a few weeks later, when some three hundred guests were defrauded of a wedding. The bridegroom had spent the morning at a magistrate's court, being fined the mandatory sum of ten shillings on account of an argument, in which he and three friends had become embroiled, with the commissionaire outside the Palladium. When my mother read of this, and recognized one of my friends among those in court, my line of defence was that for a bachelor's eve of wedding party to be ejected from the Palladium was almost a *sine qua non*. I did, however, have the sense to refrain from describing a more lively bachelor's last fling at the Slippin' night-club where a bottle of champagne cast to the ground had punctured the glass floor from which revolving coloured lights cast rainbows over the dancers. I was glad of my restraint when my mother denied, with indignation, that such riotous dinner parties had taken place at the period of her own wedding. At that date my father had been thirty-five years old, and so probably may have felt that the time was already past for hearing the chimes at midnight, but I found it hard to believe that every bridegroom approached the altar without a trace of hangover. Always avid for histories of my parents' early days together, I inquired as to how the evening before their wedding had actually been spent. From my mother's reply I learnt that the occasion had not been one of celebration, but had been devoted to material considerations. The time had passed, she said austerely, in signing marriage settlements.

10. East End, West End

EVEN TO THIS DAY I marvel at the paradox by which my mother's unreserved approval of every doing of her brother Arthur should have led her to permit her daughters to attend parties which would have caused her a profound shock had she realized the nudity and violence involved. The Eton Manor Club in Hackney Wick had been founded by my Uncle Arthur in conjunction with various friends, and was regarded by his family as the main interest of his life, outside his banking activities which contributed so much to the Club's support. Over the years the Club had spread, indoors and out, with members turning from boys into men, and the range of games and sports increasing with the growth of membership. Arthur's nephews and their contemporaries helped in a managerial capacity, and it was with my brother Frank and my cousin David Rhys that I followed the trail that led to Hackney Marshes. In the words of the song it would have been easier to get there 'If it wasn't for the houses in between'. Out on the playing-fields there was little embarrassment, except for the agony of the Club's bowls enthusiasts when they saw that a lady friend of the manager's, ignoring the mat from which the woods should be bowled, was tearing strips from their green.

Indoors, circumstances were distinctly awkward. The hosts, that is to say the managers of the Club, were usually occupied by meetings, disposing of girlfriends by taking them through the rambling club buildings, and leaving them to play ping-pong with any boy unwise enough not to appear fully occupied. My skill at ping-pong had never been above the average, and I found it humiliating to be consistently beaten by sons of Hackney Wick, far younger and smaller than myself. For their part, boredom and contempt was mixed in their attitude. As soon as decency allowed I would make tracks for the Clubhouse, whose dining-room was made convivial by Arthur's invariable habit of drinking champagne for dinner. The escape route to this haven was a nightmare of stone stairs and uncharted passages, a Minoan labyrinth from which there was no exit, except through changing-rooms, where among showers and urinals boys rioted in their pink skins. So much against nudity that she had reproved her eldest son for pointing at some classical scene because it depicted 'a lady with no clothes on', and had fled when confronted in the garden at Osterley by two bathers naked but for towels round their middle parts, my mother might have found the changing-room an unexpected aspect of evenings at Hackney Wick.

Another activity, equally startling to my mother, was the mixed game of netball played in the gymnasium. As *Chin Wag*, the Club periodical, remarked, there were no rules in what was virtually a game of indoor Rugby football except that killing a member of the opposing team was not countenanced. Loyalty to her brother caused my mother to subscribe to *Chin Wag*, at that time edited by David Rhys, but she probably took this comment as more of an exaggeration than, in fact, it was. She was known to study *Chin Wag*, for, when a naïve and ill-informed article on the subject of birth control appeared over a pseudonym, the magazine suddenly ceased to lie on the hall table, available to be read by all. It was never, I think, revealed to her that this was my first appearance in print, my purely theoretical knowledge of the subject having been gleaned from a hasty reading of *Married Love* by Doctor Marie Stopes.

Each July, for three successive years, David Rhys organized a social at the Eton Manor Club, in which the West End, represented by the more beautiful and athletic of David's girlfriends, competed against the girlfriends of the Club members with similar qualifications. The evening began to hot up with the three-legged race, in which the problem of matching partners according to both size and speed led to uneven results. My sister Julia, never much of a one for a sprint, was twice paired with running champions but did not allow this to influence her rate of progress. It was perhaps as well that these socials ceased after three years, for the number of casualties were increasing, and *Chin Wag* had to report that, to the ladies who retired hurt from netball at half-time, there had been added painful injuries to the large and beautiful girl chosen as anchor man in the ladies' tug-of-war. Whenever either side showed signs of wavering, male supporters made an illegal but reinforcing rush for the end of the rope, squeezing the anchor woman like a tube of tooth-paste pinched in the middle. My mother's confidence in the correctness of all her brother's doings must have been shared by his fellow managers of the Club, for the legitimate protest by the poor girl's father at his daughter's maltreatment was scoffed at as a piece of unwarrantable wetness from someone famous, as the father was, in the tough world of motor racing.

Dances at the Eton Manor Club were less physically violent than the evenings of games, but the element of humiliation was only too apt to be present. The first time I had been taken down to Hackney Wick happened to have been on a Sunday afternoon in summer. Childhood stories concerned with the horror of East End tenements had led me to expect a drive through noisome alleys, hidden from the sun, peopled by ragged urchins in caps and mufflers. On the contrary as one drew near to Hackney Wick the streets of low built houses might have belonged to an Irish country town, only the get-up of the corner boys being of an un-Irish sophistication. Each gang guarded its own corner, and, though all wore brown felt hats, separate loyalties were marked by suits of brightest ultramarine or richest mulberry, coats very tight and Oxford Bags at their widest. Strictly grouped in their sapphire and ruby uniforms, whose immaculacy perhaps enforced peaceful behaviour, these peacocks were distinctly at variance with popular ideas of the East End of London forty-five years ago. They did not, however, seem to patronize the Eton Manor Club, for when grey flannel shorts, the great leveller, had been changed for an evening's dancing, I looked in vain for a potential partner in a brilliantly bright suit. Instead I learnt that, in serious ballroom dancing, there is no need to clutch a partner, but that unity can be maintained by the light touch of the male's right hand in the middle of the female's spine. Complimenting her partner on his skill, the wife of one of the managers was put in her place by his reply that he, in fact, did dance rather well, but the trouble was she knew nothing about modern dancing. This would have been even more true as a criticism had it been addressed to me.

In her own dancing days, as I have said earlier, my Aunt Markie had whirled through the evenings, passing from partner to partner. At Hackney Wick she was distressed by the etiquette which dictated that the girls, brought to the dance by their young men, should languish in a neglected cluster for long periods, while their cavaliers sought refreshment and the solace of masculine conversation. Surely, Aunt Markie suggested, it would increase the gaiety of the evening if the patient girls, waiting on their partners' whims, could be introduced to other chaps. She was quickly given to understand that, whatever promiscuity might be permitted in West End ballrooms, fidelity for the evening was the rule among the members of the Eton Manor Club. This point was underlined at another party when the night was fine enough to dance in the garden of the Club. My brother Frank's efforts to bring me together with several partnerless males was greeted with shocked refusals, almost excessive for the offer of a sister made to a missionary on the dock at Port Said. Earlier in the evening there had been a concert at which the star performer had given a display of slow-motion tap-dancing. He danced facing the wings, his body bent forward, his feet twisting and snapping. With a mass emotion that was almost palpable, the audience sang with the dancer,

> 'You're the one I care for,
> The one I love and therefore,
> I hope you care for me.'

with presumably the understanding that no change of partner would be tolerated. The last photograph of the Eton Manor was taken in 1968, when the complex of underground changing-rooms lay open like an ancient site, waiting for the flood of concrete which has now flowed over it, the wheels of juggernaut rumbling above the ghosts of the dancers and singers.

The owner of the private zoo on whose llama I had ridden during the general election was, naturally, an active Fellow of the London Zoological Society. Entertained by him at a luncheon party for his friends and officials of the zoo, I found that I had perhaps more in common with the animals and humans of Regent's Park than with the sporting lads of Hackney Wick. When A. A. Milne wrote of the origin of the name Winnie given to the teddy bear of his son Christopher Robin,

I realized that the Milne family had shared the secret known to my Nanny. By whispering to a keeper that one wished to see Winnie, the magic words opened a door into the catacombs behind the Mappin Terraces, which led on to the rocks of the terraces themselves. Here, watched by crowds not in possession of the password, we were permitted to feed Winnie, a brown bear, from a tin of golden syrup, bearing the trade-mark, peculiarly appropriate for the zoo, of a swarm of bees emerging from the mane of a recumbent lion, with the Biblical quotation, 'Out of the strong came forth sweetness'.

At the Fellow's luncheon which brought back these recollections, I found myself seated next to a Civil Servant, an official whose tentacles stretched deeply into the world of museums. He opened the conversation by telling me a story of a German professor, who insisted that English was an easier language than German, 'Because in Germany we have three sexes, but in England you only have one'. Forty years later, I discovered that this story had a bizarre relevance to one of the guests at the table. To me just another bowler-hatted gentleman of an older generation called Mr Julian Sampson, he had, in fact, been a compromisingly close friend of Aubrey Beardsley. On his own account, he had been photographed in court dress, with a probably transvestite friend, in a hat trimmed with ostrich plumes, leaning over his shoulder. My neighbour was also able to help my curiosity as to how old age was treating Winnie, by referring me to the supervisor of all the keepers at the zoo, who happened to be sitting directly across the table.

News of the brown bear was so dismal that, in communicating it, my informant's eyes filled with tears, a phenomenon more often met with in Victorian story-books than in real life. Winnie, I grieved to hear, was at that moment not expected to last the night, and I saw in the next day's newspaper that she had not. I hope the keepers who mourned her had some consolation from the knowledge that her name, even allowing for a sex change, had been perpetuated in *Winnie the Pooh*, a commemoration later to be translated into a multitude of living languages, achieving a final apotheosis in the dead tongue of Latin.

After luncheon the Fellow's guests were led behind the scenes, where the tangle of water pipes and the rich aroma were reminiscent of the Eton Manor changing-rooms. In this keepers' world the less ferocious mammals and reptiles were passed from hand to hand. These residents, essentially uncuddlesome, included a mandrill with a particularly vivid rear colour scheme, a small size alligator and a boa-constrictor. I had a toleration of reptiles that may have been partly hereditary, for there was a legend that my mother, at an early age, had accosted a visitor with the words, 'Watch me kiss this frog'. (The frog did not turn into a prince, which may have disillusioned my mother with the habit of casual kissing. As I have mentioned elsewhere she had reduced her morning greeting to a bump of cheek on cheek.) Brought up in Ireland whence St Patrick had banished snakes, and in Oxfordshire where the guide-book assured one that there were no adders, though without specifying the reason that the county boundaries were so respected, I had no horror of serpents. Without hesitation, I draped the boa-constrictor round my neck as though it had been the black boa of cock's feathers which I wore with evening dress. A photograph taken at that moment does, however, suggest from my expression that the boa had begun to constrict, and the clammy scales to grip my skin.

More weird examples of natural history than any shown by the zoo were exhibited in the Fun Fair in Coventry Street, a few yards from Piccadilly Circus, which among the attractions in its tangle of alley ways, advertised a pair of mermaids. More correctly they should have been called a merman and a mermatron, for they belonged to that species of aquatic mammal that has exterior sexual organs. As they lay in rigid death, side by side in a double coffin, gender was emphasized by the merman's organ wired in a permanent erection. But the most rough and tumble of the delights offered by the Fun Fair was indubitably the dodgem cars, though the rough and tumble was greater than the delights on an evening when I was incited to take a ride alone in one of these bronco-like vehicles. A girl alone in a dodgem car was, I found, a target for approaches which frequently took the form of a head-on collision, the crash of the colliding cars being punctuated by screams from the electrical connections overhead. At the end of the session I was entering a state of physical disintegration, ears singing from all-embracing pandemonium, legs cockling from shocks caused by clashes with my pursuers.

Across the street in the Café de Paris the noise was less strident but the dramas more complex. It was said that the layout – a double staircase leading from a circular gallery to the restaurant below – reproduced the first-class dining saloon of the *Titanic* in such detail that, on his first visit, a man who had lost his wife when the *Titanic* suffered shipwreck, fainted from the shock of recognition. Less nice feelings prevailed in later days, the shock being more apt to come from recognizing a living spouse rather than from awareness of the ghost of a dead one. Like the laws governing the living and the dead, those in the restaurant below could ascend to the balcony, but those in the balcony could not return below. In the balcony it was permitted to wear day clothes and to dance on a curious little dance floor that did resemble a boat deck. Although Douglas Byng in his various metamorphoses, Flora Macdonald, Nana of the Manor, Vivette the Vestiaire, was immensely popular, the melancholy songs of Chick Endor and Charlie Farrell also brought the customers crowding in, to applaud 'My Consolation (I hear you're happy . . . I'll let that be my consolation)' and 'I Got Her Off My Hands (Now that she's off my hands, I can't get her off of my mind)'. Unlike the Club at Hackney Wick, which survived until attacked by planners, the Café de Paris had only ten years more of existence, before a bomb falling directly on to the restaurant wrote a savage end to the story of these singers and dancers of the 1930s.

11. By the Waters of Dynevor

MY MOTHER TOOK ME ON my first visit to Dynevor Castle in Carmarthenshire in the summer of 1911, when the heatwave which celebrated the Coronation of King George V had baked the grass of his realm to a dusty yellow. The exception, my mother told me, was the rain-washed Vale of Towy, which viewed from the ramparts of the Old Castle of Dynevor remained a luxuriant green. This phenomenon I had to accept on hearsay evidence as, not being born until the following March, I was in no position to make personal observations. In later summers I became part of the army of my aunt's nephews and nieces, who, welcomed with infinite toleration by her husband Walter Dynevor, only ceased to arrive at his castellated porch when autumn began to set in. Journeys to Dynevor in school holidays seemed always to start from Oxfordshire and end in Ireland, which gave my mother splendid opportunities for that manipulation of time-tables in which she delighted. It was a happy day when she discovered that, given notice, the station-master at Chipping Norton had the power to halt an express from the Midlands on its way to South Wales. It was grimmer business when my mother's planning dictated that the *massif central* of Wales should be circumnavigated in the most conscientiously local of trains, with the object, when Crewe was reached, of effecting a union with the Irish Mail. Four slow hours had by then blunted the fine edge of travelling hopefully, no encouragement coming with the knowledge that it would be two hours more before Holyhead would claim its victims, with the prospect of a wet sheet, a flowing sea and a wind that might be following only too fast.

Although, as I have mentioned, my mother habitually shunned local trains on her own behalf, she would not, I think, have accepted defeat as easily as one of her sons who, perhaps owing to a confusion over the geography of Wales, found himself at Caernarvon rather than Carmarthen. In the manner of a children's game with dice, when an unlucky throw may send a player back to start, he returned to London and began again from the beginning. Such delayed arrivals were treated by my aunt as all in the day's work of a hostess, provided the day's work of her domestic staff was not thereby increased. In August, soon after the last and most violent party at Hackney Wick, David Rhys, youngest and most beloved son of the house, announced that he would be arriving on the wings of a Gipsy Moth, piloted by a friend. As I now see, the non-appearance of the aeroplane at the expected hour made for more jumpiness in David's parents than simple distress at the idea that the servant's off-duty hours might be impinged upon. We were chewing our way through the particularly delicious food which made every meal at Dynevor a feast, when suspense was lifted by a hum in the sky, and from over the Black Mountain, twenty miles away, the Gipsy Moth came flighting in towards the park's flattest area. With, it subsequently turned out, over-confidence, David had assured his pilot that, as an airman cousin had more than once landed in the park, there must be at least five hundred yards of unobstructed ground. Like a disappointed seagull the aeroplane circled round our heads, and then swooped away towards the watermeadows, the pilot afterwards explaining that had he landed he would have been unable to take off without grave risk of impalement on the conductors that protected the towers of the house from the lightning-flash.

Anxious to follow the drama, the more energetic among the house party ran across the park to a promontory overlooking the flat fields beside the Towy. They were rewarded by the spectacle of what appeared to be the entire population of Llandilo, streaming out of the town towards the spot where the aeroplane had landed, with the unanimity of the children of Hamelin Town in pursuit of the Pied Piper. Usually calm, Uncle Walter for once lost his self-control, storming off in search of his wife to expostulate on the thoughtlessness of the pilot for parking his flying-machine in a spot where the townspeople would inevitably tear it to pieces. This was an unnecessarily depressing view of the wrecking propensities to be expected from Llandilo, for the Gipsy Moth was sufficiently intact to be flown to Pendine Sands on the following morning. Here the pilot gave flights to his friends, before a crowd which showed a flattering interest in our takings-off and landings, an interest perhaps increased by the fact that my cousin Joan and I flew in bathing dresses, mine borrowed from Joan, and particularly exiguous when climbing into a small open aeroplane. Sea and sky dissolved into one element, when the Gipsy Moth turned and banked over the town of Laugharne, whose fame as the Llareggub of *Under Milk Wood* lay thirty-five years below the horizon of the future.

When I came to read the lyric in *Under Milk Wood* which begins 'Dear Gwalia!' and which Dylan Thomas called the Reverend Eli Jenkins's morning service, I remembered the rides at Dynevor. These rides could take the riders 'By Golden Grove 'neath Grongar', on a long morning's amble through lanes, when I marvelled at the ingenuity by which my conducting cousin brought me home at the exact moment when luncheon had begun to make its need acutely felt. Almost better were the rides starting at eight, which from being so far west and from the incidence of summer time must have been more like six-forty-five in the eyes of the sun. These early morning sorties were led by my cousin Imogen, with pauses to shake hands with the tenants when we rode through the yards of white-washed farms. Imogen rode with complete mastery of a by no means easy horse, while I was happy to trot behind on a farm cob who played no tricks. My training in opening and shutting gates in the Vale of Aylesbury was not as helpful as might have been expected, for gates at Dynevor had to be locked as well as shut. After a ride alone one morning, I was reduced to the humiliation of sneaking back on foot to lock a gate that had defeated me from the saddle. But with Imogen in command there were no problems to mar the delight of cantering along the banks of the 'Towy broad and free'. It was in the Towy's waters that the most silver of sewin were caught, for one of which, in an exchange of pre-monetary simplicity, David, returning from shooting, had once swopped two duck.

Although she had left tennis and riding behind her, my Aunt Markie took exercise whenever she had the opportunity for a walk. From her expeditions into the town of Llandilo, she would return with vivid stories of her encounters, being particularly pleased when she passed one of the town's curates locked in an embrace which was still in progress on her return up the drive an hour later. She had a gift for mimicry, which she exercised on anyone who struck her as absurd or affected. From the tone of voice of a cousin who, though famous for her amorous adventures, kept up a pose of unselfish motherhood, my aunt changed in an instant to a take-off of the unmasculine tones of her own couturier. This gift came in handy when she wished to give a picture of local squabbles. To these she was ever prepared to lend a sympathetic ear, though the disgruntled Welshwoman, who began her tale of discontent with, 'It is mean you are in Llandilo', could not have chosen a less mean person to attack.

It was my aunt who took me on the kind of picnic walk over the hills which Kilvert used to record in his days on the Welsh border. She found great spiritual refreshment from these expeditions. Her lack of meanness was displayed when it transpired that I had, hamfistedly, allowed the plums intended for dessert to roll down the hillside. This discovery was made when we were sitting in the lee of the stone ramparts of an ancient camp, looking down on the castle of 'Carreg Cennen, King of Time', to quote once more from *Under Milk Wood*.

After dinner I played games of patience with Uncle Walter, under the painted regard of ancestors who were sometimes his and sometimes mine, my father's mother having been born at Dynevor of a line that ended in daughters. However, the eighteenth century brought the two lines together in the shape of an ancestress painted by Allan Ramsay. The family portraits of Walter, his wife and children were less aesthetically pleasing, and were excused by my uncle as having, in some cases, been painted in a hurry for the information of posterity. When Uncle Walter died, more than twenty years later, my sister Julia said, as an epitaph, that there were so few people with whom one's relationship had been absolutely cloudless, but with him there was nothing except kindness and affection to remember. His deafness, which came from a hunting accident as a young man, when he had also lost the sight of one eye, was a barrier to social life which grew higher with the years, but at the tea-table in the hall of his castle he was happily at ease. There was a tradition that the cook always made a chocolate cake for my visits, and, eating the melting slices, there was nothing pleasanter than to hear Uncle Walter tell the story of the harp that stood at the foot of the stairs. An aged harper had brought it to the house in Uncle Walter's boyhood, and, having played a farewell tune of the greatest beauty, declared that the pain of saying good-bye to his harp would be softened by the knowledge that its home would be at Dynevor Castle.

Uncle Walter lived beside this harp for the rest of his life. At his funeral the townspeople of Llandilo, who had, he thought, been such a threat to the visiting aeroplane, packed the church, reinforcing the harmony of their voices as they sang 'Abide With Me' with an emotional fervour that seemed to lift the congregation to a level when 'earth's vain shadows' did indeed flee. This outpouring seemed also to be an almost tangible offering to Aunt Markie, who, struggling with a cruel combination of illnesses, found the strength to make a final appearance among those who had been her friends for half a century. At her own funeral the same congregation came to fill the church. Even on the way there some wept, as they left their houses, carrying bunches of garden flowers to add to the lines of formal wreaths. But the cards on these had their own poetry in the cadences of the Welsh names, and no bard could have conceived a more touchingly evocative title for a ballad than that which appeared on one particular card, respectful sympathy being offered by 'The Fishermen of Dynevor Waters'.

12. Bats and Brickbats

IN THE MONTH OF AUGUST, in 1932, my sister-in-law Elizabeth was expecting her first child, for which event she had become a tenant of my Aunt Cynthia's house in Sussex Gardens. Occupied as ever with the necessity of emptying her home during staff holidays, it had occurred to my mother that Elizabeth might find in me a companion in the desert of London in August. At least that was what August in London was remembered as by my mother, when she had been in a similarly expectant situation. Elizabeth having agreed to this arrangement, my mother then became concerned that my maiden mind might be sullied, and even worse that I might be discouraged from matrimony, by too close an acquaintance with the miracle of birth, so I was instructed to move out before the midwife moved in. This warning caused a tenseness absent from my earlier sojourn in Sussex Gardens. There was a nervous moment when Elizabeth and I were seated in the Empire Cinema, Leicester Square. She may have welcomed a pang which she felt, as a sign that her time of waiting was over, but I felt less eager, as our only acquaintance in the vast auditorium was the writer of a gossip column, more adept, I thought, at delivering news than assisting in delivering babies.

Sussex Gardens, besides being handy for Paddington Station, had a proximity to the less well-trodden reaches of Hyde Park in which Cynthia exercised her Pekinese. In fact she may have been influenced in her choice of the house by this convenience. My mother would sometimes be driven to these same unfrequented paths, so that she could walk without feeling that her acquaintances might be witnesses of her lameness. In this unfashionable area she had once met, she told me, a cousin of my father's with a wife close to her time, who were adhering to the already old-fashioned tradition that, in the last weeks of pregnancy, exercise should be taken at dusk in secluded places. If my mother imagined that my companionship would include gentle strolls with Elizabeth in the hinterland of Hyde Park, she had made a wrong estimate of her daughter-in-law's enterprise. London was far from a desert as far as Frank and Elizabeth were concerned, and their social round was so busy that I had time not only to go out in the evening with young men, who sometimes gave me beer and sometimes caviar, but even to spend a Saturday night as far away as Minehead. This was an excursion of extreme respectability, but I did not feel it would square with my mother's idea of keeping Elizabeth company, so I did not mention the matter. I was, however, nearly betrayed by my own idiocy in leaving my camera in the train. My address was written inside the camera case, and with an honest efficiency belonging to a quieter age, the Great Western Railway sent the camera back wrapped up in brown paper. To my mother parcels arriving by rail in August only signified grouse, and, as I was still away from home, she thought it wise to investigate. Luckily her contrition at having inadvertently opened a private parcel made her overlook the unscheduled journey on which I had lost it.

Elizabeth's daughter, Antonia, avoided distressing her grandmother by arriving while I was still under her parents' roof, postponing her birth until I had, in an exercise in zigzag, set off once again for the West. This particular journey to Holyhead was cheered by the affectionate greeting of the steward who served me my breakfast. Not only did he inquire after Julia, with whom he had been accustomed to seeing me twinned, but, noblest of gestures, carried my luggage on board. Some of this protectiveness would not have come amiss in my own home, for the summer visitors included a more active persecutor than was usually to be found in the bosom of my family. In kindness to literary ambitions, Edward and Christine had invited an Oxford undergraduate called Richard to stay. This boy also shared with Edward the experience of having been thrown into Mercury, the fountain in Tom Quad, Christ Church, though Richard's immersion had been brought about by the unpopularity of his personal attitudes, not, as in Edward's case, by the unpopularity of his political opinions.

It happened that Richard and I were the only two members of the house party to relish bathing in Lough Derravaragh, which not only required a pilgrim's penance over the sharpest of stones before entering the lake waters lapping with low sounds upon the shore, but needed the most active of circulations to keep afloat once the icy waters had received the bathers. These agonies were softened by the Elysian beauty of the peninsula from which we bathed. When Julia emerged from the rushes it seemed as if a nymph painted by Renoir had strayed into a grove painted by Corot. Richard was a less satisfactory companion than Julia, for he dwelt with boring detail on his plans to become not only a great novelist, but also a complete man. In my family, at that date, there were at least four novelists, like volcanoes in more or less active eruption, so I treated the idea of the paramount importance of the novelist with a derision which provoked something approaching a free fight, with me in tears of exasperation. Fate ordained that, in my married life, a novelist was to be of paramount importance, so on this point Richard might be said to have had the last laugh. The question of being a complete man was another matter, for to his fellow guests Richard was not so much a complete man as a complete *enfant terrible*.

The holiday season had also brought the Lambs to Pakenham, with their daughter Henrietta, who was not yet entirely weaned. The actual suckling took place in the Rose Room, a bedroom that had kept its name from the rose-patterned chintzes of my mother's time. It had also retained a bed so wide that it could accommodate three pillows, but had been otherwise transformed by the brighter colours favoured by Edward and Christine. Richard had no opportunity to study Pansy's nursery routine, but it transpired that at the age of nineteen he had only the haziest conception of the reproductive processes of mammals. None the less, his imagination had been caught by the idea of Pansy's baby being fed from what Mr Micawber called the founts of nature. At dinner one evening it was suggested that the game of Truth might be played, which on the whole did not usually involve anything worse than one player trapping another into an undeniable lie. Tense with excitement, Richard could hardly wait till the end of the meal to begin a round of questions on the sexual feelings and habits of the company. Stuttering with eagerness, he asked one of the husbands present if he – this husband – felt a 'six-sexual' diminuendo towards his wife compared with the time of their engagement to marry. The answer was, I think, ambiguous, but the expression 'six-sexual' so delighted the one questioned that he used it ever after when announcing the score at Slosh. It was towards me, however, that Richard directed his heaviest fire, and, having received an unsatisfactory answer to a question about possible love affairs, went on to ask me if, should Pansy be absent, I would be prepared to feed her baby. Foolishly, I replied that I would not, rather than I could not, and, as none of those present saw fit to enlighten Richard as to the steps necessary for lactation to be established, he was left to welter in his misapprehensions.

Such an attack in public seemed to me a poor return for the loan of my pyjama trousers when we went swimming in Lough Derravaragh, but one of the many vengeances life inflicted on the unhappy Richard, which included excommunication and pitiless ragging by older intellectuals, followed with almost embarrassing speed. My brother Edward had always relished legends concerning vampires, though insistent that true vampires never took the shape of bats. Pakenham could put on a fair display of these flying mice, though never, to my knowledge, equalling the record set up at Dynevor, where seventeen were counted in the bathroom of an aunt, their nightly exit having been blocked by some roof repairs. A few nights after the unhappy game of Truth, I was woken, in my bedroom on the top floor of the house, by wild screams from the floor below. Cries for Edward and Christine were mingled with the barely intelligible words that the screamer was being attacked by vampires. Transferred to a bat-free room, Richard, who was the screamer, explained that he had woken to find seven bats flying round his head. Assuming in his terror that his host's insistence that vampires never took the shape of bats was a sinister double bluff, he thought that the flapping, slithering creatures dancing round his head were emissaries sent by his host and hostess to make a blood-sucking meal on their behalf.

My current financial arrangements with my mother had included the proviso that I should pay for my own journeys. Previously she had advanced me money for railway fares on a generous scale, supplying more funds unmurmuringly, even when it was only too clear that I must have been siphoning off journey money for other purposes. Now I no longer received a hidden subsidy, and in this low ebb in my affairs I thought it would be prudent to economize. I baulked at a cheap sea-passage from Dun Laoghaire to Holyhead, but from there on I decided to spend the night sitting up in a third-class carriage. September being a popular month for weddings, the autumn sailings had a romance all their own. Groups of friends gathered on the wet planks of the pier, mingling their encouraging cheers to the bridal couples with the screams by which the seagulls accompanied their swoops for the edible garbage floating round the ship's hull. The cheering friends receded, the seagulls returned to base, and the mail-boat sailed out past the Kish lightship, headed for Wales, England and, for the honeymooners, the unknown territory of marriage.

Had I been able to spare a thought for anyone's comfort except my own, I would have been glad that no pair of honeymooners were sharing the carriage in which I had picked a corner seat. Irish fleas have always been much prized in flea circuses for their agility and balletic grace, the Irish Mail train, even in the white-sheeted berths of a first-class sleeper, being one of their happier hunting-grounds. On this economical journey I realized only too soon that a flea circus talent scout would have had a bumper evening. Curled up against me, a girl with the sandy hair and yellow ochre skin that belongs to one particular Hibernian strain, slept with maddening concentration, while a legion of fleas, offered a choice of dishes, settled on me as presenting a larger area of pinker skin. Their meal lasted for six hours as the train passed through the landmarks of my childhood, Chester, Crewe, Stafford, Bletchley, until dawn and Euston brought release. My unwanted guests were eventually drowned in the bath, fed by a ferocious geyser, at my sister Mary's studio. Grateful as I was for early morning welcome, I felt she had rather overstated the case, when she asked the housekeeper to light the geyser on my behalf because I had never had a bath before.

My grandmother was fond of quoting from Madame de Sévigné, 'Rise up daughter, and go to thy daughter and tell her that her daughter's daughter is crying', but she recognized she was unlikely to be able, on her own behalf, to issue such a command. She was, however, a visitor at Peverel when Antonia, a wool-wrapped bundle absorbed in the privileged sleep of the new-born, was wheeled over from Stairways to pay a call on her ancestresses. At eighty-three the great-grandmother was distinctly more mobile than the grandmother. The latter had, however, made an effort to increase her range by buying a small motor-car and constructing an asphalt track round the paddocks which she owned. Legally there was nothing to prevent her from driving this vehicle, its gear-box modified for easier handling by someone of her infirmities, on the public road, as she had punctually renewed a driving licence acquired in the dawn of motoring, no subsequent legislation having rendered it invalid. Mercifully she limited her outings to her private track, which wound its way unexcitingly through the fields to end in the stableyard. Another plan had also been concocted by my mother during the summer. By some means she had learnt of a house in Kensington which was available for the tail-end of its lease, with the attractive bait that dilapidations would be paid by the previous leaseholder. This house struck her as a bargain that would obviate the need for casual rentings and borrowings on her own behalf, and provide me with a base from which I could lead a London life, one day's hunting a week having become inadequate to pin me within the red-brick walls of Peverel Court.

13. Inept at Economics

WHEN I TRESPASSED, NOT LONG AGO, into the hall of the house in Bryanston Square which had belonged to my parents and in which I had been born, I found that it had become a hostel for students from the Far East. A levelling institutionalization had obliterated faint childhood landmarks within the house, but had I climbed to the nursery floor I would have been able to look down on the drinking fountain at the end of the Square gardens. This still stands, though its only connection with thirst quenching comes from the empty mineral bottles cast into its fluted basin, above which rises a plinth topped by a garlanded urn. Time, and the acid London soot, have eroded the garlands, so that the urn now appears as a lightly decorated egg, but on the medallion below can still be read an eulogy of the virtues of William Pitt Byrne, whose friends had erected the fountain from a design by his widow. After a rehearsal of Mr Byrne's intellectual powers and charm of character, the inscription ends with the words,

> '... rendering this refreshing fountain
> a suitable memorial of his worth.'

Gone with the refreshing quality of the fountain is the line of hackney cabs that stood beside it, the horses chumbling in their nosebags, while their drivers waited for the whistle blast that would summon them to their next fare.

In all well-equipped front halls there hung a whistle, whose shrill blast would bring a cab clop-clopping to the door. From Bryanston Square to the more fashionable end of South Kensington the journey took twenty minutes, a fact that came to my notice when reading a detective's evidence in Roy Jenkins's account of the divorce proceedings that ruined Sir Charles Dilke in the 1880s. I mention this not as an example of the more reliable traffic flow in the past, but because it was in Bryanston Square that I first inhabited a London house with my mother, and in Rutland Gate, South Kensington, that she and I finally parted. This journey had taken twenty years rather than twenty minutes, but, in spite of sojourns in eight or nine other London houses, there were still a few traces in Rutland Gate of what might be called my mother's Bryanston Square epoch. She had retained three pairs of brocade curtains from those opulent Edwardian days, and these gave the drawing-room an air of elegance for those who did not cast their eyes down to the carpet which had been chosen by my grandmother as a *Hausgeschenk*. Demonstrating once again that the Aubussons on which her feet had so often trod in the days of her marriage had had no effect on her own taste, Grandmama assured us that it would go with anything, though to my ungrateful eyes it appeared that anything was the equivalent of nothing. This carpet's powerful pattern was more fully displayed than would have been usual in a conventionally furnished drawing-room, on account of my mother's attempt to placate her conscience at launching out into a house that could only be described as medium to large in size.

She proposed to employ one housemaid, so pictures were banned as dust traps, and the drawing-room itself looked as if it was awaiting another load of furniture. Bedrooms, distempered in non-committal pinks and blues, were furnished with a rigour only too reminiscent of boarding-school. On the credit side was the charmingly irregular view over the grounds of Bolney House, between whose trees peered the Italianate tower of All Saints, Ennismore Gardens, a church which was to come in handy in two years' time. My mother's new rules adumbrated that this house was not to be regarded as a pleasure dome, like those from which the London Season had been enjoyed in the past, when I had been at liberty to invite friends to luncheon and tea. Clearly, from its furniture alone, this was no house in which to loll about, but my mother and I were not in agreement as to how I should, so to speak, not loll.

My mother's suggestion that I should attend an art school was unsympathetic to me for more than one reason. In my eyes the world of art study was already over-crowded by my sisters, and in a mood of rebellion I had allowed my own drawing and painting to lapse. Additionally, the school my mother suggested was associated in my mind with a technique which I had long ceased to wish to emulate. My tastes were far from *avant-garde*, but, passionately admiring Corot's Palace of the Popes at Avignon and Oudry's Still Life, where a white duck hangs on a white wall, and the almonds of a trifle in a Luneville dish stand up like the Alignements de Carnac, I spurned the idea of a school whose founder had painted a long way after the Pre-Raphaelites. Contrariwise, my mother's response to my suggestion that I should enter the London School of Economics was unenthusiastic. She did not actually forbid me to go there, but she withdrew her offer to finance my studies, believing that money so spent would go to stoke the fires of revolution, a point of view only thirty years ahead of its time.

With this modified blessing and an introduction from my brother Frank I presented myself at the office in the LSE where the future Lady Beveridge reigned as secretary. To enter the School, delicate handling was needed to bolster my shaky academic qualifications. In excusing my failure to pass the School Certificate, it was necessary to avoid appearing on one hand as having been too lazy to do the required work, and on the other as having been too obtuse to reach the standard exacted by the examiners. At the time, I had only been depressed by my failure because it separated me for a term from my closest friends. I was well aware that my home education had left me with the area of mathematics untilled, while other areas, it might be said, were double-dug. Genuine surprise attended my discovery that a member of my family circle had taken my lapse so seriously as to consider that I was now to be graded for life as intellectually substandard.

In practice all that the LSE required of this aspirant was to write an essay on the Industrial Revolution, which had already been required of me at every stage of my education. Trotting out my stock piece, I did not fail to mention Crompton's Mule and Arkwright's Spinning Jenny, which had, for me, acquired personalities of their own, causing me to wonder if Crompton's Mule had ever remarked 'Spinning Jenny kissed me when we met'. Judged adequate by whoever read this essay, I was enrolled at Houghton Street. This street, as it happened, lay close to a building which commemorated one of the founders of the fortunes of my mother's family and not far from a pattern of streets which bore the names of another. Villiers, Duke and Buckingham Streets (with Of Alley between the last two) celebrated the beautiful boy of dazzling complexion, who raised his family to aristocratic heights by fascinating the first two Stuart kings, among those upraised being an elder half-brother from whom my mother descended. East of Houghton Street, under the shadow of Temple Bar, the Child family of bankers had made the fortune which helped to ornament the palace of Osterley, where, finally, a marriage brought together the lines of the man of business and the sexual adventurer, united in the family of Child Villiers. Child's bank building had its own claim to immortality, or so my mother was happy to tell me. When Dickens wrote *A Tale of Two Cities*, he explicitly placed Tellson's Bank on the site of Child's, with Jerry Cruncher the bank messenger outside the door in his daytime avocation, his nights being reserved for the more arduous, but profitable, trade of Resurrection Man. I suppose, in my mother's eyes, students at the London School of Economics were working towards a world in which Jerry Cruncher would be superfluous, both as a Bank messenger and a Resurrection Man.

The waters of the past have long since drowned my reasons for wishing to study at the LSE. Perhaps I felt that I should there obtain a firmer grasp of politics than I had acquired by rather dilettante electioneering, for I cannot suppose I was solely activated by opposition to my mother. She, unhappily, had not become aware that, after the periods in which she had so frequently required me to dispose of myself, it was hardly reasonable to attempt to contain me once more in a social box of her own shaping. An additional complication came from the coincidence that my life in West End night-clubs was passing through an unusually active phase, not only providing a poor foundation for intellectual effort, but increasing the practice of deception to a point that induced brain fag from the manufacture of alibis and excuses.

In the Slippin', the night-club – called by a legal quibble a bottle party – that I most frequented, the customers were fed on such curiously innocent dishes as smoked haddock and eggs and bacon. The management being largely in the hands of a family of well-brought up sisters, the place gained in sedateness from their habit of addressing the undeniably *louche* waiters as if they were devoted family retainers. Only occasionally was the atmosphere ruffled by such events as the arrival of the bachelor party I have mentioned earlier. I had never been able to regard the Slippin' as a daring haunt of vice, since on my first visit I had found there two former schoolfellows. One I had last seen when she had earned reproof, as a recently confirmed Anglican, from the Chaplain of Queen's College, Harley Street, for offering me a sweet, dyed blue in an ink-pot, during a Scripture lesson. Now, in the tightest of skirts and the highest of heels, she was dancing a tango of infinite complication, while my other schoolfellow was swooning cheek to cheek with her partner, a far cry from the day when we had together endured a French *viva voce* at St Margaret's, Bushey. Both the schools I attended had been founded with the noblest intentions of sending girls out into the world equipped for life, which in these cases seems to have included night life.

Descending the spiral of pleasure by way of the Bag o' Nails, where the attraction was the entertaining conversation of the cashier, rather than the charms of the professional hostesses, the bottom might have been said to be reached at a club in Gerrard Street called Smokey Joe's. Vice can seldom have worn a dirtier face than it did in this squalid cellar, where ladies in check coats and skirts did not hesitate to dance aggressively together, and anyone foolish enough to visit the lavatory would deserve all that they would undoubtedly get. When the police finally brought the manager of Lousy Joe's, as it was unaffectionately called, before the Bench, it was explained that this was the end of a long hard hunt, the quarry's evasion of the licensing laws having been both crafty and long-standing.

On moving into Rutland Gate, my mother had remodelled part of the ground floor as a bedroom and bathroom for herself, which, as she still insisted that her daughters should register their re-entry with her, meant that her nights were those of a concièrge. Having, as it were, clocked in on the ground floor, I would climb to my bedroom, with the hope that I had not brought with me a too powerful aroma of cigarette smoke and mixed drinks. When Henrietta, Pansy's daughter, paid her grandmother a visit, the nanny temporarily in charge of the baby would deposit her on my bed, while descending herself to breakfast in the basement, where a snugness, noticeably absent from the rest of the house, prevailed. An amiable chicken in a yellow dressing-gown, Henrietta could be amused by turning on and off the electric light switch dangling above my bed. When this game palled, tiny fingers were quite strong enough to swing the egg-shaped switch in an ever-widening circle, until it cracked on to my forehead aching from late hours and bad air. But this early morning romp earned me recognition as a friend by Henrietta, and allowed me to show her off to a coven of her great-aunts invited to view my mother's first grandchild. For this event she was decked in pink muslin frills with her hair curled elegantly. 'Quite a drawing-room child,' said my mother, paying her granddaughter the highest compliment she knew. Certainly, judging from photographs that survive, her own children had seldom attained this state of soigné perfection, their well fleshed limbs and fine heads of hair being equally out of control.

That winter weddings among my friends began to multiply, and I was booked as a bridesmaid for three in quick succession. This caused a gossip-writer to tip me as likely to head the list of the Season's bridal attendants, but I could have spared the quotation of the old adage, 'Three times a bridesmaid, never a bride.' Unexpectedly, the world of the LSE overlapped with the world of weddings, as I stood among the sombre columns by the west door of St Margaret's, Westminster. The bridesmaids were being linked together by chains of white flowers, and, as I waited to join the end of the procession, I was startled to recognize a fellow student from the London School of Economics. An earnest girl, she had, the week before, tried to recruit me for a discussion group which proposed to study the philosophy of H. G. Wells, to me only the writer of a novel, *Ann Veronica*, in which the heroine took a swipe at a policeman. Social curiosity, rather than the study of any philosophy, must have led my fellow student to edge her way in among the bridesmaids, who were themselves decked in wreaths and veils that would have been deemed adequate by many a bride. She had not gone so far as to disguise herself in a wedding garment, indeed it was her lecture-going clothes that enabled me to recognize her. Her face, as she looked at me, wore the expression of someone who dismisses as fantasy a resemblance belonging to a denizen of another world.

Almost immediately I followed another bride, my cousin Joan, up yet another aisle. It was while helping her to change into her going-away outfit that I found myself in a state of tearfulness, that I partly put down to losing the cousin with whom I had lived on sisterly terms, and partly to the after-effects of a party which Lord Lonsdale, famous throughout the world of sport and friend of Joan's late father, had given the night before. In my childhood, in Bruton Street, one of the sights had been the morning departure of Lord Lonsdale in his canary-coloured motor-car, which shared with its owner's bowler-hat the quality of being at the same time round and square. Check-suited, his cigar levelled like a lance, he would seat himself in the yellow motor-car, while a footman in a long fawn overcoat would wrap his employer in more checks, before he was whirled away to some sporting destination. At his pre-wedding party for Joan, Lord Lonsdale naturally wore evening dress, but, as he presided over tables decorated with his racing colours, his cigar was still levelled and his wide smile nearly met the curls of his gingery whiskers. He had good reason to smile as he had long since burst like a clown through the paper hoop of mere boastfulness, never hesitating to explain that he had out-ridden, out-shot and out-boxed the champion of each sport. He slipped, but only for a moment, when a guest inquired if he had ever tasted vodka, not then a drink easily come by in England. Having absentmindedly said he had not, Lord Lonsdale quickly returned to his customary attitude of a poker player who always has a royal straight flush to beat a full house, assuring the company that not only had he in his cellar some bottles of superior potency, but that he had more than held his own in a pre-Revolutionary vodka orgy in St Petersburg.

It was, in fact, neither Joan's departure nor Lord Lonsdale's hospitality that had reduced me to a tearful condition, but the beginning of a famous influenza epidemic, a lethal wave that scythed through the country. To my mother doctors and nurses belonged to the abhorred territory of invalidism, in which she had no wish that her children should become, even temporarily, resident. I acquiesced when Annie Reason, as my mother's emissary, remarked, 'We don't want to make this a doctor's case, do we?' but I found the long column in *The Times* death announcements which reiterated 'from pneumonia following influenza' far from reassuring. A visit by my mother to my sick bed gave her the opportunity of examining photographs displayed of friends close and closer, but she politely refrained from comment, confining herself to saying how my arms were thin. This was at variance with her more usual complaint that I was 'too full on the shoulders', an euphemism for too big in the bust. George Du Maurier's unnatural curves were for her still the most admired figure, ignoring that, to be the shape that Du Maurier drew, the out-thrust bottom had to be balanced by pointing the toes in the second position. For breasts to be marked, my mother regarded as an almost voluntarily obscene gesture on the part of their owner, Du Maurier's heroines' lower dorsal curve being duplicated by an equally smooth curve of chest in front.

There was a failure to link cause and effect in my mother's nostalgic references to the pleasure she had taken in the chubby legs of her infant children, particularly when clad in brown woollen stockings, and her disapproval when these children, nourished as it seemed to them on an exclusive diet of roast mutton, grew to a size she regarded as reprehensibly large. On the other hand, provided that her canons of good taste were not outraged, she took pleasure in pretty faces and gay clothes, unlike many of her contemporaries; a carping generation, critical of the efforts of their own or other people's daughters to display to advantage the looks that God had seen fit to bestow on them. Handicapped by difficulty in communicating her feelings, my mother was inhibited from complimenting her daughters to their faces. Weeks, even years, might pass before kind words bestowed by third parties worked their way round to the object of praise. Pansy, she told me, had looked a little love, in her first Season, dancing round with a rose in her hair, a charming picture, only recorded when its subject had torn the rose from her hair and danced far away from Mayfair. It is true that pleas that lips might be less red and nails less scarlet, were sometimes supported by praise from others of the natural beauty of complexion that her daughters possessed, but she also found that she over-estimated the dedication of followers of the fashionable in make-up. My eager acceptance of ten pounds as a bribe to moderate the colour of my nails was almost a shock, though later she complained of her bad bargain as my nails rapidly regained their gaudiness, except for one thumb-nail, kept unobtrusively pale for passing dishes to my mother at mealtimes.

A sad deterioration in my relationship with the London School of Economics was halted, while my tutor and I were both disabled by influenza. I had already become increasingly depressed by the sordid conditions of the women's cloakroom, which reminded me of a description of below decks on board *La Martinière*, as that ill-famed ship transported convicts to Devil's Island. Whenever I was in conversation with a fellow student an old acquaintance seemed to surface at my elbow, to spoil, with esoteric allusions, attempts at new friendships. From a more personal angle, I began to feel that I was describing a circle, when a talk on Juvenile Courts by a Probation Officer began with the stirring words, 'First of all we have that splendid J.P., the dear old Dowager Countess of Jersey.' Splendid I knew my grandmother to be, but it seemed a long way to go to be told so.

When I had first entered the LSE I had been asked if I had had any experience of social work, to which my reply was that I had often attended a club run by an uncle in Hackney Wick. This was accepted as experience, presumably the East End address being sufficiently convincing to make superfluous inquiries as to what I did when I got there. I was, however, given a leaflet concerning another place of good works, at which it was suggested that I might gain experience in social science, but I was never to discover if this would be beyond the ping-pong principle, being daunted by the succession of buses and trams by which it was to be reached. It may have been this failure that caused my tutor to remark that my last essay, written in purple ink, was, to put it mildly, on the slight side, and that I appeared to be wasting the school's time and my money. I was in agreement, but at least I had had the foresight to pay by the term, instead of putting down a year's fees in advance, which caused other drop-outs to emerge the poorer from Houghton Street.

My tutor had always been patiently kind to me, though she was not prepared to accept my suggestion that my knowledge of village life might have given me anything of a grasp as to the lives of those poorer than myself, regarding rural poverty as irrelevant, and presumably mitigated by fresh air and the fruits of the earth. This view was not shared by Doctor Eileen Power, who not only filled the LSE's theatre with her lectures, but had the strength of character to insist that latecomers should get to hell out of it again, a gift for discipline that lecturers in later days must have wished she could have transmitted. Doctor Power had no illusions about the ease of country life from the eighteenth century onwards, and read extracts from Cobbett's *Rural Rides* to prove her point.

Thirty years later I found myself in the state capital of Hyderabad, at a party given by the Director of Archaeology, sampling young Indian whisky against a musical background supplied by three singers who accompanied themselves on a drum, a portable harmonium and a flute. Somewhat surprisingly, I learnt that one of the songs was a translation of 'Come into the Garden, Maud', which is not perhaps so remote from Indian love poetry as one might think at first glance. Another surprise was to find that I must have sat in the theatre of the LSE in company with one of the guests, while we both listened to Doctor Power's exposition of the ups and downs of English economic history. Nostalgia is a plant that grows upas-like when one is far from home, but even the charm of meeting a fellow student in the middle of the Indian subcontinent raised no yearning for the days when I travelled from Rutland Gate to Houghton Street. There was a choice of routes, but I never thoroughly mastered any of them, for if I shunned the murky branch line to Aldwych, itself a prevision of Avernus, I was only too apt to find myself on an omnibus which swept off in a right-hand hook down Great Queen Street. Nor did I feel a regret for ham sandwiches and coffee eaten in a tea shop where rivers of condensation ran down the tiled walls. The only memory that still warms my heart is of sitting snugly in the incense-laden warmth of St Mary le Strand, whose spire seemed to be pointing to different objectives than those sought at the London School of Economics.

My months as a student did little to improve my grasp of my personal economics, particularly in connection to my indebtedness to my mother. As 13 March 1933, my twenty-first birthday, approached, it seemed to me that there would be no way of preventing my mother from getting a sight of the passbook, which registered that the allowance she paid me was not only overdrawn, but had been largely dissipated in cheques made out to the Berkeley Hotel. To avert painful inquiries, I walked down from Houghton Street to Child's Bank, under the shadow of Temple Bar, in order to suggest that there might be some way of keeping my passbook a private affair. This no one was prepared to do, but all my acquaintances in the bank were delighted at such a proposition and, with unfeeling mirth, gathered round me to advise that in future if I wished for financial anonymity I should be well advised to make my cheques out to Self and no other. There was, as a matter of fact, a family precedent for this, one of my mother's forbears never making out a cheque to anyone except Self throughout his entire life. On the day that I calculated that the passbook would be in my mother's hands I presented a guarded front at luncheon, not least because I had arranged a party at the Berkeley Hotel to celebrate my majority, and I had no wish to draw my mother's attention to the time and money that I spent there. To my surprise the matter of my overdraft was not mentioned. It was only when my mother's affairs were finally cleared up did I realize that for her to condemn my overdraft would have been the equivalent of a very large pot calling a very small kettle black.

Although my birthday party did not come to my mother's

notice (she failed to remark that I was leaving the house in a new pink outfit topped by pink orchids) my coming of age gave her the opportunity of some of vicarious shopping on the Stock Market. This was a pleasure that she enjoyed at the majority of each of her younger children. Her eldest son's patrimony, larger and more complicated, required the advice of professional men of business, who were apt to lack my mother's sporting financial approach. To her prospectuses were detective stories, and she even followed the fate of shares she had decided against. Gamages' attempt to outshine Selfridges in Oxford Street she had regarded with a suspicion that, from her post of vantage in Norfolk Street, Park Lane, she was able to see justified. Gamages' colossal illuminated Christmas sign, in which Humpty Dumpty, Tom the Piper's Son and other merry men chased each other across the store's façade, brought gaping crowds who halted all traffic in Oxford Street. The Metropolitan Police intervened, and a sad notice reading, 'We are so sorry but . . .', hanging below a myriad unlit coloured globes, might have been the epitaph of the whole venture, which quite soon went over the hills and far away.

14. The Rufus Stone

THE PINK ORCHIDS WORN AT my birthday party had been given me by Ty MacRae, a friend made during the term I spent at Queen's College, Harley Street. A famous Old Girl of this school had been Katherine Mansfield. I fancy that the founders of the College, called after Queen Victoria its patron, would have thought Katherine Mansfield's subsequent career even farther from their ideals than the frequenting of night-clubs by Old Girls, which I have already mentioned. I only became aware that I had shared, briefly, the same educational advantages as the writer from New Zealand when my son Tristram made a television film about her, and included a photograph of a garden of girls studying with concentrated gravity in the Library of Queen's College. I recognized that the Library had retained its elegant plaster-work and panelling down to my own day. Ty MacRae used the library table as an exercise ground for her tortoise Percy, an unusually lively four-legged reptile, which, tempted with lettuce, could be induced to surmount a volume of *Who's Who*.

Percy did not, I think, survive Ty's schooldays, but she was a natural zoo-maker, round whom animals thickened as oil thickens mayonnaise. When her animal establishment increased beyond what her London apartment could comfortably contain, she decided to move two borzois, a white pekinese and a canary called Canute to the New Forest. Here she had found a house that was to let, a mile or so from the stone that marks the spot where Tyrrell shot his arrow and William Rufus cried, *'Per vultum de Lucca'* for the last time. (This was, traditionally, William II's favourite oath, an invocation of the portrait of Christ at Lucca, begun by Nicodemus, and said to have been miraculously finished, so it is not unreasonable to assume that it would have been his reaction to a mortal wound.) Until I agreed to be a co-tenant with Ty in the neighbourhood of the Rufus Stone, all I knew of the area was learnt from the history books of my childhood, with their emphasis on the wicked kings who condemned to death and torture any villein caught poaching game, which did not, incidentally, prevent Rufus's brother and nephew from also meeting their deaths hunting in the Forest that has been called New for a thousand years.

Built on the lip of the Forest's plateau, the house we lived in looked over wooded slopes towards Southampton. On the newly built tower of the City Hall a red light glowed by night. By day in a gap of the far-off trees we could see what we thought to be the chimneys of an Elizabethan mansion, to realize when the gap suddenly became empty that the chimneys had belonged to an ocean-going liner. It was only, I suppose, for seven or eight weeks that Ty and I lived in this house. Sometimes it must have rained, and sometimes we must have had moods of nervous exasperation with each other's whims, but I remember it as a time replete with sunshine and jokes. The one wet day that I can recall was made bright by putting up a woodcock in the course of a rain-defying tramp across the top of the Forest, and finding its nest with newly hatched young at my feet. Primroses and anemones were succeeded by bluebells and appleblossom. Canute the canary was an early casualty, but the house seemed still to be full of livestock, Winkie the white pekinese providing a rather sinister sideshow by falling physically in love with a small black toy dog, which he attacked in an erotic frenzy he never displayed towards any other object or animal. Winkie's passion had to be suppressed when Ty's mother drove down to visit us, although she was accustomed to giving almost unlimited hospitality to the dogs her daughter chose to send to the MacRaes' Highland home. Without conceit, I think I can say that I habitually got on well with the mothers of my friends, finding it easy to be a good daughter to almost any mother but my own. In particular Ty's mother was always affectionate towards me, but on this occasion she carried her kindness too far in allowing me to sample her slimming pills. The owner of the house had left a calendar hanging on the lavatory door which provided a helpful quotation for every day, one of our more frequent visitors never making a decision without first consulting this oracle, but the effect of the slimming pill obliged me to become overfamiliar with too many of the quotations.

Appropriately during Holy Week, Ty added two bottle-fed lambs to the establishment. Both were called Joe, but too soon they passed from the charmingly skittish stage into the actively destructive, until one died from swallowing a teat off his bottle, and the other passed to a more conventional destiny. Serge, the elder Borzoi, was quietly moving towards old age, but he still retained the gift of jumping five-barred gates from a standstill. Boris, the younger dog, was clumsier, both at surmounting obstacles, over which he often needed to be helped, and in his human relationships. Boris's curiosity led him one day to thrust his long black and white nose into the face of a chance caller, kindly engaged in helping with some gardening job. Eyes goggled as this unhappy man was seen, by an almost magical flight, to have put the lily pond between himself and Boris.

Besides startling cynophobes, Boris had already disgraced himself in connection with the lily pond, by ostentatiously wading in to retrieve some peculiarly uneatable pudding, which had been cast upon the waters in order to spare the feelings of its maker, Ty's German maid Berta.

It soon after appeared that Berta's feelings, far from needing consideration, were of a kind to be controlled or released at will. This she demonstrated by throwing a rather suspect fit on a Sunday evening. Discovered stretched theatrically on the floor, she was carried up to her attic bedroom by two kind young men. There I sat quaking beside her, watching with apprehension as her torso curved in a rigid arc, until a doctor arrived in a very Sunday evening humour. His temper was not improved when he was impeded in his examination of the patient, first by Berta's modesty, and then by what seemed to be a chest protector of goat skin. Having told the doctor that her fiancé (a character previously unmentioned) was himself a medical man, and had prescribed some special potion for these attacks, the English doctor still persisted in his examination, remarking querulously that Berta ought to be used to the ways of doctors by this time. Next day, slightly shamefacedly, Berta excused the fact that her collapse had left her apparently uninjured, by explaining that these attacks insulated her from all sensation, reminding me of the poor electric maiden at the Oktoberfest in Munich. Berta's immunity was such, she told me, that she had once rolled unharmed 'down marble steps in Düsseldorf hotel'.

Down on the common below our house spring was celebrated by a fair, at which Lavengro and the Flaming Tinman might have slogged it out with bare fists. The glow from the flares belonged to an earlier age, and so, indeed, did the swing boats. Ominous cracks from the crossbars caused more and more of them to be put out of service, until the last serviceable boat was slewed across the uprights of the swing by an injudicious push from one of our party, just as I and a powerful Jugoslav were sailing through the air in a parabola in which the night sky and the Forest floor changed places too quickly for my liking. The keeper of the swing-boats took the incident with the philosophy of someone who had a summer season of such accidents to which to look forward. Meanwhile, on the top of the Forest, the coming of Thomas Hardy's 'mild airs that do not numb' had brought about the dispersal of a circle of caravans, leaving their winter harbour among the pines an empty space, while the gipsies set off on their summer trek.

The melting of the infinitely gaudy camp had been watched in the course of rides that ranged from the purgatorial to the idyllic. The purgatorial ride was in early days, when I had been lured into going out with the New Forest Stag Hounds on the last day of the season. Coming from a country of fences, I was surprised to find no obstacles to be jumped, other than an occasional stream, but blazing sunshine overhead and heavy going below soon reduced me to a state when I would have welcomed Tyrrell and an arrow to put an end to my pains. These were increased by the aggressive behaviour of my hireling, which, having been hunted the previous season by the first whip, had learnt to keep up with hounds in what Somerville and Ross called that school of adversity known to the hunt servant's horse. The idyllic rides came later, when the hunting season was over, and hounds no longer met at the Rufus Stone. On the last day of our last party a cavalcade six strong rode out along the sandy tracks, on horses only less ill-assorted than the clothes of the cavaliers. Less than ten years ahead lay the horrors of war fatal to three of the riders, but on that afternoon cantering through the Forest, itself new-born in the month of May, there was only agreement with the one who cried, 'These are the days!'

So hot was the continuing fine weather that, back in London, I suffered no chill when posing in the nude for my sister Mary and her friend Primrose, in the studio which had provided me with so many a useful alibi. This studio, on the top floor of a house in Jubilee Place, had a charm that was only marred by the intemperate habits of the house-keeper's husband, who, in pursuit of drink, had broken open cupboards, forced a tantalus apart, and had only been foiled by a heavily padlocked chest. Across the road the Alvis motor-works had a depot. It was the house-keeper's daughter who reported to her mother that, both in the butcher's shop, and in the newsagent's round the corner in the King's Road, she had been told that the mechanics from Alvis were making ribald remarks about 'the young lady they could see undressing in Lady Mary's studio'. By one of those coincidences with which life is far more lavish than any writer would dare to be, we knew that among the mechanics was a former childhood playmate from Oxfordshire, a past companion in rough games of hockey and rougher games indoors. Whether he was among the workshop voyeurs was never revealed, but my natural exhibitionism was sufficiently strong to prevent any crisis of modesty. Having been obliged to read *Paul et Virginie* in the schoolroom, I was aware that an over-civilized shrinking from nakedness could, in extreme cases, lead to death by drowning.

At my coming of age my grandmother had sent me a cheque for £10, with the wish that I might from then on lead a happy, useful life. In her next letter, however, she had already seen signs that I was failing in usefulness, for she wrote to say that she thought it sad that my mother, now possessed of two houses, seemed to find none of her children prepared to inhabit them with her. In my rather evasive reply, the glow from the £10 still before me, I was supported by the knowledge that any criticism from her mother towards her children roused my own mother to a defensiveness not usually displayed. 'Spoils them when they are children, and then expects me to keep them in order when they are grown-up,' was my mother's line when she learnt that Grandmama had launched a letter, protesting at social or political behaviour, and directed at a son or daughter of my mother's. I must admit that my mother herself had begun to complain that, although I had declared that I did not wish to leave my home I might at least be seen to be in it, rather than all too often departing to a house that Ty had now taken on the Beaulieu River. Here the shining waves lapped the grass at the garden's end and we sailed in a dinghy downstream. On either bank boat-owners were doing the things that would be regarded as fiddling nonsense in anything except boats. We sang 'I've told every little star', a tune that hung in the air that summer, and as we sailed home the boat lovers on the shore whistled the last bars of the refrain, 'Maybe you have known it too, Oh, my darling, if you do, Why haven't you told me?'

When I was in London I found it difficult to strike a balance between going to a party that my mother applauded, such as a ball at Norfolk House, where the ducal footman wore knee-breeches and powdered hair, and such parties to which those bidden were told to come in the clothes that they felt most sympathetic. This led to a mixture of dress, Lord Alfred Douglas being perfectly turned out in white tie and tails, while an American guest had felt his mood required him to appear in a Tyrolean outfit, with a chamois beard in his hat. Lord Alfred Douglas melted away with the dew of the midsummer morning, but the Tyrolean, a soldier, a sailor, and myself, found it appropriate to seat ourselves on the ground in the middle of Hanover Street, Mayfair, while the soldier unrolled his umbrella and held it ceremonially above the head of the sailor, as the latter read aloud from James Joyce's *Portrait of the Artist as a Young Man*.

The fog of deception with which I ordinarily covered my comings and goings had now to be more widespread, as I had become involved in a scheme for introducing women into the game of polo. This I felt obliged to conceal from my mother, not so much because she might, reasonably, consider the game as dangerous, but for fear she might inquire as to how I was financing my participation. From the writings of Lord Mountbatten, I later learnt that no one should take the field in this most arduous of games until they had become so much at one with their mount that all their attention could be fixed on marking their man in the opposing team, hitting the ball being a minor part of the strategy. Far from qualifying for this ideal state of equitation, my principal use to my team came from my ability to whack the ball a fair distance, getting possession of it when the more dashing riders had galloped ahead.

The heat of the game, and of the ponies, induced such a drenching sweat that I went to the Men's department at Fortnum's in search of woollen shirts, which, I thought, might avert sudden chills when a chukka was over. On the same mission my brother Frank had, a short time before, found himself being measured alongside the monumental boxer Carnera. On this occasion, as I made my choice, I looked round to find that Ivor Novello, a star in a variety of musical firmaments, had flung open his coat for the tape-measure to be drawn round his chest. Frank assured us that his measurements had been read out as a counterpoint to Carnera's, so I thought it wise to retire before mine could be compared with Ivor Novello's. Consequently I do not know what he chose, but the shirts I bought travelled far, one of them ending up as a gift to a female conductor on the train between Kiev and Leningrad, a gift rewarded with an embrace of the hottest Russian gratitude.

Under the imposing title of the London Ladies, my team

played a match at Brighton, but the publicity was not striking enough for my mother to remark on my début on the polo field. However, when I arrived for a second match to be played at Ranelagh the cameras of the national press were massed in front of me, and I realized that, like a secret agent, my cover had been blown. An appeal that my name and picture might be omitted from reports was met with astonishment, from those more accustomed to having subjects angling for the eye of their cameras. It would have been, in fact, impossible to have left me out without conveying the impression that my team had only fielded three players. It was the month of August, and reporters seized on this, the first all women's match to be played at Ranelagh, with the thankfulness of desert travellers arriving at an oasis. I was not troubled by pictures of myself sinking a long drink which appeared in papers my mother did not see, but in *The Times* there was too much coverage for her to overlook. In the knowledge that my mother did not usually reach the back pages of the paper until the afternoon, I snatched the small silver cup given to each player in the winning team, which mine had been, and drove home at speed. When I entered her bedroom, cup in hand, she allowed her pleasure at the idea of one of her husband's children winning a trophy at Ranelagh to overcome any doubts of my rather rocky explanation as to how I happened to be there to win it. The cup joined a silver ash-tray commemorating a victory of a team, captained by my father, in a polo handicap at Ranelagh a quarter of a century before.

15. The Beetle's Droning Flight

ELIZABETH'S DAUGHTER ANTONIA WAS ONLY eleven months old, but her position was already threatened by the imminent birth of a second child. The heat-wave shimmered on, and in the last days of her expectancy, Elizabeth, who had swum for her college when at Oxford, felt a strong need to plunge into any available stream or pool. There was a pool that we had regarded as peculiarly our own, concealed down a lane and overhung by a Pre-Raphaelite exhibition of flowers, through which midges danced and beetles wheeled their droning flight. Fine weather had, however, led to its discovery by a large proportion of the population of Aylesbury, so that grassy bank and the stream itself became more and more to resemble a bathing-place for hippopotami. On these balmy nights Elizabeth and I slept out on the gravel sweep outside her front door, to be awakened at eight each morning by a squeal of brakes from the gardener's bicycle. His name was Beetle, and, as he invariably forgot that we were reposing in his path, I always expected that he would one day brake too late and wheel his droning flight over our heads.

Finally, when even if we left for the river when Beetle woke us, we found that a crowd was building up, Elizabeth suggested that we should bathe higher up the River Thame, where it ran through the Terrys' fields, thinking that proximity to the main road from Aylesbury to Bicester would be counterbalanced by the pleasure of spreading ourselves uncrowded on the bank. This was a miscalculation, for a party of tough chaps were already wallowing in the stream, and, undeterred by the presence of a brother of Elizabeth's, let fly assorted ribaldries as we crossed the field. Suddenly Elizabeth's condition became apparent and the jeers ceased, so abruptly that something was seen to spring from the mouth of one of the jeerers. As we splashed in the chilly water, heat-waves making little impression on the temperature of English rivers, we were aware that gloom had descended on the previously rowdy party along the bank. Seldom can revenge for insult have come more swiftly, outpacing even the speed with which Richard, at Pakenham, had found himself attacked, he supposed, by vampires. In a few minutes we were approached by a chastened envoy, with an appeal for help. 'Can any of you dive?' he asked. 'A fellow here has lost his top plate.'

My mother had never followed the march of fashion except, as it were, in the rear ranks. Like many of her contemporaries, her style of dress had been so firmly crystallized before the watershed of 1914 that concessions to less rigid fashions seemed to sit uneasily on the wearer. Thus I was accustomed to taking her somewhat outdated appearance for granted, seeing it as belonging to pattern still prevalent among the mothers of many of my friends. It was only when she ventured for a stroll to the Eton and Harrow match that I had become aware of how much her pallor set her apart from the friends with whom she was talking. She had always been stimulated by social occasions, and before her widowhood her circle had been far flung, so that when she made a foray into the world she soon gathered round her a cluster of figures from the past. Pleasure in these meetings was mutual, but to me, an onlooker, the comparison of her paleness with the robust complexions of her friends made a deeper, more ominous, impression than the half understood warnings from the more indiscreet of her nurses. There were, in addition, signs that she might be abandoning some of the outposts she had held so tenaciously in the face of pain and disease. No longer was her uniformed nurse segregated at meals from her daughters, and she even invited Julia to visit her when she was spending a week in a nursing home.

A few days after the incident of the lost top plate, Elizabeth gave birth to the only grandson my mother was to see, her delight being increased by his being called Thomas, after his paternal grandfather. Between my mother and myself a better understanding had grown up during these days of sunshine. This process had begun on a night of alarms, when I became aware that a doctor had been summoned at midnight. Well-disciplined not to interfere in any medical process, I remained hidden, but alert. On the following morning, the emergency passed, my mother for the first time accepted that it was not unreasonable for me to have been alarmed. On my side I found that by asking her if she would like to be told my plans, she reacted more sympathetically than if she was asked for permission to carry them out. I did not know that this was the last summer in which I should be accountable to an elder generation, but I did speculate that, had I handled affairs more adroitly in earlier days, I might have been able to establish a less deceitful way of life.

For both my eldest sisters the first step after leaving their mother's roof had been to live as *pensionnaires* with Miss Baillie in Halsey Street, on the edge of Chelsea. This charming lady welcomed not only Pansy, until she moved to share a flat with a friend on whom she was supposed to be a benign influence, and Mary, who remained as an adopted daughter of the house for nearly five years, but also Frank, who immediately collapsed with pleurisy. Miss Baillie's *sang-froid* was, however, equal to this, and indeed to any, domestic emergency. I was particularly impressed with the charm of the establishment when, at tea time, the aged Scotch terrier was found to have made a mess on the hearthrug. To my mother the threat of such a disaster taking place, and even worse the possibility of having to tell a butler to dispose of the excrement, caused her to refuse to allow any but visiting dogs indoors. Miss Baillie, on the other hand, merely bade her parlour maid fetch a shovel, and had she employed a butler I am sure she would not have hesitated in telling him to do likewise.

Retirement having taken Miss Baillie back to her native Ross and Cromarty, Mary suggested to my mother that she might take over the top floor of the house in Rutland Gate as a flat for herself, my mother's plan for an economical London life having left these attics unfurnished. Prepared to welcome back a daughter, my mother was unaware, as far as I know, that she was also receiving the third novelist thrown up by her immediate family in the space of three years. Pansy had written her first novel during her engagement. It was compared in style by one reviewer to Rabelais, not a writer that one would have expected my mother to have studied, but she was delighted with the grotesque inappropriateness of the compliment. Pansy's second novel appeared at the moment when Christine, my sister-in-law, produced her first, but after that Pansy abandoned novel-writing as a means of self-expression. In the meantime Mary's books were published under the esoteric nom-de-plume of Hans Duffy. Consequently it was never possible for my mother to read novels which had been boiling up in the years of her daughter's misanthropy, a pitch of gloom that a younger sister depicted by a Christmas card of Albrecht Dürer's 'Melancholia' in Mary's own image.

I am writing exactly forty years after the autumn that I now describe, when the first growling hint could be heard that the brew mixed in Hitler's Brown House was beginning to bubble. Coming out of *The Song of Songs*, one of Marlene Dietrich's more disastrous films, in which the betrayed heroine smashes the betrayer's statue of herself with a heavy stone mallet, Hamish Erskine and I were faced by posters announcing that Germany had left the League of Nations. This indication that Hitler, German Chancellor since the previous spring, had started on a collision course seemed to echo grimly like an additional blow from Marlene's stone mallet.

The visit to the cinema had been a measure of convalescence, after an evening when Hamish and I had been entertained by a friend of some eccentricity, whose London life was based on the Cavendish Hotel. This host had hired a box for a musical show, where I was suddenly conscious that, from the orchestra pit, the pianist had turned from his music to bow and smile as he played, not just at our party but at me in particular. He was, I realized, the pianist of the band that had played at my coming-out ball, and ever after had played devotedly whatever tunes I requested. Flattered by attention that I did not often get from musicians, I was in an elated mood for supper at the Cavendish Hotel in the sitting-room of its ruler Rosa Lewis. On this, my first visit, the apartment struck me, as it did many others, by its resemblance to the housekeeper's room of a large country house, not only by the furniture covered in cabbage rose chintz, but by the feeling that all present, dogs included, were refugees from the constraints of drawing-room life. Among a welter of photographs on the mantelpiece, there stood a chalk drawing of one of my cousins, dated the day before, which increased the feeling of having passed through a magic green baize door into a world where children were able to sample, without prejudice, the dissipations of grown-ups. The cousin whose portrait welcomed me was a well-known frequenter of the Cavendish, but Rosa was untroubled by lack of personal acquaintance with many of the subjects of the photographs she cut out for display from the illustrated papers. One of my friends, never known to be out after midnight and with a record of academic success at the LSE, suddenly found herself installed in Rosa's Pantheon, because her brother, in the Brigade of Guards, was an habitual guest in Mrs Lewis's sitting-room.

Casting her eye over the party, as she circulated among the champagne bottles, white Pekinese at her heels, Rosa, imposing in white satin, drew me on one side. Her object was to separate me from another girl in the company, who she rightly judged would be an unsuitable auditor for the story Rosa wished to tell. This concerned an episode which had taken place 'the other night', a period of time which with Rosa might mean yesterday or twenty years before, when she and her guests had painted a face on the stomach of a young man, a favourite known from childhood, she having cooked gastronomic meals for his parents. The artistic experiment had been finished off by sticking a cigarette in the mouth which had been painted round the navel. Pleased though I was at this tribute to my sophistication, I was secretly glad to be rescued from the necessity of finding a correct response by the mother of our host, as tall as Rosa and also dressed in a sculptured white robe. With the confidence of someone famous for written works of piety, she swept Rosa on to one of the cabbage rose sofas, and, leaning her eagle countenance towards Rosa's pink cheeks and blue eyes, remarked firmly, 'And now, dear Mrs Lewis, tell me all about the famous adulteries that have taken place in your hotel.'

After such an evening it will be understood that bleak news from Germany was no help to convalescence, but I did admire the resilience of Hamish, subsequently proved in a gallant wartime escape to be endemic in his character. When I made some speculation as to what part of the armed forces he might find himself a member, he announced that he proposed to raise a regiment of his own to be called The Black Erskines.

16. The Blue Train

REMEMBERING THE ADVERSE COMMENTS ON the subject of my desertions from home during the summer, it was with a guarded approach that I told my mother that I had been invited to keep Ty MacRae company at Cannes, where Ty's mother was going in a Will-o'-the-wisp pursuit of health. Unhesitating approval of this plan so much surprised me, that I checked with Annie Reason as to whether there was some immediate alarm about my mother's health. This was denied, with a confidence that I subsequently discovered to be ill-founded, but at the time I assumed that Mary's installation on the top floor had made me, as it were, more expendable. Her object being to seek medical advice, Ty's mother showed an Olympian disregard for the fact that she had chosen the depths of the off-season in which to install herself at Cannes, the patrons of the South of France in summer having fled before autumn's chill, while those who clung to the idea of a winter in the south had not yet begun their migration. In addition the Depression was lying like a fog across Europe, which was immediately apparent when the Wagon-Lits coach in which we had travelled from Calais was, at Paris, attached to the Blue Train. It was only by luck that Ty and I were *en voiture* to be attached with it, for feeling the need to fortify ourselves before the night journey, we had left Ty's mother at the Gare du Nord to be conveyed round to the Gare de Lyon by the *ceinture* that girdles Paris.

We were, we explained, going to see a schoolfellow who lived with her parents at an address that sounded of the the utmost respectability. Whether it was or not, we never found out, our real objective being the Ritz Bar. When I read of the wild doings, both in novels and in biographies, that to Scott Fitzgerald and to Ernest Hemingway seem to have epitomized the Ritz in Paris, I find it hard to collate either their fiction, or their real experiences, with a place that I remember as sedately muted in atmosphere. Admittedly, we had little time to do more than snatch down a drink before calling a taxi in which to rejoin the Blue Train. Had I been able to linger I might have found the couples murmuring in the half-light were more dramatically fascinating than they appeared to a casual glance. As the taxi proceeded, in the style which has made Paris taxis famous as sparks in the bright eyes of danger, I suddenly recognized an advertisement, a scarlet aeroplane in high relief on a vast hoarding, which I recalled as having been ominously adjacent to the Gare du Nord. Inquiry revealed that Ty had absentmindedly given that as our destination. Train fever gripped our pulses, as the taxi-driver, though prepared to race against time, needed to fill up with petrol before he could do so. When, with a rather shaky nonchalance, we had caught the train, we found that the long trek to the *wagon-restaurant* was made gloomy by the sight of carriage after carriage in which the beds were not even left as seats, but strapped down like mattresses in a barracks. Dijon and Lyon, names cried so mournfully by the porters, were suitably melancholy as greeting for the ghost train that ran, empty, down to the blue sea from which it had taken its name.

The hotel in which we stayed was on the steep road that

climbs through the old town of Cannes, and of an emptiness which bordered on the eerie. Ty's mother had been drawn to this battered caravanserai by the presence of a pair of friends, the B's, continental nomads, who had settled in Cannes on account of their faith in one of the local medical practitioners.

Years of experience had given the B's skill in probing the secrets of fellow residents that approached second sight. Hardly worth their attention was a young lady who had come for a holiday in order to repair a broken engagement with a local chap. More worthy of discussion was a less young lady, who was said to be pensioned by her family on condition that she resided in a place of which they approved, drug addiction being the reason for her exile. These were Englishwomen, and essentially prosaic, compared to a French family of a mother, a daughter and two grandchildren, the children's father being the secretary of Maurice Chevalier. Before the breakdown of his employer's marriage, the secretary's family had lived in Chevalier's villa, but with the departure of Madame Chevalier (Mr B. suggested a reason which reflected sadly on the hero of *The Love Parade*) the females had been ejected, and were now living in that uninhibited domesticity which the French have the gift of importing into hotels. As a child I had been teased for pronouncing Mont Blanc as 'Mong Blong' in the manner dictated by an ancient geography primer, but though my own accent was not much improved I was struck by the fact that the B.'s, long resident in France, conducted conversation with the pronunciation favoured by my long disused geography book, calling their white fluffy dog 'Fifi de Mammong'.

Alongside the dining-room in which this ill-assorted company ate, there was a salon that housed both a ping-pong table and, new to me as a game, a Russian billiard-table. It was at the latter that Ty and I filled in the space which yawned between dinner and bedtime, this three weeks' practice giving me an efficiency that impressed onlookers when, shortly afterwards, Russian billiard-tables sprouted, mushroom-like, in the saloon bars of the south of England. On one night only was Chevalier's secretary allowed a connubial evening. His mother-in-law tactfully made herself scarce, and, to celebrate this off-duty, he led his wife, voluptuously plump as a seductress on a French postcard, to the ping-pong table. As she picked up her bat, the secretary's wife dissolved into incapacitating giggles, which she kept up throughout the game, and which not unnaturally prevented her from returning the ball to her husband. From his expression he did not appear to find this manifestation of wifely excitement unpleasing, though he was not so absorbed that he could not spare an occasional *œuillade* for the English girls at the billiard-table, from whence the rumbling of the balls into pockets made a bass accompaniment to his wife's soprano giggles.

Along the Croisette what picture postcards called *les grands hôtels* were shuttered and sad, so empty being the sea-front that I was able to undress for a bathe uneyed except by the blank windows above me. Beside the harbour the plane trees, tailored to reproduce the convolutions of the bandstand, were, as Roy Campbell wrote, stripped of their 'sun-clouding' foliage, while in the harbour itself yachts rocked in their winter sleep. In the general vacancy it seemed that the only diversion would be to have our last summer's wardrobe overhauled by a local dressmaker. This was not exactly an exhilarating experience, for the *couturière* was depressed by one of my less happy choices, a garment made from a kind of tweedy string, which like old elastic, gave without contracting, and she was totally defeated by a suit of Ty's whose crinkled glazed surface – *un tissu affreux*, said the dressmaker – gave and gave again. Having no need for ball gowns in her present circumstances, Ty included a white satin model in a bundle that was deposited with the cleaners next to the hotel. She failed to notice that it had not been returned, and only after several days came to realize that it had been retained by the shop as an advertisement for the service offered. Spread out in the window it seemed to be of a size infinitely too vast for Ty, whose pet name was a derivative of tiny.

Anxious to find some entertainment for Ty and myself, Ty's mother and Mrs B. set the concièrge to work in search of a diversion that had not been closed by the dead season and financial depression. The golf-club at Mandelieu, it was rumoured, was open. There we proceeded, to find ourselves in sole possession of the restaurant, the course and the boat, chief charm of Mandelieu, in which players hauled themselves by means of a rope over one of the streams that empty their waters into the Golfe de La Napoule. Attempting to identify these landmarks of the past, I have only been able to consult a French *Guide-Joanne* to Provence, published in 1884, and an English Blue Guide published seventy years later, the former being fifty years too early, and the latter twenty years too late, for my purpose. The *Guide-Joanne* was, in fact, the more useful, supplying me with the forgotten name of the Hôtel du Pavillon, and the information that it stood in the 'Quartier Anglais... se compose surtout de villas separées par de grands jardins et de vastes hôtels'. That fashion would abandon the sequestered charm of the Quartier Anglais for the glare of the Croisette must have seemed, in 1884, as improbable as that the steep road climbing through the old town of Cannes would be renamed rue Georges Clemenceau.

During the summer months I had been cheered, in a moment of depression, by finding an ex-library copy of Hemingway's *Fiesta*, as *The Sun Also Rises* was originally called on its publication in England. I think the message it conveyed to me was that others had sadder lives than I did, but also that there were still some pleasures to be enjoyed. In Cannes I had the good fortune to find another novel reduced in price, Somerset Maugham's *Cakes and Ale*, perhaps the only book in which this writer allowed gaiety to break through, and certainly a much-needed antidote to the two French novels which my faint desire for self-improvement had caused me to buy. The first of these was *Aux Abois* by Tristan Bernard, in which, if I remember rightly, the hero commits a murder in order to pay alimony to his ex-wife, his mistress commits suicide while he is in prison and, reprieved from the guillotine, he poisons himself, having no desire to live. After this merry tale Céline's *Voyage Au Bout de La Nuit* might be said to have faced a challenge in tenebrosity, but I found that there was a photo-finish in gloom between the more obscure and the more famous of these two works of fiction.

A rainy season now settled down on the Côte d'Azur, blotting out the jagged shapes of the Esterel and fogging the windows of the taxi in which we drove up to Grasse to visit a friend of Ty's mother's mother. This ancient Maltese lady lived out her widowhood in a house that on a fine day must have been enchanting, hanging as it did on a cliff, with a vine-covered trellis shading a terrace and the fields of jasmine that fed the scent factories of Grasse lying below. But in rainy October hostess and guests groped their way through dimness to a dining-room even darker. Round the table moved a man-servant to orders issued by his employer in a Maltese *patois*, his cast of countenance being a reminder that Malta was the home of an ancient people, whose religious practice was as sinister as it was mysterious. The hostess was, herself, of an extreme devoutness, so that Ty's mother was hard put to it to avoid a commitment to spend All Souls' Day in an orgy of reminiscence of departed dear ones. The Depression had dealt a cruel blow to the products for which Grasse was renowned, scent and crystallized fruits, but, while the jasmine fields lay unharvested, it was still possible to send boxes of *fruits glacés* freshly crystallized from the factory. These delicacies were one of the few luxuries that my mother had ever allowed herself to enjoy, so I dispatched a box to her address, at the same time writing a tentative letter to inquire if it was permitted to ask how she was. In her reply, she was enthusiastic about the *fruits glacés*, reminiscent about a childhood's visit with her parents to such a factory, and actually went as far as to admit that she grew no better, a relaxation of her guard which struck me as both unprecedented and ill-omened.

Wet as the day at Grasse had been, it was merely showery compared with the day picked for a visit to Monte Carlo. This was accomplished in the sort of motor-car described by Anthony Powell, in his novel *From a View to a Death*, as designed for an Edwardian Swiss Family Robinson. On the back seat Ty's mother and Mrs B., both in some degree lame, spread themselves, while Ty, Mr B. and I sat in a row on subsidiary seats, which seemed to sprout from the body of the automobile. At Monte Carlo the Casino was practically deserted, the official at the door only rousing himself to query the birthdate on my passport, the 2 of 1912 being written carelessly to resemble a 3, which would have barred me from entry as under twenty-one. After the fresh cold rain outside the accumulated vapours of the gaming-rooms hit the nose like a blow from a rotting sock. At one solitary table what must have been the sweepings of the gamblers of Monaco were clustered round the only croupier to be spinning a roulette wheel. It was not thus that I had pictured Monte Carlo, where my mother's eldest brother had been well-known, until he decided to abandon the tables. His reason for ceasing to play was the somewhat unusual one that his persistent good luck caused him to be plagued by a train of followers eager to stake where he staked. On such a low ebb afternoon as that of my visit, I find it hard to imagine scenes of high excitement as those stimulated by my uncle's good fortune. After losing most of the money which Ty's mother had generously given me to stake, I retreated to the fruit machines, where I managed to control my own fortunes to such an extent that a handful of francs tinkled into the receptacle designed to catch winnings. Driving home, the befogged interior of the ancient vehicle became emotionally charged by Mr B.'s inclination to treat Ty's knee as though it belonged to Fifi de Mammong, and could be stroked accordingly.

Leaving the atmosphere to cool off, Ty and I set out for Carcassonne, which was to be our staging-post in an effort to reach Andorra. To me this minute mountain enclave was only familiar as the scene of the opening chapters of Rose Macaulay's novel *Crewe Train*, read on housebound afternoons when rain attacked the walls of Pakenham as it might be with javelins. Ty, on the other hand, had been attracted to Andorra by reading of its joint control in the past by France and Spain, and of the ceremonial hats, or possibly crowns, kept in case one or other of the rulers of the giant neighbours should choose to pay a visit to their pigmy vassal. Inquiries showed that only a rather tenuous omnibus service linked the more sophisticated towns of the Pyrenees with the valley of Andorra, so it was from Carcassonne that we had decided to launch our attack. After a night in *couchettes* we cannot have looked very appetizing guests at the Hôtel de la Cité, or so the manager thought, for we were offered dank, cell-like bedrooms gazing on to blank walls. Protests swung us to the other end of the scale of accommodation, into vast chambers below whose windows the Department of Aude lay spread like a carpet. When the sun rose, the bugles from the barracks beyond the city walls greeted the dawn with their sudden music.

Walking the ramparts of Viollet-le-Duc's masterpiece of

reconstruction, I remembered that his name had first come to my notice in a story from *Stalky and Co* called *An Unsavoury Episode*. I had taken a personal interest because Beetle had referred to 'A Frenchwoman . . . Violet something'. It was now strange to reflect that it was the creator of the pepper-pots and machicolations around me who had written a book of architectural exposition, a book which had given Beetle the expertise to turn the tables on his enemies by insinuating the decayed corpse of a cat between the joists of a dormitory floor. Cased as it was among the battlements, the hotel carried out the spirit of Viollet-le-Duc to the extent of policing the banqueting hall with suits of armour, the only company present to watch over our meals.

When the management had bestirred itself sufficiently to provide a car and a driver to take us through the Pyrenees to Andorra, Ty, perhaps as a precaution, suggested that we should attend mass for All Saints' Day before setting out. We found that the service was mostly for the benefit of the local schoolchildren, the preacher conveying with considerable force his idea that few embryonic saints were likely to be among his listeners. His low opinion of his congregation cannot have been improved by the behaviour of the two English grown-ups, who got the legs of their chairs entangled when turning them round before the sermon. The next time that Ty and I attended a religious service together, it was forty years later. By chance we were seated side by side at a cathedral carol service, grandmothers in spectacles, as Ty herself remarked.

As we approached the Spanish border our driver assumed an air of increasing distrust, as though he was advancing into a territory where attacks by bandits might hourly be expected. He was unmollified by a knockabout scene at the frontier itself, where women returning with market baskets were jocosely threatened with confiscation by the customs officers. However the driver relaxed slightly when we arrived in the valley of Andorra, remarking 'C'est un pays de gangster, mais d'honnête gangster' as he waved away a passing Andorran, who offered an assortment of smuggled cloth caps and silk ties, dangling from a pole slung over his shoulder.

Mountain air of crystalline purity gave a spurious sense of well-being to me, who had imported a gastric infection from the Alpes Maritimes to the Pyrenees. This trouble did, however, prevent me from seeing what surely must have been the last European display of *The Love Parade*. The film was showing in Escaldes, where we were staying at an inn whose simplicity would have been an interesting contrast to the palace in which Maurice Chevalier courted the Queen, Jeanette Macdonald. After following the film from London to Munich, it was a sad disappointment to have missed whatever adjustments might have been thought necessary for Andorran tastes. My affection for this film was, I thought, completely vindicated ten years later, when the serious-minded critic of a Sunday newspaper urged the members of the Film Society on no account to miss a showing of one of Lubitsch's early masterpieces, *The Love Parade*.

In Rose Macaulay's novel *Crewe Train*, the heroine, rescued from Andorra by highbrow kinsfolk and transplanted to Chelsea dinner parties, was found to be conversationally uninspiring. Asked about the architecture of Andorra, she replied that the buildings were houses, barns or churches, a true if prosaic assessment, the local habit being that, if a building became unduly decayed, another should be built nearby on the same pattern. This custom meant that an eleventh-century church was barely distinguishable from a twentieth-century cow-shed. A few more ambitious citizens had colour-washed their houses, giving a glowing background to the swags of drying tobacco leaves, which would supply the smugglers, les honnêtes gangsters, with the raw material for their trade. At the inn the proprietor knew enough French to inquire which of us wished to share a room 'avec le chauffeur', but otherwise limited himself to bows and smiles. As we sat eating our way through a meal at whose commencement there had been a pile of seven plates before us, the proprietor reappeared and gave a particularly low bow, adding two words of Spanish to his salutation. Six strange courses had each been put on to a separate plate, and we were now engaged on the seventh and last, which was jam all alone. Ty's knowledge of Spanish happened to be Andalusian, so it was somewhat speculatively that she put forward the theory that the words had not been an inquiry if we found the jam to our taste, but rather the humble greeting, 'I prostrate myself'.

Shopping, except for the smuggled ties and tweed caps, was limited to picture postcards, on to one of which I crammed an entire issue of Andorran stamps for my mother's benefit. She had never subscribed to the idea that stamps in their virgin state were more to be valued than those that had passed through the rigours of posting and delivery, an attitude which somewhat depreciated the value of her own collection. After two nights the driver was only too anxious to ferry us back to civilization, and to escape from what he called 'le boût du monde'. Eager to regain the safety of France, he refused to pause for luncheon in Spain, claiming, with some reason, that by Spanish standards it would be far too early to hope to find a meal. We, on the other hand, were apprehensive that by the time we reached France it might well be too late. This fear was aggravated by delays on the twisting mountain roads, constantly blocked by carts transporting barrels of wine up to homesteads, where the winter hibernation was, it appeared, spent in a state of chronic fuddle. One of the brighter sons of the region, so our driver said, had gone out into the world and, while making a fortune, had been impressed by the economic prescience of Swiss peasants, who occupied their snowbound winters in carving toys to be sold in the summer. At his own expense he had brought tools and samples to the Pyrenees, only to find that the sober industry of the Alps did not export. Besides this tale of excellent intention that did not turn to good, the drive was made memorable to me by the sight of nineteen magpies, assembled on a plateau that lay between the hills. Superstitious at any sight of these pied birds of mixed omen, I never failed to offer an incantation to ward off misfortune, but this number far exceeded the runes at my disposal. When we finally stopped for a meal, before each person was placed an anonymous bird, and though hunger dictated the hope that these were a variety of partridge, inescapable was a nagging feeling that we might well be lunching off magical magpies.

At the age of thirteen, taken abroad for the first time, I had found solace when journeys grew tedious in the study of the Continental Bradshaw. Beguiled by the idea of expresses tearing across Europe, with only a brief hesitation at frontiers, I had taken a particular fancy to a train which ran from Barcelona to Ventimiglia, sweeping round that curve of the Mediterranean which still re-echoes with the marching feet of ancient armies. To return to Cannes, Ty and I had to join a train at Narbonne, or rather wait in a *wagon-lit*, until a conjunction was effected at some midnight hour. Sleep was shattered when the link-up took place, and as we chugged through the night additional rattles seemed to be coming from the region of the top bunk in which I was stretched. I was impolitely uncooperative when Ty wished to summon the attendant to see if the racket could be reduced, and from above I heard her settling down for a night to be rendered sleepless by my obduracy. Her wakefulness, I am glad to say, lasted for not more than five minutes, but in the meantime I suddenly realized that I was travelling over the line that I had picked out in childhood as the most picturesque to be found in the Continental Bradshaw, a lyrical journey along the shore of the blue inland sea. Now, as in a wish granted by a malicious fairy, I found I was indeed travelling on the train of my choice but in the total blackness of a November night.

In Cannes faint symptoms of a winter revival could be perceived. Down on the beach at La Bocca, reached from the Hôtel du Pavillon by a tunnel that ran under the railway line, the Culture Physique establishment had begun morning sessions. At school gymnastics had been my most unfavourite lesson, ineptitude exposing me to continual pain and humiliation, but I was persuaded to join Ty on the various racks by which the class was tormented. This strange group had, as its oldest member, an Englishman so skinny that it seemed cruel to inflict exercises on such a frail skeleton. The youngest member was a rubbery little French girl, the star of the class, or so the Englishman assured us, although Ty, fortunate possessor of double-jointed hip bones, displayed an elasticity which came near to threatening French supremacy. Her virtuosity so impressed one of the onlookers that he joined us at a rest period, and attempted, unsuccessfully, to get into Ty's good graces by dribbling handfuls of sand over her bare feet. Some compensation came for earlier agonies at the end of the session when the owner of the Bains-Culture-Physique, his own well-developed physique covered with a tawny pelt, led his victims at a run up a springboard from which they landed on the vast rubber ball, whose slogans advertised the establishment, and bounced off into the soft sand before splashing into the waves.

A more enjoyable symptom of seasonal revival was the reopening of the bar of the Carlton Hotel, although the bedrooms above remained under dustsheets. Ty and I flew there like homing pigeons, with a frequency that caused even Ty's uncomplainingly generous mother to express wonder at the size of the concièrge's bill on which our taxis were entered. Beyond consuming two costly cocktails and eating the squares of cheese that were at least provided free, our evening hour in the Carlton Bar lacked, one might say, dramatic incident.

I occupied myself in beating down the barman's idea that 12 francs was the price for a packet of twenty cigarettes, clearly marked 'Prix de vente en France 8.50'. A compromise of 10 francs was arrived at, but I marvel still at what tough genius for negotiation I then possessed. Unlike so many places we had frequented that autumn we were not the only evening visitors, three other habitués, at two separate tables, added undeniable quality to a scene short on quantity. Every evening Michael Arlen, a character retreated into one of his more melancholy novels, sat solitary in front of a single drink. We never arrived before he was in position, and he never left before the early dinner hour of the Hôtel du Pavillon summoned us home, so the length of his sojourn remained for ever mysterious. I had first read *The Green Hat* at an age when I had been too ill-informed to understand the implications of the narrative, even needing to consult the dictionary over the medical details of the 'death for purity', but this had not impaired my enjoyment of a rattling good tragedy. To me it was sad that active enjoyment seemed to have fled from the creator of such an animated commedia del'arte.

Mr Arlen's melancholy was, however, a light mist compared with the fog that hung over the only other table to be occupied in the Carlton Bar. Here, as companion and possibly bodyguard, Maurice Chevalier's secretary sat in silence beside his employer. If, sequestered in the Hôtel du Pavillon, the secretary's wife felt a jealous pang that her husband was frequenting smart bars unimpeded by his family, her anxiety would have been unfounded. Remote indeed seemed the bubbling gaiety of *The Love Parade*, at that moment being shown to the smugglers of Andorra. The pall of gloom that hung over M. Chevalier obliterated any professional sparkle. The mind boggled at what the misery of his domestic interior must be, if sitting in such public depression could be preferable. Even the speculation that he might have switched himself off, as it were, for lack of public acclaim turned out to be erroneous.

On the last Sunday of my visit, our party drove down to tea at the Winter Casino, due to open its season with a concert whose programme has fallen through a hole in my memory. The audience was mostly made up of noisy young Canneois, whose vitality was refreshing after the empty melancholy of the recent past. Noise began to get out of hand when the audience had absorbed the fact that, with a few friends, Maurice Chevalier was drinking tea at the table next to ours. Like hounds singing in kennel, the young men broke into a chant, which must have had significance in the Chevalier canon, but which to my dull English ears sounded like the surf on the beach outside. Whatever the chant's import its object sat immobile and unresponsive, his face a rigid mask. Long afterwards, in Wiltshire, I came to know a taxi-driver who had been a fellow prisoner of war with Maurice Chevalier in the First World War. Both had taken part in the camp concerts, in which Chevalier was said to have developed his expertise, though the taxi-driver hinted that at the time he himself was the more popular performer. In any case, had he been in the star's position at the Winter Casino, I am sure his response to such a gale of admiration would have been more obliging.

Next morning Ty's mother was disturbed by her lugubrious maid, who burst in to announce that 'The Chevalier' was in the garden of the hotel, discipline having been sufficiently relaxed to allow the secretary to say good-bye to his wife before departing on a journey. This was also the last of my days at the

Hôtel du Pavillon, as I was due back in London to be, yet again, a bridesmaid. No sooner had I left than a gruesome murder took place in the hotel next door. About this drama Ty kept me informed by frequent telegrams, which explained that the excitement engendered had led to a conspicuous lowering of moral standards among the guests of the neighbouring Hôtel du Pavillon.

My journey home was made physically unpleasant by the heavy cold into which influenza had degenerated, and darkened by a hint, in a letter from my sister Mary, that my mother's condition had not merely remained unimproved. I was still struggling to read Céline's *Voyage au Bout de la Nuit*, which did nothing to raise my spirits, and I viewed the bumpy walk to the wagon-restaurant with no enthusiasm. As I set off towards dinner, I was approached by the Wagon-Lits attendant belonging to the through coach to Calais, in which I was travelling.

Although my mother had an esteem for these officials, christening them 'chocolate men' from their uniforms, she had also instructed me in the unorthodox ways by which they augmented their incomes, creating awkward situations which a *pourboire* would be needed to rectify. The simplest of these was to place a female of obvious modesty in the same compartment as a male unknown to her, a bribery gambit which might be described as picking money up off the floor. As the Blue Train was, if anything, emptier than on the journey down to the south, the question of such profitable manipulation of berths seemed unlikely to arise. I was all the more surprised when the 'chocolate man' asked me if I wished to be alone. With as much force as my cold-thickened voice could convey I assured him that I did, assuming that he might have hoped to earn a tip by an introduction between fellow travellers. On further reflection, and consideration of the emptiness of the train, I did begin to wonder if he might not have been making an offer of his own company. If that was the case my rebuff did not sour our relationship, and he was civil enough to listen to my reminiscences of childhood holidays in the Pas de Calais as we steamed through the pine-covered sand-hills on the last lap to the Channel. Cold-ridden and feverish, I reached Victoria Station and decided to abandon my registered luggage which was still loitering at Dover. The following day Annie Reason volunteered to retrieve it. Loving to travel she found even such a faint connection with foreign parts to be enjoyable. Her pleasure was increased by being able to have a good laugh with the custom officer over the jumblesale effect that was revealed when my suitcases were opened.

17. An Ending

WHILE AT CANNES I HAD written to suggest that my mother's cave-like bedroom on the ground floor, practical in her more mobile days, was gloomily unsuitable for someone increasingly bedridden. On my return I found that my mother had indeed been installed in brighter surroundings, but this was only one of the revolutionary changes that had taken place in my absence. As well as the move to a better room, she was now surrounded by luxuries of invalidism which she had never before encouraged. Tall vases of carnations, an impressive radio set, and a silk counterpane were so unexpected that I gaped in surprise even in the midst of my first greeting. The carnations, my mother explained, had been presented by Edward and Christine, over on a visit from Dublin, while the counterpane and the radio had come, respectively, from my grandmother and from an old friend and admirer of the days of her youth. This latter had remained in her life, partly on account of her friendship with his sister, and partly because his position as a stockbroker gave her an opportunity to consult him as an extra opinion, when she was engaged in investing the inheritances of her children, as I have earlier described. In addition to these tokens of a less Spartan régime, it now appeared that nurses were in attendance day and night, so that, when Mary revealed that no hope of recovery was left, tears, though of shock, were hardly those of surprise.

Having failed noticeably to set myself up as a serious student, it seemed to me that I might find a job in a more frivolous world. My mother's objections to those not in need competing in the labour market would no longer have to be considered, a question-mark also hanging over the future of her daughters' finances. Consultation with a friend, who combined a Grecian profile with skill in the marketing of hats, led me to an interview with the proprietor of a hairdressing salon, as a candidate for the post of receptionist. At that age I had an embarrassingly good memory for faces, so I might have been of some help to the business, but whether I should have given satisfaction or not was never put to the test, the march of events cancelling my availability.

At home, the tragic tenseness of the situation was kept at bay by my mother's own cheerfulness, when, as had always been her custom, she gave interviews to her family. Clinging to her prerogative of privacy, she saw no reason why she should now be treated as someone who could be intruded on at will. The time before her had been set at a possible two months, but ten days after my return the end came abruptly. In the afternoon as I left the house, I heard her laughing in unforced cheerfulness with Edward and Christine. When I came in I was told that a turn for the worse had taken place, an euphemism for the termination of her suffering. Her last contact with the world she was leaving was to tell the nurse on duty that it was time for her to go down to her tea, and such was the force of my mother's character that the nurse did so without argument.

With my mother's death it seemed that much of the emotion which she herself had kept at bay was released. In her own family her deepest affection had been given to her younger sister and brother. It was this sister who felt her loss almost to prostration, while her brother's gently enigmatic attitude must have concealed the knowledge that he had lost a loving admirer.

After I had made what seemed to me an inordinate number of lugubrious telephone calls, those most concerned were gathered together in Rutland Gate, where the supply of beds proved unequal to the demand. Although Aunt Markie, as ever, offered hospitality it chanced that one of her spare beds was under repair. In consequence Elizabeth was bedded down on two arm-chairs, for bizarre side-effects invariably attend bereavements. In the course of the evening my grandmother sent her chauffeur to collect a representative grandchild, partly perhaps to reassure herself, and partly because she may have had doubts as to whether we were familiar with the procedure of what Kipling called Normal Civil Death. I volunteered to go round to my grandmother's house, and I was struck by the fact that in emotional upheavals it is something of a release to change everyday habits. The Dynevors were already present to comfort my grandmother, and, most unusually, the party had assembled in a little back study, to me associated with the telephone, and childhood's exile when grown-up matters were under discussion in the drawing-room.

This room featured in a story of my mother's demonstrating my grandmother's capacity for coping with any emergency. My mother had been expected for luncheon, on a day when the downstairs cloakroom had been out of order. In view of my mother's lameness my grandmother had arranged temporary lavatory accommodation in the so-called study, and, testing the key from the inside, found herself unable to unlock the door. When my mother rang the bell, she was informed by an agitated parlour maid that Her Ladyship, then over eighty, was at that moment climbing out of the study window.

Next morning the same principle of conferring in strange

rooms applied, for we found ourselves sitting on straight chairs in a *conseil de famille* in the dining-room of Rutland Gate. Having convened the gathering, my grandmother also dominated it. It was she who declared that Middleton churchyard would be a resting-place where my mother could join her father, her elder brother, and an infant sister, whose life of one day had begun and ended in the Lord Warden Hotel at Dover. (My mother's own wishes, which were not coincident, were only discovered when arrangements had gone too far to be undone.) Edward and I drove down to make arrangements with the Vicar at Middleton, and, so accustomed was I to thinking of Edward and Christine moving inseparably together, I found the drive alone with him among the strangest moments in a week wracked with strangeness. By the time we had reached Middleton the dusk of a November eve had fallen, and we were obliged to inspect the graveyard by the light of a lanthorn dimly burning, the Vicar's cloaked figure adding grandeur to the scene. Beside the grave of the infant Margaret Villiers there stood twin tombstones, marking the graves of my grandfather's bachelor brothers, who, having lived refrigerated lives as secondary heirs of small means, had at last come to rest on equal terms with the head of the family. One of them, Uncle Reginald, had been loved by my mother and consulted by her on domestic matters of which she felt incompetent, when left a widow, to judge. The cigarettes that he had recommended were ever after faithfully purchased, though my mother did once mention that Uncle Reggie himself had always smoked cigars. Uncle Robert, on the other hand, had led a hunted life, pursued by creditors. Once my mother had come across his tracks in a nursing home, where the matron remembered and appreciated the discipline he had imposed on her nurses, who were obliged to wait with his tray outside the door in order to enter exactly as his own clock struck the hour.

In the next few days complications of business left little time free in daylight. An expedition we planned to see the effigies at Westminster Abbey, which I suppose seemed an outing interesting but not unduly frivolous, failed in its object owing to the lateness of the hour, though I did manage to identify the tomb of Sir George Villiers. This was far from irrelevant in the circumstances, as it was from his loins that the 1st Duke of Buckingham and the fortunes of the Villiers family had sprung. As we left the Abbey in a crowd surprisingly thick for the time of year, Christine pointed out that anyone who accosted one of us girls with the white-slaver's classic opening, 'Your mother has met with an accident just round the corner', was going to look distinctly absurd. Apart from this sortie, we congregated in Mary's attic sitting-room, which, furnished by herself, was free of the associations dogging the furniture in the rest of the house. An additional solace was a jig-saw puzzle, which Mary had installed, and which provided distraction even for Edward who, given two interlocking pieces, declared that no one on earth could have taken longer to put them together.

Brought up to the Victorian attitude when mourning would last for months, or, in the case of the Queen and emulative widows, for ever, my grandmother was impressed by the immediate appearance of her granddaughters in black dresses, before they could have had time to spend the cheques she had pressed on them for this purpose. Black to her was strictly funeral wear, and she had failed to notice it was, at that date, fashionable for Londoners. She told me that once, as a girl dressing for dinner, her maid had passed on a message that she was to go down to dinner in mourning, the death for which she was to mourn being unspecified. She was generously prepared to help in the following of the convention that still sent the bereaved into black, but when, on my birthday in the following March, I appeared in a dress of violet hue, she made a point of telling me that she applauded my move into what used to be called half-mourning. She would have sympathized with my brothers, who had a dislike for their wives wearing black, so that, before my mother's funeral, Christine and Elizabeth were obliged to go out on hurried shopping expeditions, becoming, as Mary said, a little blacker each time they came in. To Pansy, nursing her infant daughter Felicia in the country, my grandmother dispatched a black woollen cardigan, so that should she wish to make a mourning gesture she would be in a position to do so.

With her habitual generalship, Grandmama had also arranged that a post-funeral luncheon should be prepared at Middleton in the house of a retired stud-groom. Mary and I drove down with her, sharing the car's floor space with a hamper of wine for the luncheon. We found the drive unexpectedly entertaining, because my grandmother, with whose repertoire of anecdotes we were on the whole familiar, kept up a flow of stories which lasted for sixty miles and were totally new to our experience. It happened that some of my mother's companions in the hockey games of her girlhood had buried their own mother a few days previously, so they were present to say good-bye in Middleton churchyard. As is so often felt at funerals, the sadness was in not being able to tell my mother something that would have given her pleasure, and led her along the path of happy reminiscence. Her memories of these games in the past were among the jolliest of her not always comfortable early life, the games themselves being unhampered by science or undue attention to rules. I was surprised when I learnt that to be asked to bully was more a tribute to personal popularity than the duty arising from a position in the field, where it appeared that, with the possible exception of goal, positions were not allocated. Hints from old friends suggested that my mother's style of play had been forceful, not to say aggressive, so she might have been more sympathetic to the Hackney Wick version of netball than I sometimes supposed. A telegram of condolence, conveying the news that the Westmeath Hounds had been taken home, as a mark of respect, touched me perhaps more than it might have moved my mother, whose wish for hounds must have often been that they should not only go home but stay there. I am, however, sure that she would have appreciated the attitude of an estate steward who had worked for her father, and who made no attempt to conceal that this gathering of a family, once seen daily and now long absent, was the most enjoyable he had attended for many a sad year.

When we were back in Rutland Gate, Annie Reason asked us not to wear black stockings, as she found the sight of them unduly depressing, and I suppose our agreement was the first step on a new path. Invitations suddenly became a matter of taste, and no longer problems to be presented in a manner that would convince my mother of their desirability under her rules. On the other hand, I found there was a particular gap in my everyday life that I would not have foreseen. Anxious to divert my mother from too close an attention to my comings and goings, I had trained myself to remark anything that I thought might interest or amuse her, subjects to provide conversation, and, I hoped, to make her feel less cut off by the bonds of her invalidism. In the last weeks of the year 1933 I found myself making up a daily parcel of news that I had heard and sights that I had seen, only to find that there was no address to which it could be delivered.

Two obituary notices of my mother appeared in *The Times*, the first by her brother-in-law, Dunsany, the second by her friend Olive Baring, whose brother, mentioned earlier, had been the most assiduous of her dancing partners in my mother's girlhood. Dunsany, whose behaviour was regarded as men-

AN ENDING

acingly unpredictable by some of his wife's family, had always enjoyed a cheerful give and take relationship with my mother. Literally so, for, while she was prepared to give his uninvited fox terrier hospitality, when Dunsany, at tea in the drawing-room, removed the butter from a scone to add it to one he found inadequately buttered, leaving the butterless scone on the dish, my mother did not hesitate to place the dry scone on Dunsany's own plate. She said that he had better keep them both, a rebuke he took with uncharacteristic meekness. In his obituary notice, her brother-in-law wrote of my mother's courage throughout a life cleft by tragedy and tortured by illness. His judgement that it was difficult to be certain that her qualities would be reproduced in others was somewhat unfortunately phrased, and words he had probably intended to convey doubts as to the moral stamina of a whole succeeding generation seemed to imply a suspicion that my mother's children might prove to be unworthy of their parent. Less pessimistic, Mrs Baring's tribute dwelt on the early days, when Middleton and Osterley had been the background for birthday parties, and the outdoor games she had shared with my mother.

Condolatory letters were also consoling, in that many of the writers lost sight of the widow, stoically suffering, in remembering the lively, adventurous friend. As it happened the most unexpectedly charming salute to my mother's personality did not reach me till a year later, when, among the letters of good wishes on my engagement to be married, there arrived one addressed to me, care of my future parents-in-law. Headed 'Albert Vaults' Holyhead, the letter began with a most earnest apology. My correspondent had written a letter of congratulation to my dear mother, as he was nice enough to call her, and addressed it c/o G.P.O. London. He continued, 'on retiring to bed last night I remembered that Her Ladyship, the Dowager Countess of Longford passed away about 11 months ago'.

Deepest regrets were offered for this error, and the writer went on to say that he had the most pleasant recollections, not only of the journeys made across the Irish Channel by my father and mother, but also of those made by my grandmother, whose journeys had ceased a quarter of a century before. In the past the mail-boats of the City of Dublin Steam Packet Co. had been called *Leinster, Ulster, Munster* and *Connaught*, after the four kingdoms of Ireland, and this letter came from a retired Chief Steward, RMS *Ulster*. He had been lucky in his ship, for the torpedoing of her sister ship, *Leinster*, in 1918, had been a tragic sensation of my childhood, stewards and stewardesses being among the many drowned. In his retirement at Albert Vaults, Holyhead, having settled by the sea as Kipling, in his poem The Virginity, wrote that every sailor would choose to do, the former Chief Steward continued, it appeared, to cherish the happiest memories of my family. At the period of his stewardship I could have been no more than a bundle carried on board wrapped in a red cloak, but the tone of his letter was of one writing to a bride in whom he took the most personal interest, concluding by warmly wishing 'every success' to my future husband and myself. Remembering only too vividly that my mother had invariably crossed the Irish Channel stretched flat in her cabin, endeavouring to keep sea-sickness at bay by calculating how many times she would have to make the crossing before she equalled the time spent at sea when taken to Australia as a girl, I could only salute, yet again, the courage with which she had concealed her suffering from such an expert as the Chief Steward must have been.

18. Beginning Again

EVEN BEFORE MY MOTHER HAD died Peverel Court had been put on the market, but it hung unsold, and so became a problem for her heirs. For many weeks the only nibble came from the late Nubar Gulbenkian, who was in search of a hunting-box. He would have been an appropriate buyer, because it was in composing verses about his family that Julia and I had beguiled the time on our journey home from Munich. This plum was dangled before us only to fall into the mouth of another, luckier, seller. Peverel's eventual purchaser reaped the benefit of the low property market, which had been sinking for years to the disadvantage of my family. Assisted by my mother's distaste for bargaining, there seemed to be a law that dictated that each house sold should fetch half what had been given for it, a diminishing return which left the final sellers with no roof, and little cash with which to acquire a new one. The emptying of Peverel much improved the interior of Rutland Gate. We were unable to house the billiard-table, but the piano and the ping-pong table turned the melancholy drawing-room into an apartment devoted to pleasure, with the added interest of temporarily housing some of the larger portraits painted by my brother-in-law Henry, visitors on their way to or from exhibitions.

During my mother's last illness, Mrs Baring had lent much support to my sister Mary, who had become something of an extra daughter to my mother's friend. Like my mother, Mrs Baring had had six children, though only one was a girl. Both friends had lost their husbands in the First World War, somewhat resembled each other in appearance and, curiously enough, seemed to be governed by similar stars as far as moving house or travelling abroad was concerned. They had both been born with a sense of time that was at its best rudimentary, and at its worst non-existent. At this point the likeness ceased, for while my mother's failures to catch trains or to witness the rising of a first act curtain concerned only herself, or at most an agonized daughter, Mrs Baring's mantle of unpunctuality was flung far beyond her own family, covering a train of semi-adopted children, friends of all ages and both sexes, and indeed anyone who attracted her eager benevolent curiosity.

My mother was known to shun company at breakfast, even going so far as to take the arm of a visitor, who had joined her with the kindest intentions, and place the interrupter on the far side of the dining-room door. Mrs Baring, on the other hand, was prepared to open the first meal of the day with an inquiry as to whether her neighbour considered it was Colet, rather than Erasmus, who brought the New Learning to England. In this all-embracing spirit she added Mary and her two orphaned sisters to a Christmas house party, already seven or eight in strength. Subsequently Mary drew a picture of the *dramatis personae* in which everyone's idiosyncrasies were given their due. The youngest son of the house was shown being strangled by his next eldest brother, on account of having asked the company to guess who began with O, ended with N and was his brother's only rival, which turned out to be Oberon, the King of the Fairies. Julia and I were drawn by our sister as figures in crow-like black, holding hands and singing, 'Oh do you know the Muffin Man who lives in Crumpet Lane?'

I believe the authentic version originated in Cambridge, where the Muffin Man lived in Jesus Lane, which was modified to avoid blasphemy when the song entered Mrs Baring's family. Before dinner, on Christmas Day, her daughter, who, even after years of knowing my family, had failed to appreciate the endemic tone-deafness of most of its members, had run through the tune of 'Oh, do you know the Muffin Man' on the piano, but without having made me understand that the ritual required a solo rendering of two repeats of the tune. Faced with the question of did I know the Muffin Man, my lips moved but no sound came, so the answer remained a mystery, until the song had gone right round the table and the diners shouted 'We ALL know the Muffin Man'.

The changes that marked our new life in Rutland Gate did not only include the arrangement of a sitting-room full of books and pictures, and the liberty to entertain friends in it, at all hours of the day and on into the night. Ty's dogs, who had occasionally passed surreptitious nights under our roof, now became regular visitors, Winkie the Pekinese being particularly welcomed by Annie Reason, who found in him a compensation for years of dog frustration she must have suffered when attending on my mother. Winkie came with us when Mary and I took the long bus ride to Hackney Wick, where Mary was engaged in painting the scenery for the Eton Manor Club's production of *Miss Hook of Holland*. It was the chill beginning of the year, in fact I was feeling fragile from having danced at the Chelsea Arts Ball the night before, but I thought it in better taste to leave Winkie's braid-trimmed coat at home for a journey through the East End. No sooner, however, had we reached Shoreditch than we were joined on the top of the omnibus by a greyhound, exquisitely groomed and wearing a coat of superlative smartness, far more elaborately trimmed than the model owned by Winkie. He sat beside his owner with a decorum of expression which was a rebuke to the inquisitive and snuffly visitor from South Kensington.

In the hall used by the Club for theatrical shows, Mary worked on a dazzling drop scene of sky and sea designed by herself, while I endeavoured to transform a kitchen scene from an earlier show into an inn parlour. Size was scarce, so my stern work of turning pots and pans into bottles had a ghostly effect, the kitchen ware fading-in again like reappearing Cheshire cats. At one moment I thought I had discovered a useful basin of ready-mixed red paint, only to be disillusioned by Mary, who pointed out that it was a basin of blood left over from the last boxing match. As we worked we became conscious that an audience was building up on the floor of the hall behind us, drawn, I imagine, from those employed on the maintenance of the Club. Silent though they were, the onlookers managed to give the impression that our activities were as enjoyable as the show itself. The exception was the manservant from the Manor House, a man of such unforthcoming demeanour, that I sometimes speculated if he was employed by my uncle out of sympathy for some misfortune too sad to be mentioned. On this occasion he stood for a while with his hands in his pockets, and at length by a jerk of his head indicated that luncheon was awaiting the scene painters.

In the cloakroom hung the well-known picture of a dachshund regarding with dismay a puddle that has dripped from an umbrella, the caption reading, 'Zut! On va dire encore que c'était moi!', a situation that would have not caused Winkie's conscience the smallest pang. I never saw this production of *Miss Hook of Holland*, so I never knew how effective my handiwork was as a background to the song,

> 'A little pink petti from Peter,
> A little blue petti from John,
> And one that is yellow from some other fellow
> And one that I haven't got on.'

My sister Mary has herself described how she happened to become employed in Fleet Street, where she added two more pen names to the one under which she wrote novels. Later I inherited the job attached to one of these names, and we were chastened to find how few of the advertising managers on whom it was our duty to call could tell one sister from another. On the other hand they may have been wise not to attempt to do so, for time showed that my parents had not only produced six children but also six contributors to the *Evening Standard*.

Unlike Mary, I failed to find employment, and so could not plead business as an excuse when I was asked to take the part of Britannia in a pageant that was to celebrate the Industries of the British Empire. Nothing, I was told, would be required of me, except to lead the parade through the Dorchester Ballroom, which seemed to me a star position. Here I made a mistake, the high-spot being nabbed by the Spirit of Empire, complete with torch and stuffed lion. The pageant master was a lady of formidably tailored aspect, whose boast it was that in her stage career she had never played a female part in any Shakespearian production, also emphasizing her penchant for masculine roles in private, by objecting if she was not offered a double bed when on tour with the companion with whom she shared her life. The pageant master had not, however, bargained for a Britannia so musically unresponsive that she could not be relied upon to pick up the first note of 'Rule Britannia . . .' and move forward having stood, trident raised on high, while the introductory chords were played.

To avoid the hold-up of the show, a prompter was to give me the word to start the procession moving, my immediate supporters being Ireland (Northern, and so carrying a bunch of orange lilies), Scotland (with heather and a tartan sash) and Wales (with daffodils). The outsize measurement of Britannia's skull also presented a problem, all helmets offered by theatrical costumiers rested on the top of my cranium, being designed, it appeared, for pinheads. A photograph, published under the caption 'The Most Beautiful the United Kingdom', showed a Britannia submerged in a silver coal-scuttle of papier-mâche, an improvisation that had gone too far in the other direction. The girl who was Wales, her face pasted on to the body of a stand-in many years older than herself, presented a strange example of a young head on old shoulders.

For the audience the pageant can have had little dramatic impact, except for the evocation of Coal, in which a red-haired dancer, sheathed in black, writhed and swayed through the darkened ballroom to the accompaniment of Stravinsky's 'Firebird' music. The onlookers could not know that a sullen-looking Canadian lumberjack, marching between two gaoler-like companions, had, shortly before, been whirling in an intoxicated dance along the hotel corridors. Fur cap awry, axe brandished aloft, he had appealed to Britannia – 'Britannia! Be just!' – to rescue him from the friends who were trying to pinion him, if not into sobriety, at least into a marching step.

My lack of employment made me available for an excursion to Ireland, where my Aunt Beatrice was known to be feeling forlorn at the loss of her sister, indeed so dispirited that from that moment she abandoned the diary kept from the days of her girlhood. On the way to what I hoped would be a visit of comfort, I paused in Dublin to stay with Edward and Christine, whose life was then concentrated on the Gate Theatre. With them I watched rehearsals of Molnar's *Liliom*, but my visit ended before the last act had been reached, so I was never to know what happened to Liliom, played by Micheál Mac-

Liammóir, when he had been posthumously arrested by heavenly policemen. In the play running at the moment Mr MacLiammóir had a less harrowing role, being led away into the sunset by Grace O'Malley, Grania of the Ships, this seventeenth-century dictatress of a piratical tribe of Galway, having had no difficulty in inducing her rival, a little Spanish prisoner, to jump off the castle battlements in a choice of death rather than dishonour.

At Dunsany Castle, I found that my aunt, and a visiting friend, were glad to have a third to take a turn reading aloud from *Ivanhoe*, while the two listeners sewed a fine seam, or rather in my aunt's case transferred the pattern of a Worcester plate on to a yard of silk. It should not be assumed, however, that the drawing-room was merely the peaceful background to reading and needlework. Two disrupters prowled among the gilded tables and display cases, Sultan, a vast Alsatian, and my even vaster uncle. Sultan had arrived for a visit, and had remained to become my aunt's loved companion, but his prowling, which included sweeping waves of his bushy tail, was less disruptive than that of my uncle. If the fire was unlighted he would attend to the matter by standing over the grate and striking matches continuously until chance dictated that some, not blown out on their descent, effected a kindling. More often his perambulations ended in a precipitate ringing of the bell to order a fresh pot of tea, from whichever manservant was unfortunate enough to be on duty, or to implement some other inquiry that happened to have crossed his mind, such as the whereabouts of a decanter broken years before, about which he had suddenly experienced a renewed pang.

Frequently a summons would be issued for Twomey, the gamekeeper, Dunsany conducting publicly, and without inhibition, conferences that most landowners reserved for business rooms or kitchen passages. During the visit of which

I write a tenant of the estate, much respected, had died, and Twomey was called up to the drawing-room to listen to a diatribe from his employer on the burden that the Irish custom of lavish funerals imposed on the survivors. This disapproval was an hereditary trait for, as my uncle pointed out to Twomey, two generations earlier the reigning Lord Dunsany had laid it down in his will that not more than ten pounds was to be spent on burying him. A certain reserve in Twomey's manner led me to suspect that this attempt to set an example in economical obsequies had been regarded locally as spoiling sport, both as depriving the deceased of due respect, and the neighbourhood of the interest and excitement of a wake.

Next day, driving to have luncheon at a neighbouring Palladian house, we halted at a cottage so that Dunsany could pay a condolatory call on the bereaved family. As I have said, my uncle was a tall man, six foot four or five, and though thin in youth, middle-age had brought thickening with it. Recently he and my aunt had returned from the North-West Frontier of India, where they had been to see their son, then serving with the Guides Cavalry. Always at his happiest when he had the opportunity to do some exotic shopping, Dunsany had returned with an outsize sheepskin coat, a heavily embroidered *pushteen*, which doubled the by no means inconsiderable space he required in a motor-car. On top of this he wore, as was his custom, a wide-awake hat in pale felt. Surprisingly, a faint idea that his appearance was somewhat unorthodox for a house of mourning must have crossed his mind, for he asked my aunt if she thought it would be all right for him to pay his call wearing his *pushteen*. Having learnt in her married life to discard the unimportant, my aunt reassured him on this point. He strode up to the low thatched cottage, and I was entirely surprised that he did not raise the building on his shoulders as he squeezed through the doorway.

Between Dunsany and W. B. Yeats there smouldered a literary feud, first ignited in the dusk of the Celtic twilight, and at intervals bursting into flame. To this day the rumour persists that Yeats dictated the constitution of the Irish Academy of Letters expressly to render Dunsany ineligible. More than once, on the other hand, the story has been printed that Yeats, having carefully chosen, at a cultural festival, to judge all the classes for which Dunsany might be expected to enter, suffered a setback from neglecting to keep an eye on the chess tournament, in which Dunsany, a player of championship standard, won a medal. Yeats did not, however, at once abandon his campaign, for when Dunsany's novel *The Curse of the Wise Woman* was one of three sent to John Masefield, the Poet Laureate, to be judged for an award given to the best Irish work of imagination, Yeats took the trouble to cross the Channel and travel to Boar's Hill to press his own favourite's claim. If I remember rightly, the book fancied by Yeats concerned an Irish female guerrilla leader called Tullolagh, which could hardly fail to cause surprise to those familiar with the stage, screen and private career of Tallulah Bankhead.

As it happened, taking tea with John Masefield on Boar's Hill the year before, I had produced my connection with Dunsany as a kind of literary passport. The Laureate, luckily, turned out to admire my uncle's writing, and we moved on to an enjoyable talk about what missing parts of *Macbeth* might yet be discovered, a conversation somewhat brusquely brought to an end by the intervention of Mrs Masefield, who gave me the impression that I was breaking the house rules. Consequently when an undercover agent from the Dublin literary world arrived to convey the news that Yeats had failed in his mission, I was in a position to declare that admiration, and not simply contrariness, had contributed to Masefield's choice of Dunsany's novel for the prize.

19. The Family Gets a Fright

NOT MANY WEEKS LATER I found myself once again at Dunsany Castle, but on this occasion my visit, supposedly again of comfort to my aunt, came near to adding an additional sorrow. Smitten by a ferocious sore throat I retired to bed, uneasily conscious that all around me the house was being closed down, preparatory to my aunt and uncle migrating to London for the Season. Deciding, on no evidence, that my temperature was normal once more, I took the boat, but my frail state incited me to take a first-class sleeper, the alternative being to share a carriage with two friends who were importing a whole salmon. My health seemed improved by the time I reached Rutland Gate, to find that Pansy had arrived for a visit.

After a winter as nursing mother in the country, she felt a desire for a party, so a guest list was drawn up, to include those of my friends who she considered would combine with hers. On Pansy's list was written the name of Anthony Powell, whose first two novels I had read in the Lambs' spare bedroom. His address was uncertain, but the telephone book offered someone of his name living in Brunswick Square, Bloomsbury, which sounded promising. I volunteered to ring up in the character of a parlour-maid, issuing a formal invitation to

Mr Powell from Lady Pansy Lamb. The invitation was accepted with an equal formality, but with a lack of surprise that led us to believe that we had traced the character we were seeking. This laid the first flagstone on the path leading to matrimony, but at the party no more words were exchanged than were needed for the offering and accepting of a glass of gin and tonic.

Two days later, I awoke with a feeling that the cold I had imported from Ireland was not yet defeated. This I partly attributed to over-strenuous social activities on the previous night. At the start of the evening I had found myself stranded on the doorstep of a block of flats in Jermyn Street, having forgotten the number of the apartment at which I had been invited to dine, and also the name of the host. In this predicament I had the choice of retreating to the Cavendish, where I felt I might be allowed to trace by telephone where I was supposed to dine, or seeking the same help in Jules' Hotel.

As it happened I had, for a while, kept a bottle of Fernet Branca at Jules', relic of an evening when the management had lent a sitting-room for a game of poker. Orgiastic as the party may sound, nothing could have been less wild than the gambling that took place, and nothing could have been primmer than the sitting-room. On a wall papered in pale blue stripes there hung a picture called 'Passing Fancy', in which a vaguely Regency horseman turned to cast an admiring, but respectful eye, at a modest village maiden. If other, less pastoral, passing fancies had been entertained in these prim surroundings, there could have been even less encouragement from the hard little sofas and chairs than from the management's taste in art.

On the doorstep in Jermyn Street I recalled that one of my friends, on her way to buy scent at Floris' shop, had been warned off by a professional lady claiming that stretch of pavement as her beat. Whether this was fact or folklore, I was relieved to be joined by a sympathetic man selling gardenias. From his tray I bought a wax-white flower, and in return he gave me his protection until I had pressed a combination of buttons which resulted in the door being opened by a butler. He made no attempt to hide his distrust of a guest who neither knew her host's name nor could refrain from picking up passers-by in Jermyn Street.

At that date gambling was illegal in public, even, I believe, in Jules' private sitting-rooms, but organizers raising funds for a dental charity had discovered that, if entry was by personal invitation, banks could run and wheels spin without risk of prosecution. It was to this party, held in Sunderland House, usually the scene of wedding receptions, that I proceeded after dinner. My invitation was reasonably genuine, not having passed through more than two or three hands before it reached me, but the sceptical doorman was surrounded by ticketless would-be gamblers, determined to force an entry, and risk the gold from their back teeth in the cause of charitable dentistry. Once inside, I found that the organizers' success was complete, both in reconstituting the foetid atmosphere of the Monte Carlo Rooms, and finding amateur croupiers delighted to preside over banks at chemin de fer running at three and four hundred pounds. Subsequently the success turned to failure, as it was decreed that no charity could justify such a flouting of the spirit of the law.

After this party, not surprisingly, my gardenia and I were conspicuously wilted. The flower's brown edges I trimmed with nail scissors, but more than Fernet Branca would have been needed to bring my condition back to normal. It did seem, however, that a day in the fresh air at a point-to-point in Kent, to which I had been invited, would be a remedy for the malaise left by an evening at the tables. Arrangements were, in any case, too complicated to unpick. For some reason it was necessary to make a detour to collect a strange young man, whose name I shamefully failed to remember. This was a particularly bad lapse, as he retained an impression of me at wild variance from what I was feeling. His letter of good wishes on my engagement was only second in charm to the letter from the retired steward of RMS *Ulster*, with the addition of compliments from personal acquaintance.

Arrived at the race meeting, I found it essential to remain in the car, as my legs had become untrustworthy. Assorted wines and spirits from the picnic basket brought no relief, though I craved water to such an extent that I drank dry the supply belonging to a Rolls-Royce parked alongside, which its kind chauffeur passed to me in tumblers. The plans for the rest of the day loomed before me, as unsurmountable as the tallest fence on the racecourse, but good fortune provided me with another new friend. He found my strange condition so far from repulsive that he volunteered to drive me back to London, leaving me at my door with promises of meeting again, and assurances, without foundation, that my recovery would certainly be rapid.

My bed seemed unaccountably to be swinging inches above the floor, but for twenty-four hours the philosophy that had prevailed in my mother's time, of not making influenza a case for calling a doctor, held good. Then Annie Reason became so frightened that she sent for the medical man who had attended my mother. To me he was practically a stranger, my mother's determination to keep her family and her doctors apart having been, in this instance, a complete success. As much as I could formulate ideas, I clung to the theory that I was merely suffering from having neglected a protracted cold, suggesting that it would be more sensible to finish the mixture prescribed the previous week for my sister Julia, and apparently efficacious, as the bottle was still half-full. Surely, I argued, this would save the trouble of knocking up a chemist on Sunday evening.

The nurse sent in by the doctor to a case of congestion of the lungs, which was his diagnosis, found the household unusual, even mysterious. Particularly baffling were references by the servants to 'Her ladyship' who turned out not to be the ladyship she was required to nurse. In my family, chest ailments had never reached dramatic extremes since my eldest brother had been struck by bronchitis on the day of his christening. So when Mary hastened back from a country visit, she had wild thoughts that it might be necessary to move house to Davos, the place she associated with any lung complaint. Matters, she found, were not so desperate, but when she supposed that care must be taken to avert pneumonia, she was told that this had already set in. Having recently attended my mother in her last illness, the doctor took a rather nervous view of my prospects, suggesting that my eldest brother might be summoned to my bedside, which he seemed to think was obligatory for any sufferer in that house. These apprehensions, illogical as they were, communicated themselves to my kinsfolk. I myself insisted on a sight of *The Times* each morning, not from a wish to keep up with the world, but to follow the bulletins on a friend, seriously ill after childbirth, with whose fate I had, equally illogically, decided mine was linked.

Penicillin and antibiotics were lurking in the laboratories of the future, so, uninfluenced by drugs, my temperature zigzagged across its chart, as might the needle on a seismograph in an earthquake zone. I was more informed of its ups and downs than patients are apt to be, for Annie Reason, who nursed me in the daytime, needed my help to read a thermometer. At night my nurse curled up on the sofa at my feet, to rise devotedly at 2 a.m., in order to change sheets, soaked after that fall in temperature when pneumonia retreats in order better to advance. As the week wore on towards the disease's crisis, I became an ever more expensive invalid. Grapes and Brand's Essence ceased to be palatable. Chicken tea, made daily from a whole carcass, like Henri IV's ideal of a chicken in every pot, together with peaches at out of season prices, were all I could force down. Champagne was also prescribed, with which, as it happened, we were well stocked. During my mother's last weeks her brother Arthur had sent her cases of half-bottles and cases of quarter-bottles, in the hope that she would be cheered by the only wine which he himself cared to drink.

Much as she loved her brother, my mother was not tempted to abandon the abstemious habit of a lifetime. She had no actual moral prejudice against champagne, rather did she regard it as something that bumped up the household expenses. Before her eldest son's coming of age she had discussed with her butler the amount of champagne that would be needed at the festival. Pansy, present at the conference, had reported my mother's distressed surprise at the avidity of the female guests she had remarked when the champagne had been handed round at a local wedding. Reluctantly, Pansy said, she accepted Taylor's explanation that in the country consumption must be gauged by scarcity of opportunity. Guests could not be expected to show the restraint that might be exercised by those sated at the champagne fountains of London.

In addition to a quarter of champagne administered at six o'clock in the evening, preparations were put in hand to rally the patient from the expected crisis. I watched these from what seemed an enormous distance, into which I spoke words meaningless to my hearers but intended to convey my indignation at the undue violence, or so it seemed to me, with which the doctor tapped at my lungs. With oxygen and brandy lying at hand, I passed once again through the 2 a.m. fall of temperature. Then the windows of my room grew faintly lighter as the grey London dawn edged through the curtains. Suddenly I felt limp, but almost new-born, as if an evil spirit had departed. Chicken tea from a thermos flask was ambrosial, and the glass of brandy on which I insisted was a toast to recovery instead of a hindrance to collapse. The oxygen cylinder was returned unopened to the chemist, and, in a slightly reproving tone of voice, my grandmother told me that I had given the family a nasty fright.

Convalescence was an unfamiliar condition in my home, my mother having seldom reached that state herself, and having regarded the illnesses of her children as proceeding from ill to well with no intervening passage. My last days in bed were enlivened by Mary reading aloud to the nurse and me a classic of our childhood, *Naughty Sophia* by Winifred Letts. This begins with the naughty archduchess, Sophia, biting her juvenile fiancé in the calf, the first of a series of adventures, *coup d'état* followed by encounters in the mountains with helpful dwarfs and facetious but brutal brigands. To me it was a meeting with old friends, but the nurse was so enthralled that the reading had to be speeded up so she could learn what happened before she left. She was kind enough to say how much she had enjoyed a case where the patient was still at the beginning rather than the end of life, as was more usual in her experience of private nursing. She had also relished my running commentary on the goings-on in the house opposite where what the newspaper studied by Fanny Price's father in *Mansfield Park* called 'a matrimonial *fracas* in the fashionable world' was taking place. Fortunately, from the point of view of the neighbours, much of the *fracas* took place on the balcony, culminating in the lady of the house dropping an orange on to the head of a departing guest on the pavement below, which was not, probably, the method chosen by Mrs Rushworth in *Mansfield Park* when she wished to indicate her intention of eloping with Mr Crawford.

Pneumonia had sweated a stone off my weight, leaving me with skeleton legs, and feet on which crimson toenails looked like no adjunct of the human frame. Lying on the sofa of our sitting-room, my first descent to an everyday level, I was surprised by a call from my Great-Aunt Aggie, herself said to have contracted pneumonia in middle life, though as I will show, doubts were cast on the truth of this family legend. Although Aunt Aggie was less strict in her views than her sister Aunt Cordie, I thought it prudent if discourteous to continue to recline, concealing my legs in pyjama trousers, and my lurid toenails, under a pile of sofa cushions. Aunt Aggie had just turned eighty. She had the prettiest white hair in the world, which might, I suppose, be considered a reward for having passed her life as a handmaiden to stronger-minded relations. She had once been shepherded after dinner into the garden at Osterley with a gentleman who might, it was hoped, propose. However, the manoeuvre, by which the pair were sent to walk alone under the cedar trees on a chilly May evening, failed to achieve the happy result for which my grandmother hoped, when she triumphantly closed the doors of the Long Gallery upon them. My uncle Arthur, then a small boy, had been recruited to play a part in the plan which was to isolate the couple, and it was he who ever after insisted that, though the *parti* escaped with no more than a shocking cold, Aunt Aggie subsequently developed pneumonia. Arthur, almost certainly, overstated the dire results of his mother's attempt at matchmaking, but it was undeniably an evening when the magic of Osterley failed in its potency.

Although lacking the physical stamina of her brother Lord Leigh, who piously followed the Arrangements for the Day, as announced in *The Times* each morning, Aunt Aggie was no weakling. At the end of her visit she was indignant as she ever showed herself, when I suggested that a taxi might be summoned to convey her to her home on the lower slopes of Belgravia. Taxis were, indeed, an expense against which my grandmother had seen fit to warn her three granddaughters now living in their own commune, after I had made the mistake of telling, as a comic incident, how, returning to Rutland Gate in an omnibus, I had passed my sister Mary on foot and been passed by my sister Julia in a taxi.

Determined to instil prudence into her descendants, my grandmother also preached against the wanton practice of having accounts at shops. This advice may also have been given because of the suspicion, only too justified, that we had been brought up by a mother who had kept an account at practically all the larger London stores, bestowing her patronage as her mood, and the state of her bank account, dictated. Only on one point did Nature dictate to her. The vast size of her children's heads obliged her to seek their hats in the more fashionable millinery departments, a grievance to my mother that she never learnt to accept as the irreversible will of Heaven. She did, however, experience a sensation of economy by sending us to shop for some garments, in which our sizes were less spectacular, at a store which followed fashion at so respectful a distance as to be practically out of sight, but at all emporia, modish or dowdy, the purchases could be entered to the account of the Dowager Countess of Longford. Time, it is fair to say, showed that my mother's attitude brought an unexpected bonus to those who adopted it. Had I followed my grandmother's advice to shun accounts and pay laborious cash, I would doubtless have found myself to be on a firm financial footing, but I should never have been able, in later days of clothing scarcity, to collect, and distribute as presents, a six-monthly ration of nylon stockings, allotted to account customers at half a dozen different shops.

THE FAMILY GETS A FRIGHT

A consensus of family opinion decided that I must have a formal seaside convalescence, and I obediently set off for an hotel at Hove, which was known to my elders, and distinguished by the, for those days, astonishing luxury of bathroom and lavatory for each of its bedrooms. This effort appeared to have exhausted the management's initiative, for the dishes served in the restaurant were of a uniform tastelessness which made course barely distinguishable from course. My sister Mary kept me company at first, but when she was obliged to return to her job in Fleet Street, I ate the grim meals in solitary gloom. I was accustomed to regarding any course of action proposed by my family elders as being automatically of extreme propriety, and it was only years later that I came to wonder at their insouciance in not considering that I, alone at my table, might not be thought to be fair game for a pick-up. Ty had lent me Winkie to keep me company, which he was reluctant to do, not caring for the lawns of Hove, where a police constable was constantly on duty to dog the dog walkers who might let their pets off the lead. Winks made no attempt to conceal his delighted relief when Ty and Sara, her Saluki, joined us. Locking the dogs into our suite, we went out to dinner, returning to find the manager gibbering in the hall. Sara, an animal whose diamond drill teeth could mince the stoutest lead in two minutes, had set herself to break out of her hotel prison, and the desk clerk, sent with a master key to investigate the wails and scrabblings, had fled before what was alleged to be a savage attack by Winkie. Having paid a bill for repairs, I parted from the hotel in an atmosphere of chill that not even impeccable family connections could warm. In fact, I have seldom left anywhere with a lighter heart, or under a blacker cloud.

Suddenly the days of pneumonia were gone as if they had never been. In a summer of seemingly unending sunshine, I again played polo, and danced till the rosy fingers of dawn were writing the date of a new day in the sky. It was a new experience to cross the Wiltshire Downs in a horse-drawn caravan that lurched through the rhododendron woods, liberated from the tyranny of metalled roads, while in the evening the owner sang songs concerned with the goings on of the Monks of St Bernard's and the highly unclerical bets laid between the vicar and the curate of a town on the sea-coast of Sussex. But it was with an unexpected journey to Cornwall that, for the first time, I fell into the enchanting clutches of the kingdom of the West.

It was to my mother's cousin Julia that I owed this expansion of my horizon, the invitation being to visit her in her new home, which was perched on top of St Michael's Mount. A new world to be wondered at began, for me, when the Cornish Riviera Express ran under the red cliffs of Dawlish, a world that opened out when Truro had been passed, and the traveller, new to Cornwall, sensed that the Atlantic and the English Channel were about to meet at the iron rocks off Land's End. Cousin Julia took her name from a succession of ancestresses, the first of whom had been born in Fort St George, Madras. Love and admiration had attended all these Julias, including Cousin Julia herself, with the exception of the Julia who had been daughter of Sir Robert Peel and wife of the 6th Earl of Jersey. I have mentioned earlier that the name of her lovers was said to be legion, and she was reputed also to have sent her son, my grandfather, to Eton in a blue blouse instead of an Eton jacket, while she kept her daughter Julia, mother of Cousin Julia, in childish pantalettes, practically until her wedding day. This unpleasantness was, luckily, quickly bred out of the family, and I had an additional appreciation of Cousin Julia's kind hospitality when I remembered the chill discomforts she had been exposed to when a guest at Peverel Court.

In the months that followed that visit a romantic change had taken place in Cousin Julia's life, transforming her from a Dowager Countess into the wife of Lord St Levan, owner of St Michael's Mount. This wedding between two septuagenarians was not only the union of a couple who had been parted in their youth, my mother had told me, by insensitive inquiries from the young lady's father as to the young man's intentions. The departure for their honeymoon achieved almost the quality of an elopement, when the motor-car in which they were sedately bowling towards Dover broke down dangerously near sailing time. Entirely capable of coping with this setback, Cousin Julia flagged a passing lorry. Persuading her new husband, who had a delicate constitution, to sit in the driver's cab, she herself climbed in among the lorry's cargo. The captain of the Channel steamer had been warned to expect this arrival, and as the lorry drove on to the quay at Dover the St Levans were greeted by photographers from the national press, and cheers from the passengers lining the decks.

Lord St Levan's first wife (the star-crossed lovers having each married another) was said not to have cared for the sea, which at high tide circled the rock on which her home was the pinnacle, lacking feeling for the wild grandeur celebrated by Milton and Macaulay. Fortunately to Cousin Julia the sea was a friend, and the *St Michael*, the retired Scilly mail-steamer used for fishing expeditions, sailed dead on-course when she was at the helm. The long days fishing exactly suited my temperament, though I was often disgraced by failing to detect a bit on the line I was trawling, ignominiously bringing a mackerel long dead to the surface. These lapses were only too easy when the fishers had been feasting on stew, brought to sea in a vast casserole, and followed by a glass of port. In the saloon, among packets of sandwiches marked 'Ham' or 'Beef', I was startled, one day, to see a parcel marked 'Wolf', an animal I had always regarded as more devouring than devourable, and in any case long extinct, even among the rocks of Cornwall. The parcel turned out to be magazines for the men of the Wolf Rock Lighthouse, a lone finger pointing skywards between Land's End and Scilly. A promise of going ashore there in a bosun's chair, the only means of landing, was impossible of fulfilment, as the bosun's chair had been claimed by the Trinity House boat which had called with reliefs of men and supplies. As we sailed away across an oily sea, it seemed almost beyond imagination that only too often raging storms would hold the lighthouse men prisoners long after relief was due.

Besides individual lines, the *St Michael* towed a many barbed trawl behind her, supervised by one or other of the two oldest members of the crew. They had to be put to work separately, being inheritors of a family feud dating back to the heroic smuggling days of the past. The forbear of one had been a Preventive, employed to suppress the evasion of customs dues, while the ancestress of the other had kept a public-house where the smugglers found a retail outlet, hiding, it was said, kegs of brandy under her crinoline when the Preventive arrived with a search warrant. Any opinion offered by one of these old men of the sea was at once contradicted by the other, but they both joined with the rest of the crew in derisive smiles when, in a gambling mood, Lord St Levan stuck a pin at random in the chart, and declared that there we would trawl next day. It would be nice to record that the catch was a miraculous draught, vindicating the owner's speculation, but under the smug smiles of the crew the trawl came up from full fathom five bearing only seaweed, a stray halibut, and the rainbow fish which even seagulls shun, until at last an infant shark was hauled aboard, its belly purely silver beneath a back of darkest indigo, on which the dorsal fin had already begun to take sinister shape.

After such days dinner in the dining-room, looking down on the evening sea as it turned from aquamarine to lavender, would be rounded off by crunching the crisped back bones of the mackerel which we had trawled up from the depths. Sea air and the central heating of the Mount which, in consideration of Lord St Levan's health, was kept high even in summer, caused many heads to nod round the billiard-table as the evening wore on, but the host himself found long nights in bed tedious, so that games of Slosh, under Mount rules, lasted till after midnight. Poised to add to a break that would have entitled to me to an entry in the book of honour kept for big breaks at Mount Slosh, I failed to score. Partly because I was hampered by an evening dress whose scarlet chiffon frills frothed over my cue, and partly because my eye was caught by a sudden movement from what had appeared to be an empty black leather arm-chair, but which was in reality occupied by the sleeping form of an enormous cousin. This was the last night that I spent at the Mount, and its spirit seemed to be epitomized by the masthead lights of the Penzance pilchard fleet, which that evening fished close under the island's cliffs, their lights gleaming like fire-flies dancing on the sea.

The party which my sister Pansy had given in the spring, and to which Anthony Powell had been invited by me speaking in the character of a parlourmaid, had begun a chain of events which had resulted in an invitation to him to stay at Pakenham. As it happened he was still in the house when I arrived, in company with the Lambs and their children, and he was immediately claimed by Henry as a model. While Anthony sat, I, supposedly present to entertain the sitter, followed past events in the newspapers on which Henry cleaned his brushes.

The bedroom used by Henry as a studio had once, in my childhood, been my night nursery, during a summer when my mother had thought economy in staff might be achieved by moving nursery and schoolroom down to levels more proximate to the kitchen from which their meals were supplied. The black rays of discontent sent forth by her children's nurse convinced my mother that this was an economy of which the price was too high, but to me the room remained associated with a stormy patch in nursery history, which it needed all the charm of the conversation of artist and sitter to exorcise. Out of doors I led Anthony down the steep path to the kitchen garden, and, in a manner somewhat reminiscent of the second chapter of Genesis, offered him an apple from the tree of Worcester Pearmains which had been regarded by the nursery as inviolably private to that department. Although I had been praised for a map my mother had once incited me to draw of the gardens at Pakenham and their surrounding woods, time seemed to have distorted my sense of distance. We walked through brake and briar, but never did we reach the Float Bog, where I had planned to show this new friend what Somerville and Ross, writing of a similar landscape of heather and sundew, called 'a massed embroidery of flowers'.

The bog was a mirage, but on these walks we began a conversation which has continued unabated until this day. To me surroundings known from childhood, and perhaps blurred by familiarity, came into focus as though I had been given new spectacles of a magical clarity. Looking down from a hilltop, it seemed that the white horses on Lough Derravaragh had never before galloped so dazzlingly over the steely blue water. Indoors, in the library, the leather backs of books collected two centuries before had never glowed so golden in the morning sun, as I sat in a window-seat and Anthony read aloud from the novel that was, at that moment, growing under his hand.

That September the heat wave of the summer days persisted, like an actress refusing to retire from a career of intoxicating success. Leaves drifted about the gutters in sun-dried heaps, and discarded summer clothes were snatched back from premature hibernation. On the last day of the month, a Sunday, the heat was still so intense that, lunching on guard at St James's Palace, guests were taken out to drink their coffee on to the leads among the Tudor towers. The guests, invited by the officers to enliven their guard duty, were on this occasion only two, myself and one other girl, with whom my acquaintance was of the slightest. When we had baked for a while in the sooty sunlight, it seemed churlish not to leave in her company, though I was immersed in my own thoughts of what the immediate future might hold in store. Indeed I was so abstracted that it was only when walking up St James's Street that I remembered I had forgotten to cast a glance at the scrap screen in the officers' mess, a famous furnishing said to include such skittish juxtapositions as moustached colonels gazing through telescopes at ladies unlacing their stays. My fellow guest, facing an unoccupied Sunday afternoon, stayed by my side while I exercised Winkie on the tinder dry grass bordering Rotten Row. Anthony had suggested that he might come to tea, and I had a strong feeling that a third party might be superfluous. Finally, at the turning leading down Rutland Gate, I escaped by urging Winkie into a canter, leaving my companion to peer after me with a wild surmise.

At the tea-table, Anthony and I became engaged. Two months later, on 1 December, we were married at All Saints', Ennismore Gardens, whose tower had been such a feature of the view from the windows of 12 Rutland Gate. We had a share in the splendid decorations, rose-coloured garlands and huge paper bells, with which London was hung in honour of Princess Marina of Greece and the Duke of Kent, whose wedding was two days before our own. On the dark side, we learnt long after, Stalin had chosen our wedding day to start his reign of terror by the murder of Kirov. In London it was a mild grey day, kind to those who were suffering from the after-effects of our pre-nuptial party. This celebration had got somewhat out of hand, by reason of the drinks being mixed by a pair of maids borrowed from my grandmother. In her house they had had no opportunity to learn the approved ratio, pouring out gin like water. For the evening the ping-pong table had been folded away, but the much punished schoolroom piano remained. On this an enthusiastic hand drummed out Sir Roger de Coverley, to which tune a double line of our friends danced at our wedding. Next day we left from Newhaven for Paris, the Simplon-Orient Express and the city of Athens. The four years between eighteen and twenty-two had rolled by and brought with them the new family circle that was to be Anthony's and mine.

Index

Acheson, Ladies, 85
Andrews, James, 42, 51
Arlen, Michael, 200
Austen, Jane, 76
Aux Abois, 192

Baillie, Miss, 182–3
Bankhead, Tallulah, 221
Baring, Maurice, 70
Baring, Olive, 210–11, 214–15
Beaverbrook, Lord, 101
Beerbohm, Max, 2
Beetle, 180
Bernard, Tristan, 192
Berta, 174
Beveridge, Lady, 160
Birmingham, George A., 131
Bonner, Cecil, 37
Bowra, Maurice, 117
Buchanan, Jack, 79
Buckingham, George, 1st Duke of, 160, 208
Byng, Douglas, 142
Byron, Lord, 37–8

Cakes and Ale, 192

Campbell, Roy, 117, 190
Carnera, Primo, 178
Cavalcade, 102
Cavendish, Charlie, 60
Céline, Louis-Ferdinand, 192
Chamberlain, Joseph, 21
Chamberlain, Neville, 104
Charles II, 23, 28
Chevalier, Maurice, 90, 189, 196, 200–1
Chiffinch, William, 23
Child, Robert, 109
Clare, Mary, 103
Cochran, Charles B., 79, 102, 114
Colet, John, 214
Colville, Joan (*née* Villiers), 33 passim, 40 passim, 70, 89, 121, 128, 146, 164–5
Compton-Burnett, I., 124
Corot, Jean-Baptiste, 152, 159
Coward, Noël, 64, 102
Crewe Train, 194, 196
Cruickshank, Mrs, 43
Curse of the Wise Woman, The, 221
Curzon, Lord, 21
Cuyp, Albert, 83

INDEX

Darnley, Lord, 28
Dartrey, Julia, Countess of (see St Levan)
Dedalus, Stephen, 58
Desmond, Countess of, 63–4
Devonshire, Duke of, 60
Dickens, Charles, 161
Dilke, Sir Charles, 158
Douglas, Lord Alfred, 177
Doyle, Richard, 83–4
Du Côté de Chez Swann, 125
Dunsany, Beatrice (née Villiers), wife of 18th Baron, 27, 33, 56, 75, 116, 128, 218, 220
Dunsany, Edward, 18th Baron, 33, 51–5, 82, 118, 210–11, 219–21
Dürer, Albrecht, 97, 183
Dynevor, Margaret (Markie, née Villiers), wife of 7th Baron, 22–3, 75, 111, 122, 138, 144–9, 206
Dynevor, Walter, 7th Baron, 122, 144–9

Edgeworth, Maria, 30
Edgeworth, Richard Lovell, 43
El Greco, 97
Endor, Chick, 142
Erasmus, Desiderius, 214
Erskine, Hamish, 126, 184, 186

Farrell, Charlie, 142
Farrère, Claude, 50
Fitzgerald, F. Scott, 188
From a View to a Death, 193

Galloway, Lady, 24
Gough, Hugo, 3rd Viscount, 79, 80
Goya, Francisco, 97
Grahame, Kenneth, 92
Greece, Princess Marina of, 237
Green Hat, The, 200

Gulbenkian, Miss, 98
Gulbenkian, Nubar, 213

Hare, Augustus, 21
Harman, Elizabeth (see Pakenham)
Hatto, Bishop, 84
Hay, Ian, 131
Heine, Heinrich, 84
Helen!, 114
Helm, Brigitte, 87
Hemingway, Ernest, 188, 191
Henrietta Maria, wife of Charles I, 28
Hitler, Adolf, 88–9, 184

James, Henry, 17, 20–1, 118
Jenkins, Roy, 158
Jersey, George, 8th Earl of, 38
Jersey, George (Grandy), 9th Earl of, 33
Jersey, Julia (née Peel), wife of 6th Earl, 232
Jersey, Margaret (née Leigh), wife of 7th Earl, 2 passim, 19 passim, 25–6, 34, 69, 109–15, 118, 156, 167, 176–7, 206 passim, 228, 230, 238
Jersey, Sarah Sophia (née Fane), wife 5th Earl, 37, 109
Jersey, Victor Albert George, 7th Earl of, xi, 20, 25–6, 232
Jock o' the Bushfeldt, 131

Kaiser William II, 80
Kaufmann, Angelica, 23
Kent, Prince George, Duke of, 237
Keys, Nelson, 71
Kipling, Rudyard, 206
King George V, 74, 80
Kirov, Sergei, 237
Kitchener, Lord, 21

Lady Chatterley's Lover, 72
Lamb, Henry, xii, 49, 153, 235
Lamb, Henrietta, 118, 132, 153, 163
Lamb, Pansy (*née* Pakenham), xii, 76, 100, 101, 105, 153, 182, 222–3, 227, 235
Lang, Alöis, 83
Lavengro, 174
Lawrence, D. H., 72
Lawrence, Sir Thomas, 79
Leigh, Agnes, 110, 113, 229
Leigh, Cordelia, 23, 111–14, 229
Leigh, Dudley, 3rd Baron, 112, 229
Letts, Winifred, 228
Lewis, Rosa, 184–5
Lieven, Princess, 37
Liliom, 281
Lisieux, Sainte Thérèse of, 16
Longford, Christine (*née* Trew), wife of 6th Earl, xii, 41–51, 60, 153 passim, 204 passim, 218
Longford, Edward, 6th Earl of, xi, xii, 8, 41–51, 60, 153 passim, 204 passim, 218
Longford, Mary (*née* Villiers), wife of 5th Earl, xi, xii, 1–14, 19 passim, 24 passim, 39, 57–8, 77, 94, 101 passim, 116 passim, 144–5, 151–8, 181 passim, 227, 230, 235–6
Longford, Selina (*née* Rice-Trevor), wife of 4th Earl, 27–8
Longford, Thomas, 5th Earl of, xi, 4, 13, 17, 25–6
Lonsdale, Lord, 164–5
Lowell, James Russell, 21
Lubitsch, Ernst, 196

Macaulay, Rose, 45, 194, 196
MacLiammóir, Micheál, 218
MacRae, Lady Margaret, 173, 187 passim

MacRae, Ty, 171 passim, 187 passim, 231
Mansfield, Katherine, 171
Mansfield Park, 24, 76, 228
Marie de Medici, 28
Married Love, 137
Mary, Queen of Scots, 28
Masefield, John, 221
Maugham, W. Somerset, 192
Milne, A. A., 139
Miss Hook of Holland, 215–16
Molnar, Ferenc, 218
Monolulu, Prince, 126

Napoleon III, 126
Naughty Sophia, 228
Nicodemus, 172
Nordau, Max, 44
Novello, Ivor, 178

O'Donovan, Gerald, 45
Oh! What a Lovely War, 103
Opie, John, 55
Oudry, Jean-Baptiste, 159

Paget, Dorothy, 127
Pakenham, Antonia, 151, 156, 180
Pakenham, Charles Reginald (later Father Paul Mary), 50
Pakenham, Edward Michael (Bingo), 130–1
Pakenham, Elizabeth (*née* Harman), 77, 95, 101–5, 117 passim, 150 passim, 181–2, 206
Pakenham, Frank, xii, 9, 10, 95, 101–5, 117 passim, 135, 151, 178
Pakenham, Julia, xii, 30, 39, 66 passim, 81–99, 100, 106, 114–15, 125, 128, 152, 215 passim
Pakenham, Mary, xii, 11, 74, 77, 95, 107–8, 176, 182, 187, 230–1

Pakenham, Pansy (*see* Lamb)
Pakenham, Thomas, 182
Pakenham, Violet: birth, 11; in Ireland, 39; in Bavaria, 100; in Wales, 144; at London School of Economics, 157; in France, 187; marriage, 237
Palmerston, Lady, 37
Paul et Virginie, 176
Pepys, Samuel, 61, 74
Piggin, 40
Plunkett, Randal, 52, 128
Pope John XXIII, 72
Portrait of the Artist as a Young Man, 177
Powell, Anthony, 193, 222, 235–8
Power, Doctor Eileen, 168
Prince Regent, 29

Rabelais, François, 183
Raleigh, Sir Walter, 64
Ramsay, Allan, 148
Rawlins, Miss, 68–9
Reason, Annie, 5, 71, 73, 123, 165, 187, 199, 210, 215, 222–3
Renoir, Auguste, 69, 152
Revelstoke, Lord, 113
Rhys, David, 107, 135–7, 145–7
Rhys, Imogen, 147
Rosée, Madame de, 118
Rothermere, Lord, 88
Rubens, Peter Paul, 97

Saki (H. H. Munro), 86, 110
Salisbury, Lady, 24
Salisbury, Lord, 21
Sampson, Julian, 140
Slessor, Cynthia (formerly Jersey), 33, 36, 100, 128–9, 150
Soest, Gerard, 23
Somerville and Ross, 65, 175

Southey, Robert, 84
Squire, J. C., 79
Stalin, Josef, 237
Stalky and Co., 195
Stevenson, Robert Louis, 22
St. Levan, John, 2nd Baron, 233–4
St. Levan, Julia (formerly Dartrey), wife of 2nd Baron, 124, 232–3
Stravinsky, Igor, 218
Stuart de Decies, Lady, 64
Stuart de Decies, Lord, 64
Sun also Rises, The, 191
Sutherland, Duchess/Countess of, 110
Swinburne, Algernon Charles, 120

Talbot Rice, David, 49
Tale of Two Cities, A, 161
Tauber, Richard, 92
Taylor, John, 119–23, 227
Terry family, 11–12, 181
Thomas, Dylan, 146
Travels of Brown, Jones, and Robinson, 83
Tristram Shandy, 30
Tyrell, Walter, 172, 175

Under Milk Wood, 146, 148

Villiers, Ann, 89
Villiers, Arthur, 19, 20, 27, 136, 227, 229
Villiers, Beatrice (*see* Dunsany)
Villiers, George (*see* Buckingham)
Villiers, Sir George, 208
Villiers, Joan (*see* Colville)
Villiers, Mansel, 38
Villiers, Margaret (*see* Dynevor)
Villiers, Margaret (d. inf.), 207
Villiers, Mary (*see* Longford)
Villiers, Reginald, 207

Villiers, Robert, 207
Villiers-Stuart, Elspeth, 56–7, 61–5
Villiers-Stuart, Ion, 54, 57, 61–5
Villiers-Stuart, Mrs, 58
Viollet-le-Duc, 195
Voyage au Bout de la Nuit, 192

Waste Land, The, 97
Watts-Dunton, Theodore, 120
Waugh, Evelyn, 117

Wells, H. G., 164
White, 41–2
Wilde, Oscar, 86
William Rufus, 172
Wind in the Willows, The, 92
Winnie the Pooh, 141
Witzell, Madlon, 81, 84 passim

Yeats, W. B., 70, 221